DEMETRI
PORPHYRIOS

SELECTED
BUILDINGS & WRITINGS

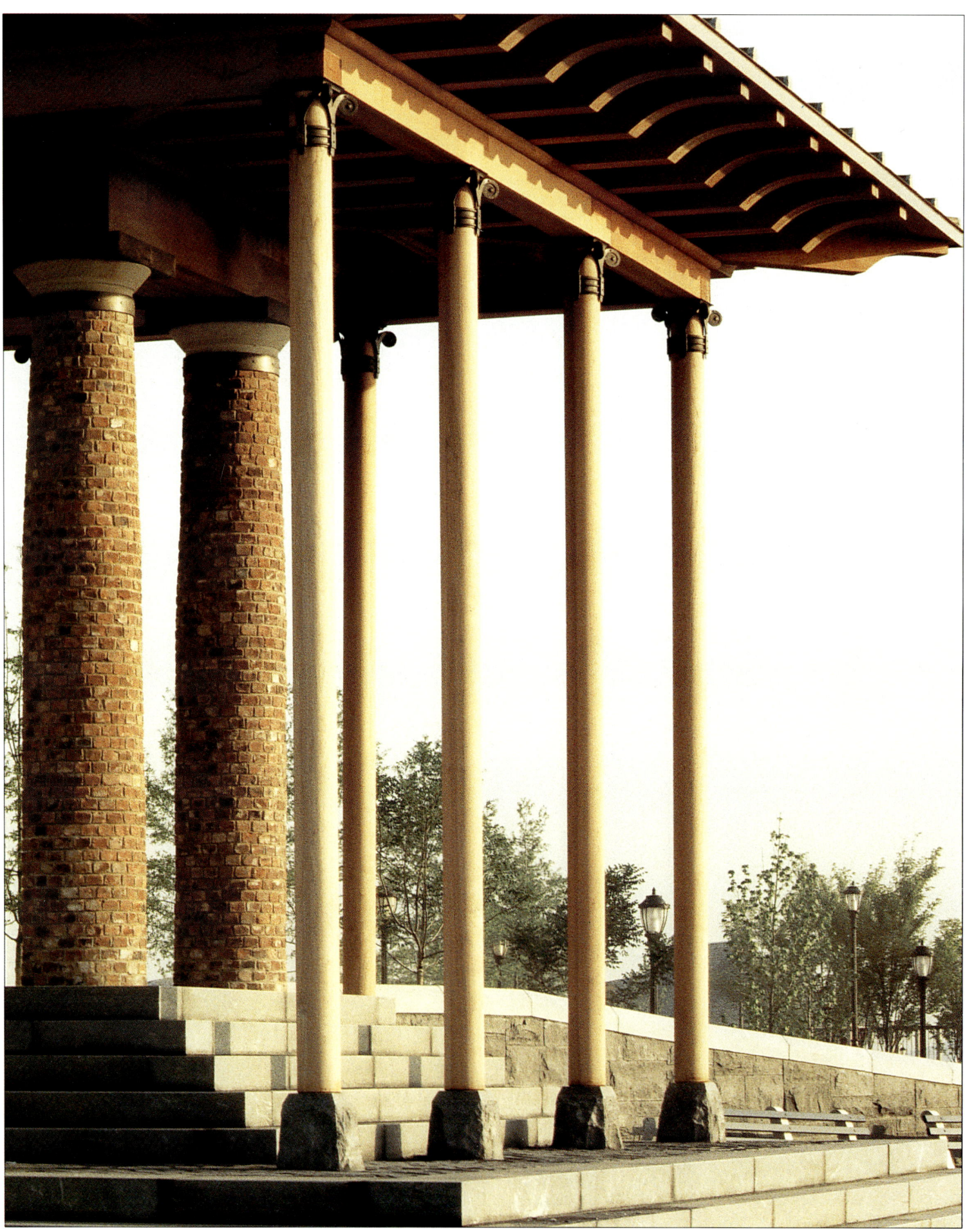

ARCHITECTURAL MONOGRAPHS No 25

DEMETRI PORPHYRIOS

SELECTED BUILDINGS & WRITINGS

FRONT COVER: Belvedere Village, detail of main barn, Ascot
BACK COVER: Propylon in Surrey; PAGE TWO: Battery Park City Pavilion, New York

This monograph would not have been possible without the contribution over the years of all who have worked in our Practice. We are most grateful to Dr Oswyn Murray, Fellow and Vice Master of Balliol College, Oxford, for writing the introduction. Special thanks are due to the publisher, Dr Andreas Papadakis, and to Andrea Bettella, Alireza Sagharchi, Jan Richter, for their editorial competence and enthusiasm.

First published in Great Britain in 1993 by
ACADEMY EDITIONS
An imprint of the Academy Group Ltd, 42 Leinster Gardens London W2 3AN
Member of the VCH Publishing Group

Copyright © 1993 Demetri Porphyrios
All rights reserved
No part of this publication may be reproduced or transmitted
in any form or by any means, whether by photocopying, recording or facsimile machine
or otherwise howsoever without permission in writing from the Publishers

ISBN:1 85490 174 5 (HB)
ISBN:1 85490 175 3 (PB)

Printed and bound in Singapore

CONTENTS

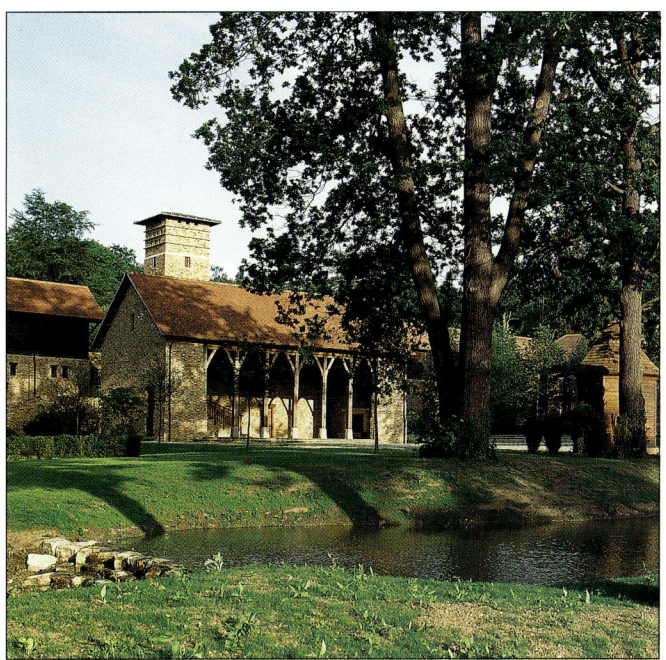

BELVEDERE VILLAGE, ASCOT

INTRODUCTION 7

PROJECTS
PAVILIONS IN HIGHGATE *10*
BELVEDERE VILLAGE, ASCOT *16*
RURAL HISTORY CENTRE, READING UNIVERSITY *44*
WORKSHOPS AND OFFICES IN POUNDBURY, DORCHESTER *50*
INLAND REVENUE OFFICES, NOTTINGHAM *52*
BATTERY PARK CITY PAVILION, NEW YORK *58*
MAGDALEN COLLEGE, NEW LONGWALL QUADRANGLE, OXFORD *62*
PROPYLON IN SURREY *72*
THE FITZWILLIAM MUSEUM EXTENSION, CAMBRIDGE *74*
VILLA IN ATHENS *78*
SHIPPING OFFICES, LONDON *88*
OFFICE BUILDING, ATHENS *92*
PATERNOSTER SQUARE OFFICE BUILDING, LONDON *94*
HOUSE IN KENSINGTON, LONDON *100*
HOUSE IN CHELSEA, LONDON *108*
CHEPSTOW VILLAS, LONDON *112*

ESSAYS
CLASSICISM IS NOT A STYLE *123*
BUILDING & ARCHITECTURE *129*
TRADITION AND THE NEW *135*

PROJECT CREDITS 142

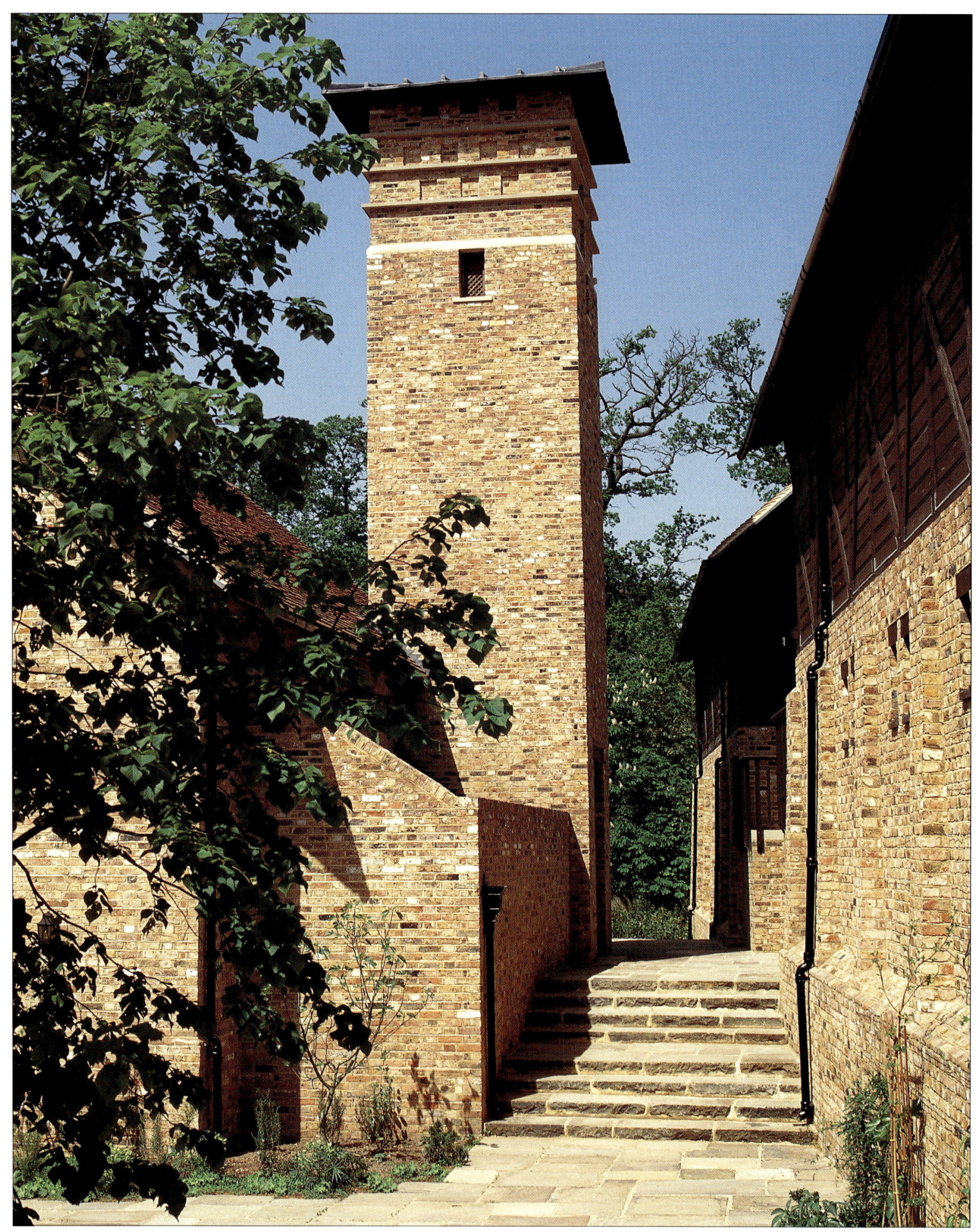

BELVEDERE VILLAGE, ASCOT, VIEW OF THE TOWER

INTRODUCTION
OSWYN MURRAY

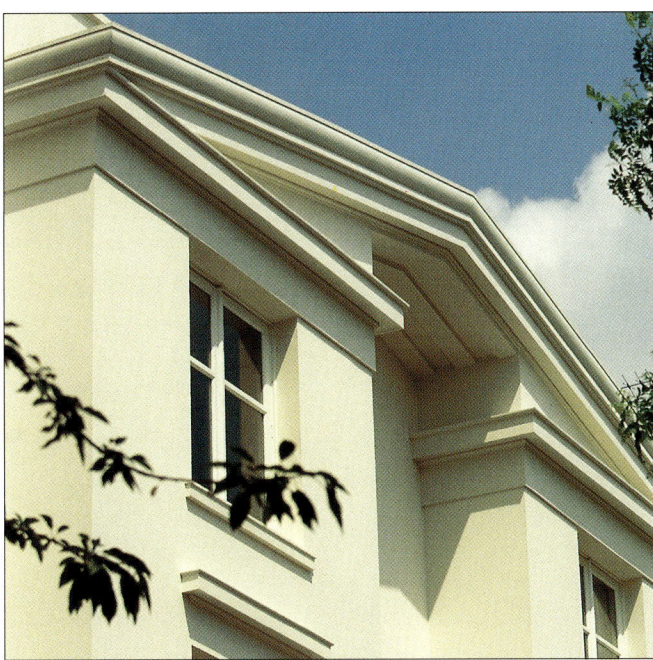

CHEPSTOW VILLAS, DETAIL OF PEDIMENT

In his buildings and in his writings Demetri Porphyrios naturally approaches the problems of tradition and innovation from the point of view of an architect and a theorist of architectural forms. But in reading and viewing his work, I am much more struck as a cultural historian by the extent to which his problems and his solutions reflect the continuing preoccupations of all artists and writers who seek to work in the classical tradition.

Tradition in all the arts is Janus-faced; it looks backwards for its language and forwards to new creations; it plays on the relationship between inherited images and creativity. Michael Baxandall has recently objected to the notion of influence: 'Influence is a curse of art-criticism primarily because of its wrong-headed grammatical prejudice about who is the agent and who is the patient: it seems to reverse the active/passive relation which the historical actor experiences and the inferential beholder will wish to take into account. If one says that X influenced Y it does seem that one is saying that X did something to Y rather than that Y did something to X'.[1]

Tradition is indeed a form of order created not by influence in this crude sense, but by a continuity in the conscious or unconscious use by the artist of the past in a new context.

But the situation is not quite so simple, for two reasons. The first is that all art involves both creator and audience. It is true that one may use tradition more or less mechanically, and so be regarded as influenced by the past; such practitioners within the tradition may even be necessary for the maintenance of a general language of art and for the continuance of its understanding. But the great artists renew tradition by a form of inspired abuse of their models. Tradition in this sense is about creativity, which is why the misunderstandings of the past in medieval or renaissance literature or art, are more important than the painstaking copying by minor scribes and the philological investigations or accurate reconstructions of modern scholarship. Nevertheless, even for the great artist, it is still important that both the artist and his audience inhabit a tradition and share a vision of the world; for one of the functions of tradition is to facilitate communication through shared values; and those values control to some extent the responses of both parties. Ernst Gombrich rightly pointed out thirty years ago in *Art and Illusion,* (Phaidon, 1960) that no painter ever paints what he sees, but rather what he perceives, and his vision is ordered by his training and mental set. Similarly, there are no writers who record reality, only realists who try with more or less success to escape from established convention towards a new organisation of perception. And equally in his response to the artist, the viewer or the reader does not 'see': he perceives, or reinterprets what the artist presents according to his own expectations.

So the sophisticated artist will play with the expectations aroused by tradition, in order to elicit responses from his audience (as Porphyrios does with his Highgate pavilions). Part of the pleasure of any art form for that audience lies in recognition; in discovering the resonance of every act and making the connections to all recorded or imagined past and future experience. To the poet and painter, David Jones, all life was a system of signs that embodied both past and present events. *In Parenthesis* reveals his experience in the trenches of the First World War as a re-enactment of the same reality as the Greeks before Troy, the Roman legionaries on the Wall and his own Welsh ancestors in the Dark Ages. As he wrote: 'Some man known to the reader may indeed appear to escape from all that is commonly or vulgarly meant by the 'sacramental', but no sooner does he put a rose in his buttonhole but what he is already in the trip-wire of sign, and he is deep in an entanglement of signs if he sends that rose to his sweetheart, Flo, or puts it in a vase by her portrait; and he is hopelessly and up to his neck in that entanglement of Ars, sign, sacrament, should he sit down and write a poem 'about' that sweetheart. Heaven knows what his poem will really be 'about'; for then the 'sacramental' will pile up by a positively geometric progression. So that what was Miss Flora Smith, may turn out to be Flora Dea and Venus too and the First Eve and the Second also, and other and darker figures, among them no doubt, Jocasta. One thing at least the psychologists make plain: there is always a recalling, a re-presenting again, anaphora, anamnesis.'[2]

The second complication lies in the claims of transcendental meaning for a particular tradition. Just as ER Curtius argued with some justification that all medieval literature was based on classical forms transmitted through rhetoric, and that this rhetoric expressed the permanent values of European culture, so Porphyrios has claimed that the forms of classical architecture are not *per accidens* the origins of Western architecture, but express its very essence: 'classicism is *not* a style'.

Porphyrios' buildings are works of exquisite beauty, which play on our pleasure in recollection; but the aim is not simply to provoke a sensuous response. There is first a respect for the craft of building in its relation to the art of architecture, which recalls many of the ideals of William Morris, a love of old brick, oak and outline detail. Then, behind the beauty of form and material, he is concerned to argue for a creative continuity in the theory and language of architecture: the evocation of aesthetic response does not disguise a deeper almost Ruskinian message, that in some way the forms of classical architecture are intrinsic to our sense of order. Thus classical architecture is not a question of decoration, but it is grounded in the fundamentals of building techniques: it has its origin in the function of shelter, and 'constructs a tectonic fiction out of the constructional necessities of building'; but it also reveals an underlying order in the laws of human nature: 'the Classical Order imitates human temperament and rank as well'.

The first of these claims is a historical one, but disguises a 'metaphysical' element: for all appeals to historical origins as justification for contemporary practice imply a Darwinian theory of the continuing importance of origins. Porphyrios would reply that his concern for tradition rests on the continuities of tectonics and the use of materials; his theoretical stance here seems to me close to that of Ruskin's *Stones of Venice*, which similarly asserted the importance of the basic relationship between natural materials, human use and architectural form. For Porphyrios, style is a fictive or mythical language created in response to the fundamentals of tectonics; such a view, as the comparison with Ruskin shows, implies a respect for the past, rather than a rigid adherence to the schemas of classical architecture.

When we consider the second claim, that classical architecture reflects the order of humanity, it is true that it does reflect the civic order of the *polis* or urban community about which Porphyrios cares so deeply; but once again this requires no rigid adherence to classical solutions. The classical model encourages the architect to move from the architecture of buildings to the architecture of the city, without being committed to the actual solutions of a particular historical period; indeed there is often a radical quality in the rationalism of ancient Greece which rejects continuity, and seeks in each generation to replan the city without regard to the sentiment of place or history. The claim that Porphyrios makes for his work is not classical in this sense, but rather in the sense that we should accept the respect of classical architecture for the civic order.

Perhaps we should not be frightened of asserting the ontological status of the classical tradition in some more extreme form; but it seems to me that Porphyrios' recent work makes less absolute claims for the value of one particular architectural language. Instead he seems to prefer an appeal to the *genius loci* and to the significance of tradition in general, as an element which predates the work of the individual architect and offers him a context. It is concern with the spatial context and purpose of buildings which has led him to adopt at Magdalen College, Oxford, a 'vernacular' derived from medieval and nineteenth-century college building, which he sees as particularly appropriate to the collegiate functions of cloistered quiet and staircase community. In this case he has rightly rejected the more obvious course, given his own classical leanings, of following the example of the eighteenth-century New Buildings which, like his own new open quadrangle, face onto garden and deer park, but which seem to deny their function as collegiate buildings in the rigid and rather sterile classicism of a misplaced English country house. Here we see Porphyrios avoiding easy universal solutions in favour of an appeal to an undoctrinaire concept of tradition.

Porphyrios writes as an architect, a creative artist intent on justifying his perception and actual use of tradition. But what fascinates me is that the same words with different illustrations (visual or verbal) might have been written by any practising painter or poet who takes tradition seriously. As a former inmate of the Warburg Institute for the History of the Classical Tradition, I recognise his preoccupations as being those of all of us who try to understand the meaning of Western culture: he is engaged in the same debate as all artists since at least the rediscovery of the classical world. For it is still an open question whether it is the concept of tradition itself which is the key to cultural expression, or whether the art which belongs to the classical tradition has a privileged position, in expressing the resonance, not of a divine order, but of the human condition as it is entrapped in a code of signs – whether that art is built from words or images, or bricks. For, regardless of its appropriateness or inappropriateness in various contexts, classical architecture still belongs to the art of a culture responsible, above all, for that creation of the rational order which is a defining characteristic of Western civilisation: a culture which for over a thousand years from the eighth century BC believed in the necessity of town planning, which practised an architecture responsive to the public order and private activities of the city, and first defined that relationship between public and private space which so concerns Porphyrios today. It was indeed this culture in which the humanist claim of Protagoras was formulated, that 'man is the measure of all things, both of what is that it is, and of what is not that it is not'.

NOTES
1 Michael Baxandall, Patterns of Intention, *Yale University Press, New Haven and London, 1985, pp 58f.*
2 David Jones, In Parenthesis, *from 'Art and Sacrament' in* Epoch and Artist, *Faber, London, 1959, p 167.*

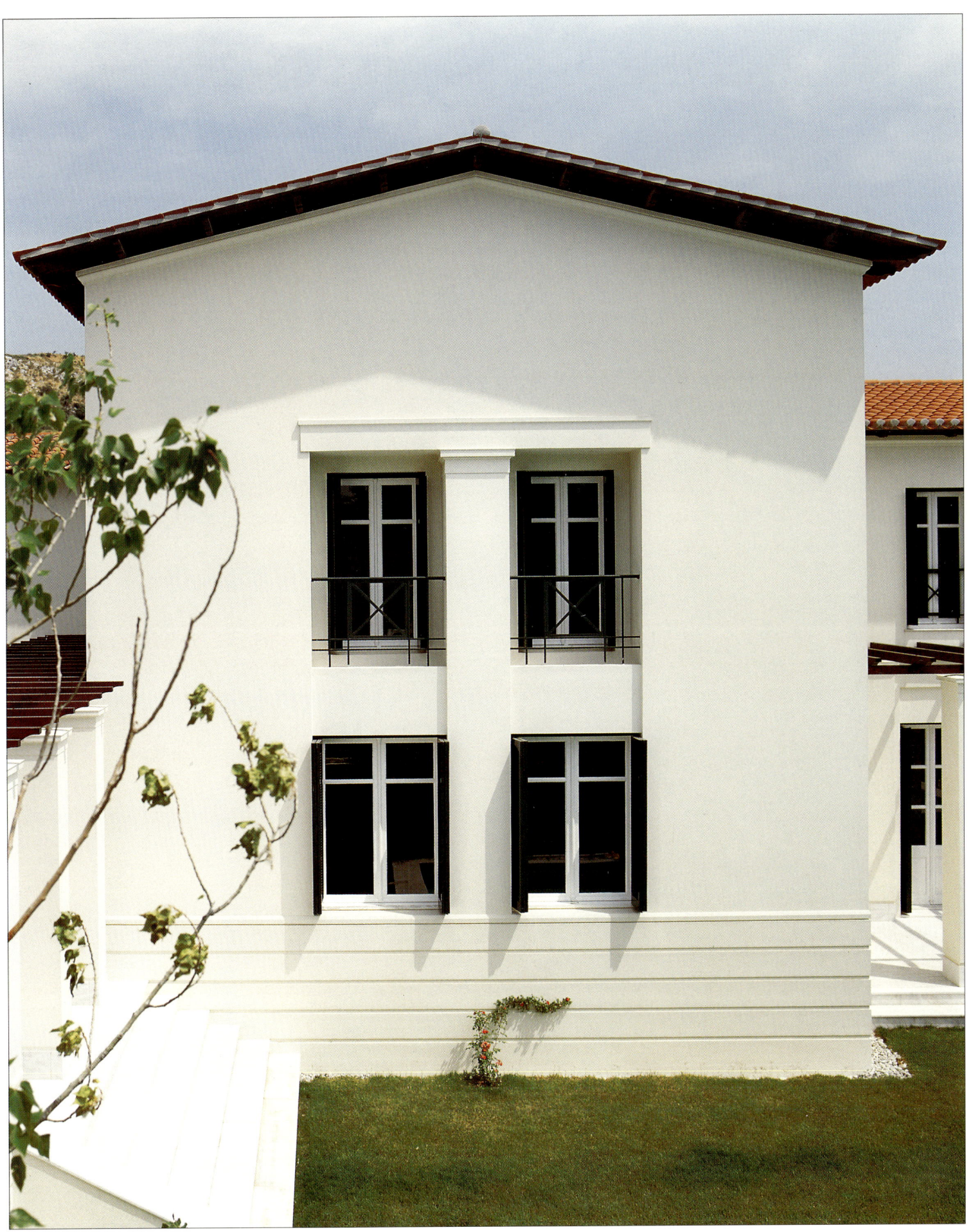

VILLA IN ATHENS, VIEW FROM THE GARDEN

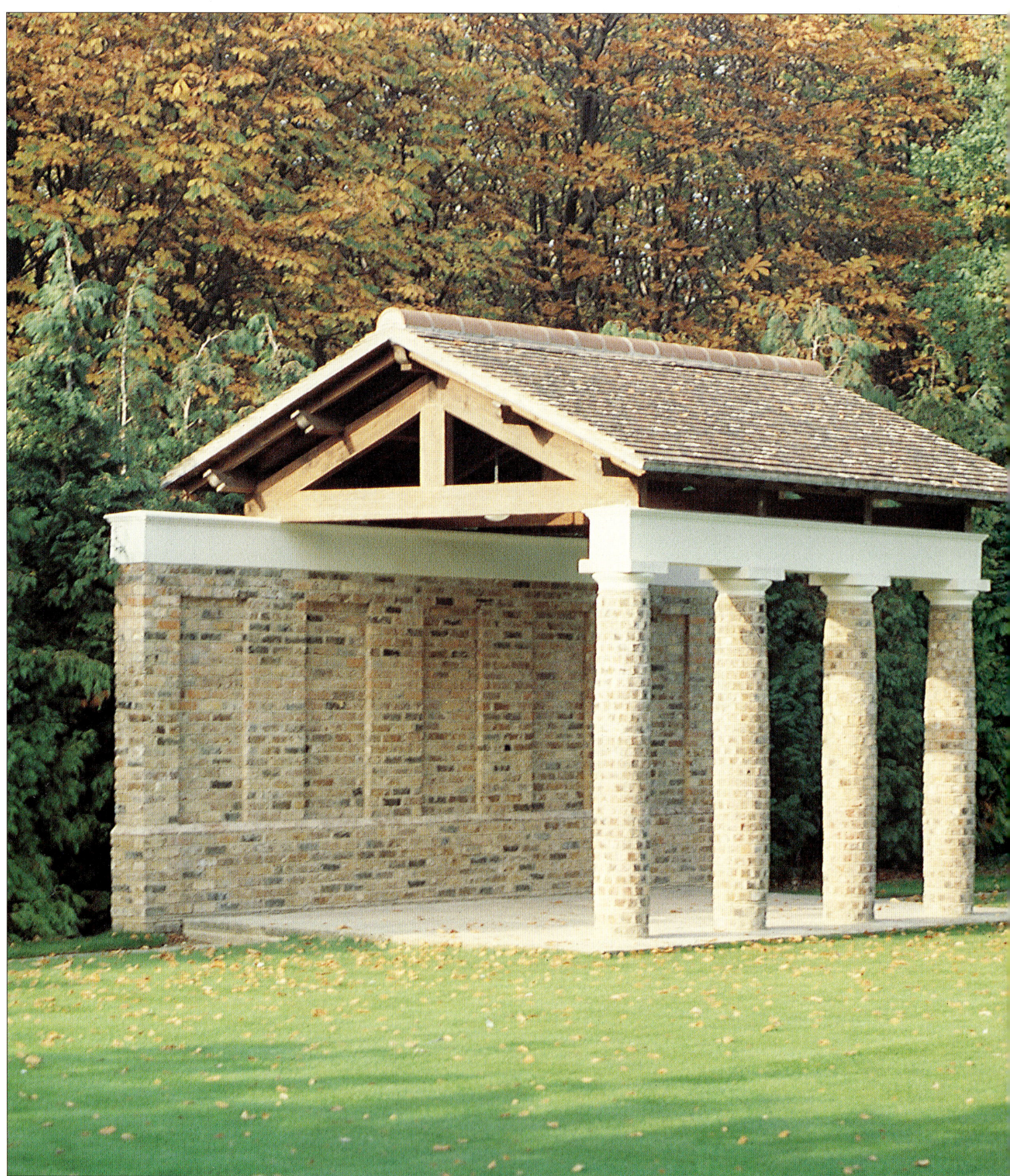

VIEW OF TEA PAVILION

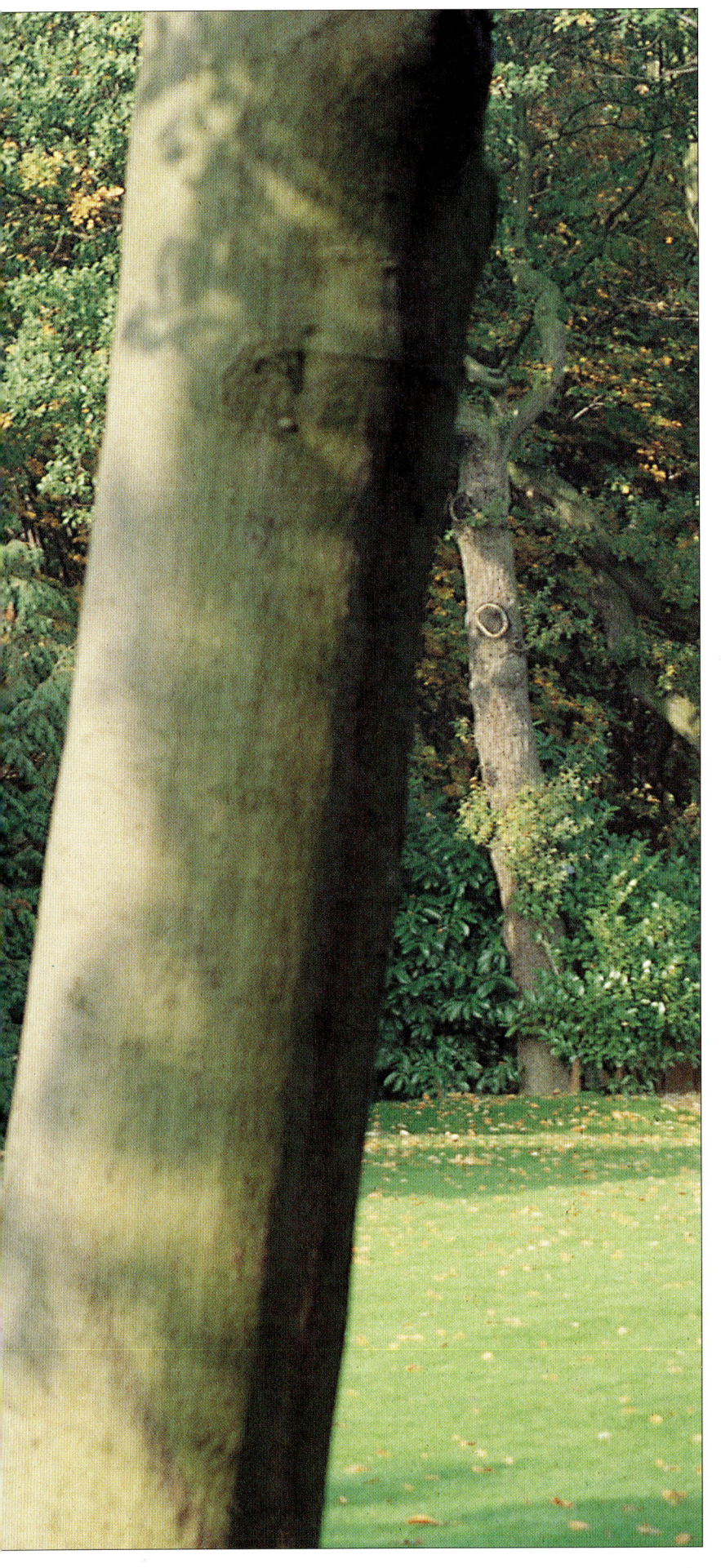

PAVILIONS IN HIGHGATE
LONDON, 1981

Today the question of architecture should be asked not from the point of view of what historical fragments we may borrow from the past but of how to establish an architecture that is common and durable – both physically and symbolically.

This project involved extensive landscape proposals and the erection of a number of free-standing pavilions and entry gates. The topography of the existing estate and the oak trees under conservation ruled out any strict geometric organisation of the site. Instead, all buildings, new and old, are related to one another by means of vistas formed in the landscape. They are sited to be seen in three-quarter perspective views, emphasising the mutual dependence between building and landscape.

The pavilion positioned centrally at the edge of the lawn court derives its composition from the constructional typologies of its elements: the wall, the trabeated colonnade, and the trussed roof. The contrast between its severe trilithic vocabulary and the detailed refinement of its capitals and lintel serves symbolically as a primer of the relationship between building and architecture.

The materials used throughout are second-hand London stocks for the brickwork; York stone for the driveway and the paths; Portland stone for the capitals and wall copings; clay tiles for the roofs, lead sheeting for flashings and tops to pediments; and stained softwood for all exposed timberwork and joinery. All lintels to doors and windows are in second-hand oak. The pavilions are constructed in load bearing brick walls and all profiles generally are formed by bricks cut on site.

Building always speaks of technique and construction. The craft of building and the commodious disposition of shelter are the first guides. Sound building shows the way to typical solutions, the formal characteristics of which acquire over the years a symbolic value: architecture is born.

Architecture commemorates its own origins by assigning symbolic value to all its time-honoured building solutions. In this sense, architecture is neither an arbitrary adornment nor the inevitable causal outcome of building technique. It is the mythic form that man gives to his building craft. Architecture makes us see the building craft from which it is born, from which it detaches itself as art, and to which it always alludes.

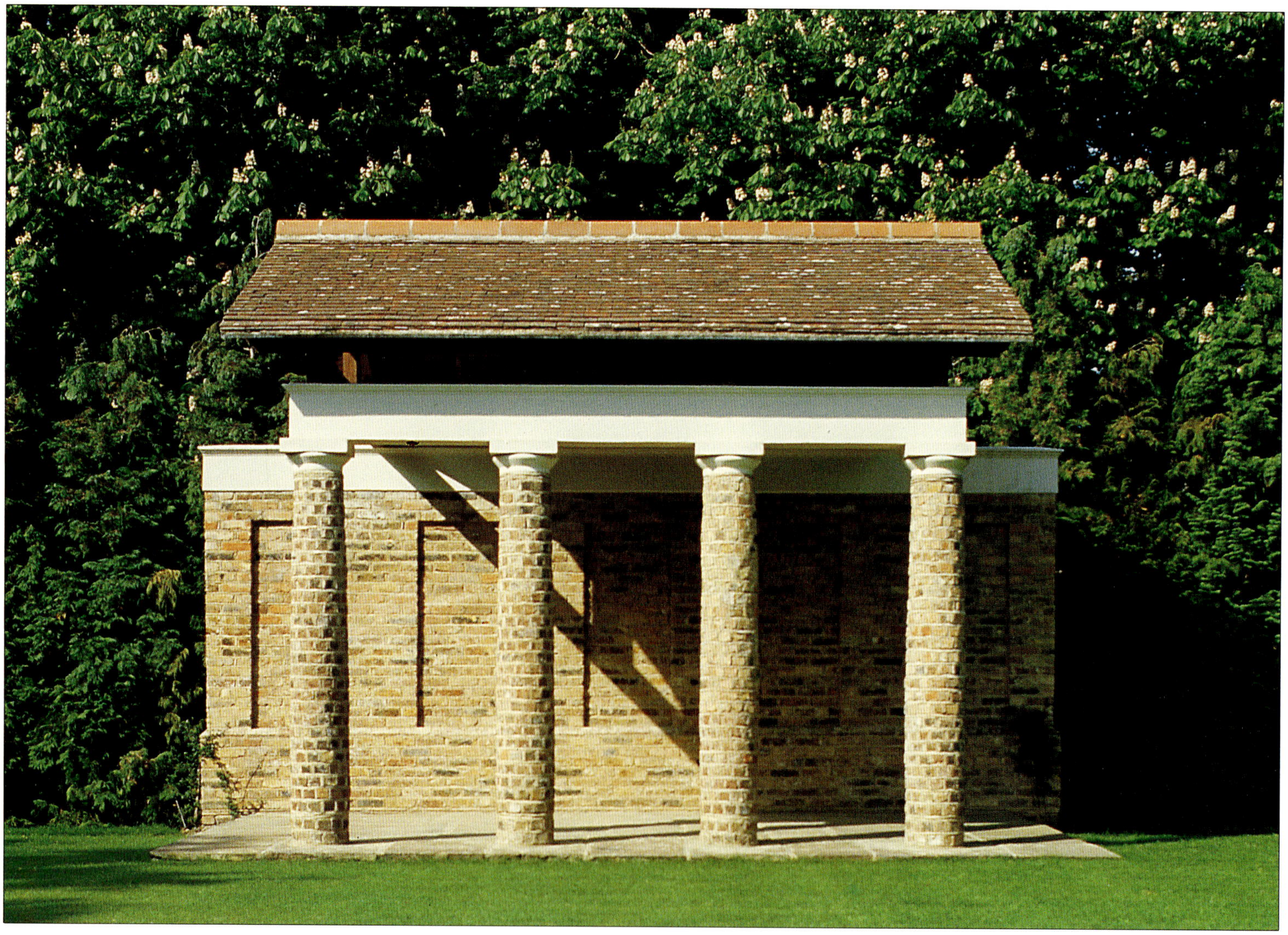

DEMETRI PORPHYRIOS

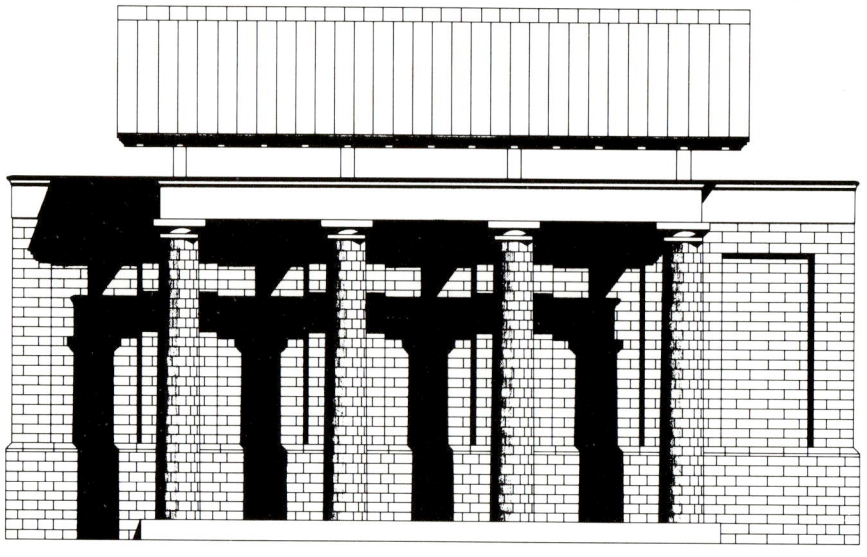

ELEVATION AND VIEW OF TEA PAVILION

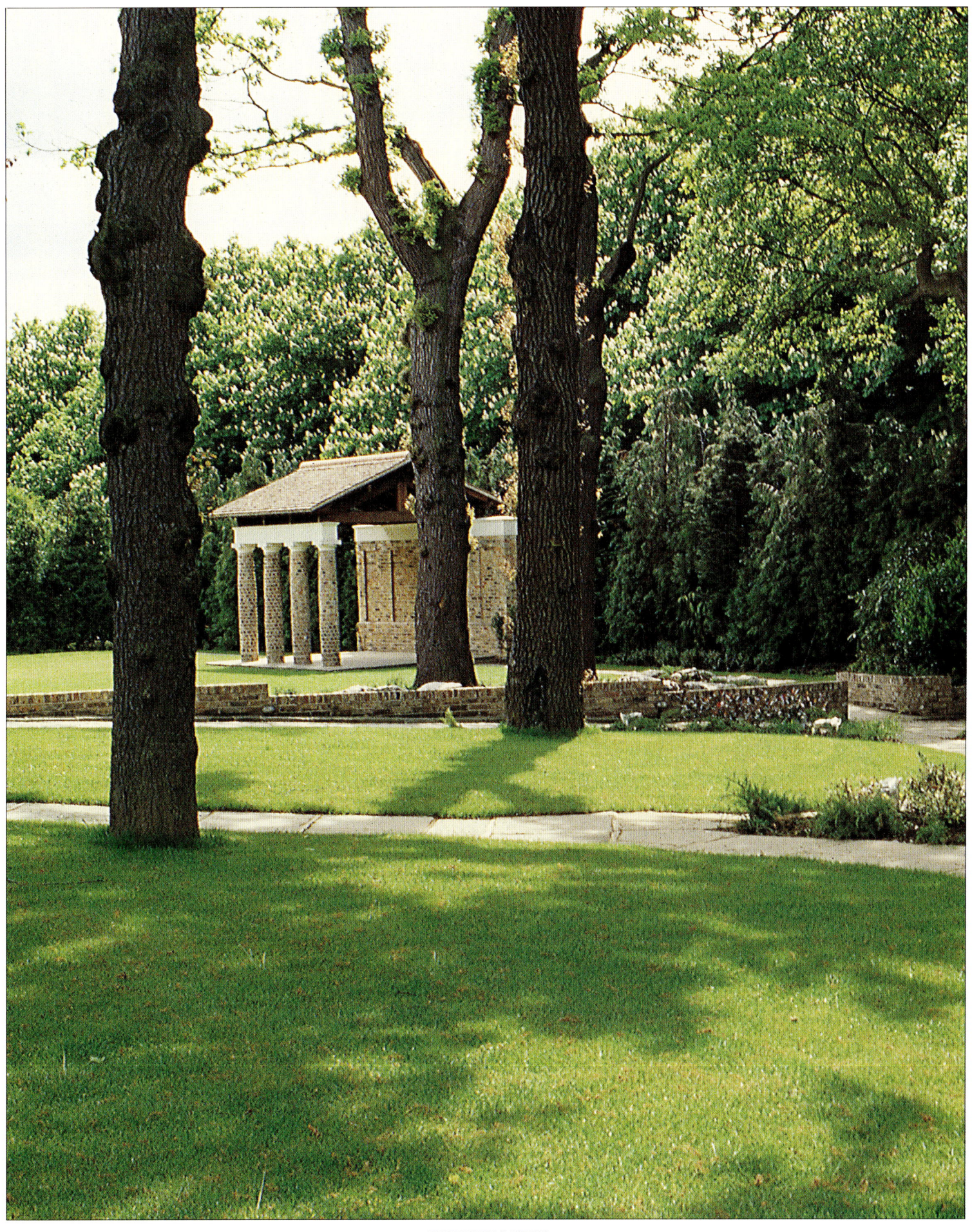

VIEW OF THE GARDENS

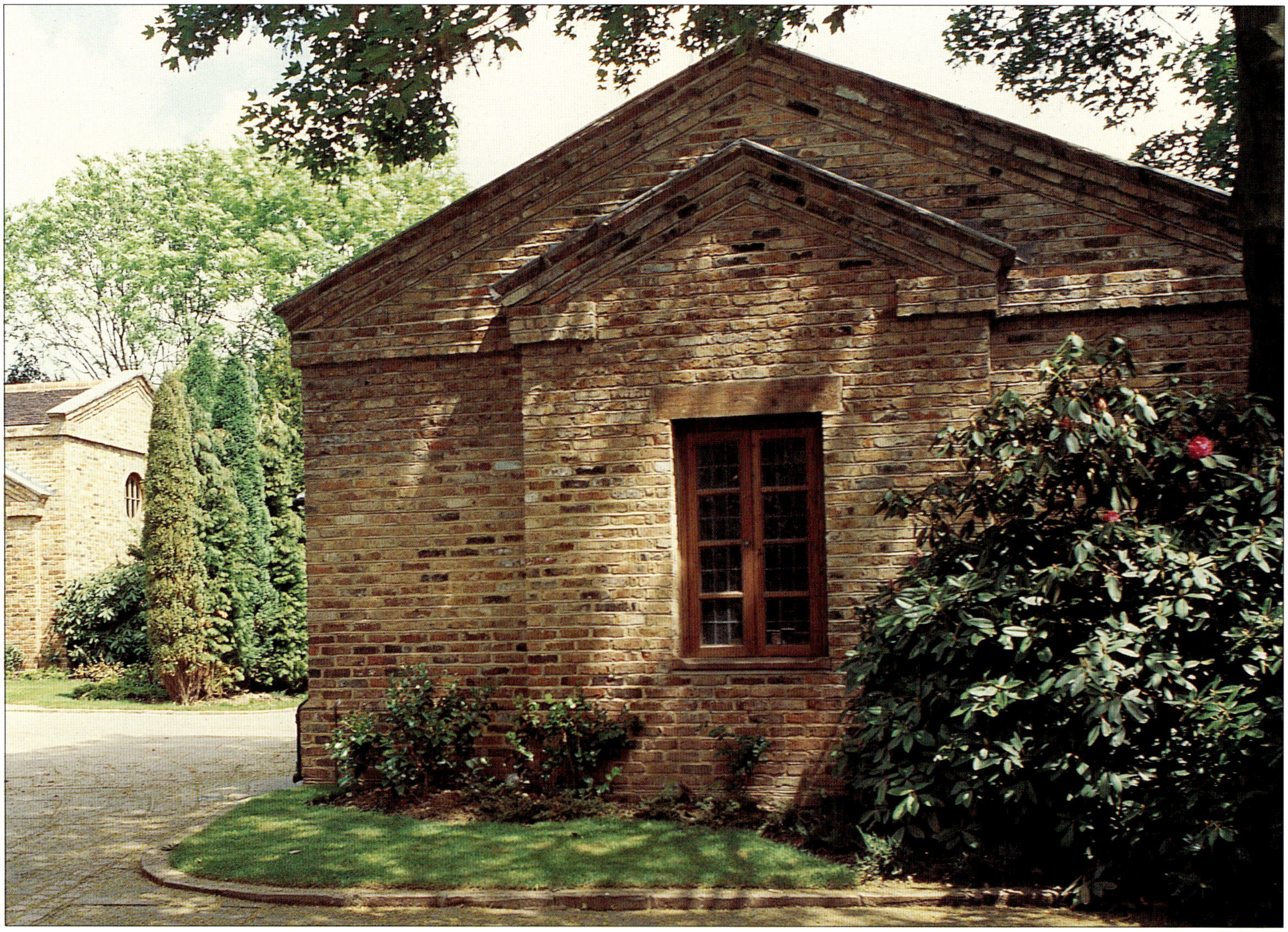

DEMETRI PORPHYRIOS

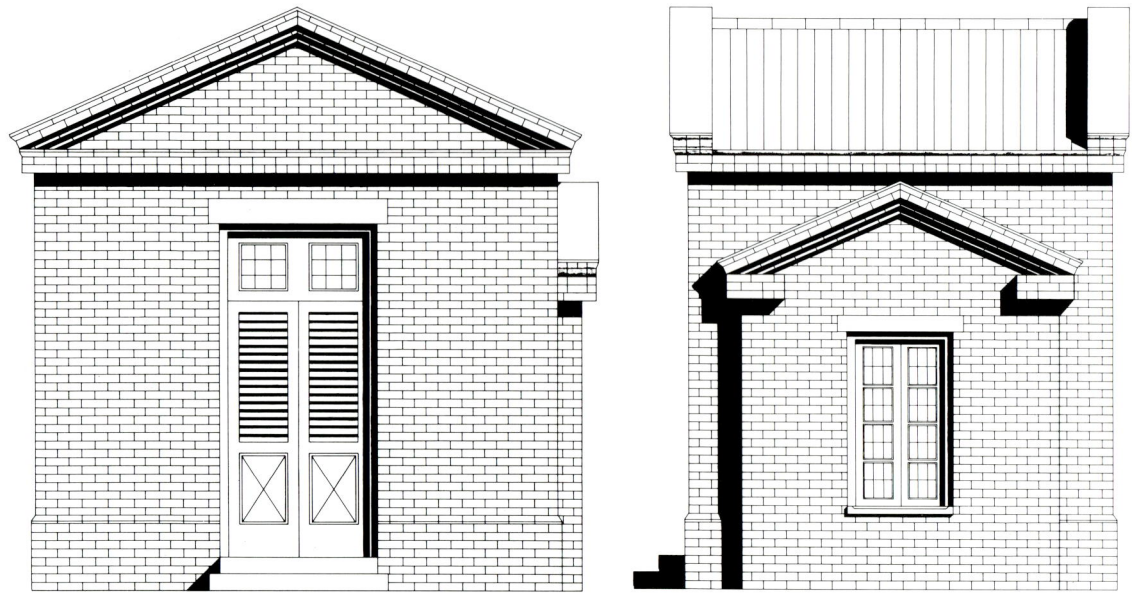

ELEVATIONS AND VIEW OF GARDENER'S PAVILION WITH LODGE IN THE FOREGROUND

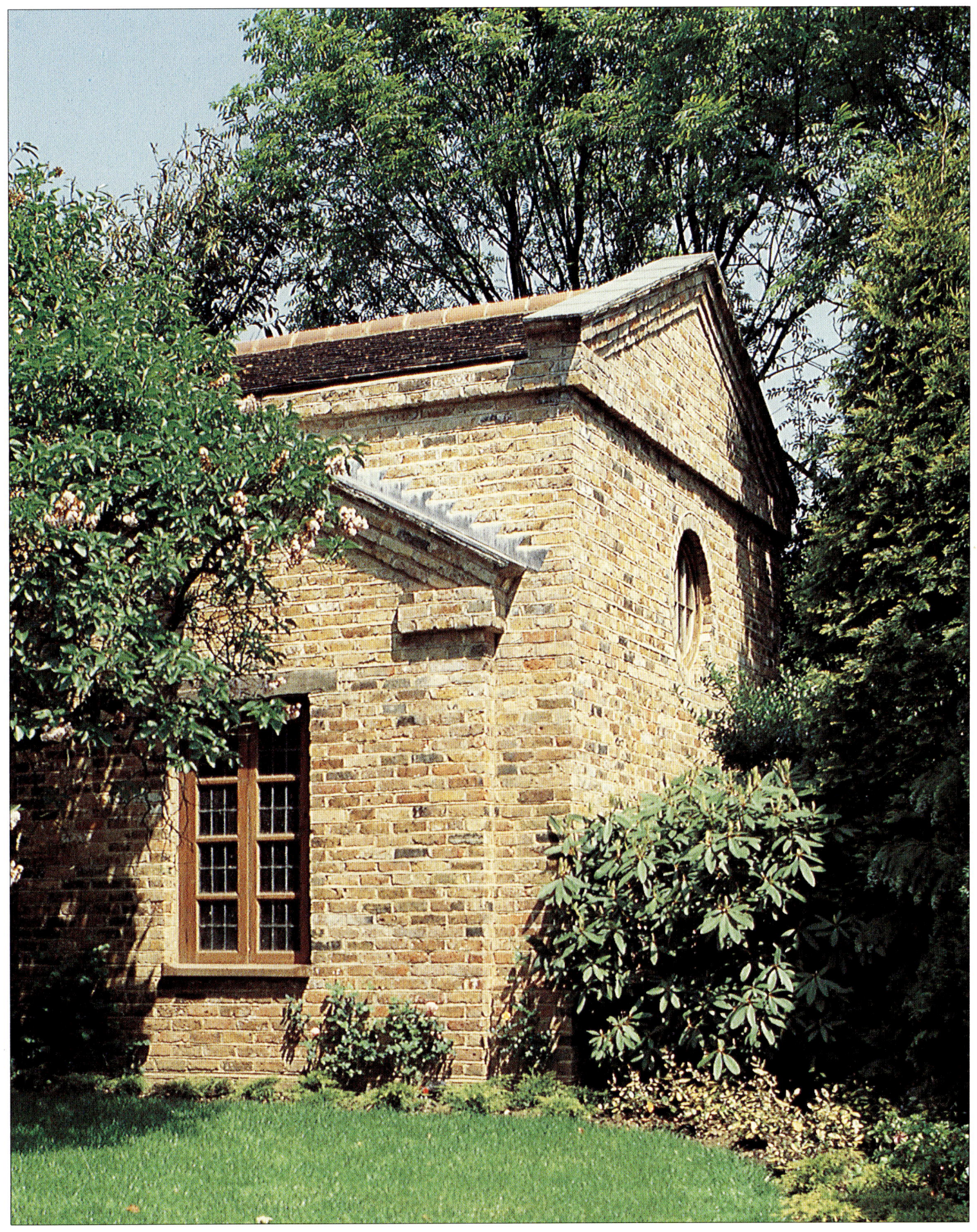

VIEW OF GARDENER'S PAVILION

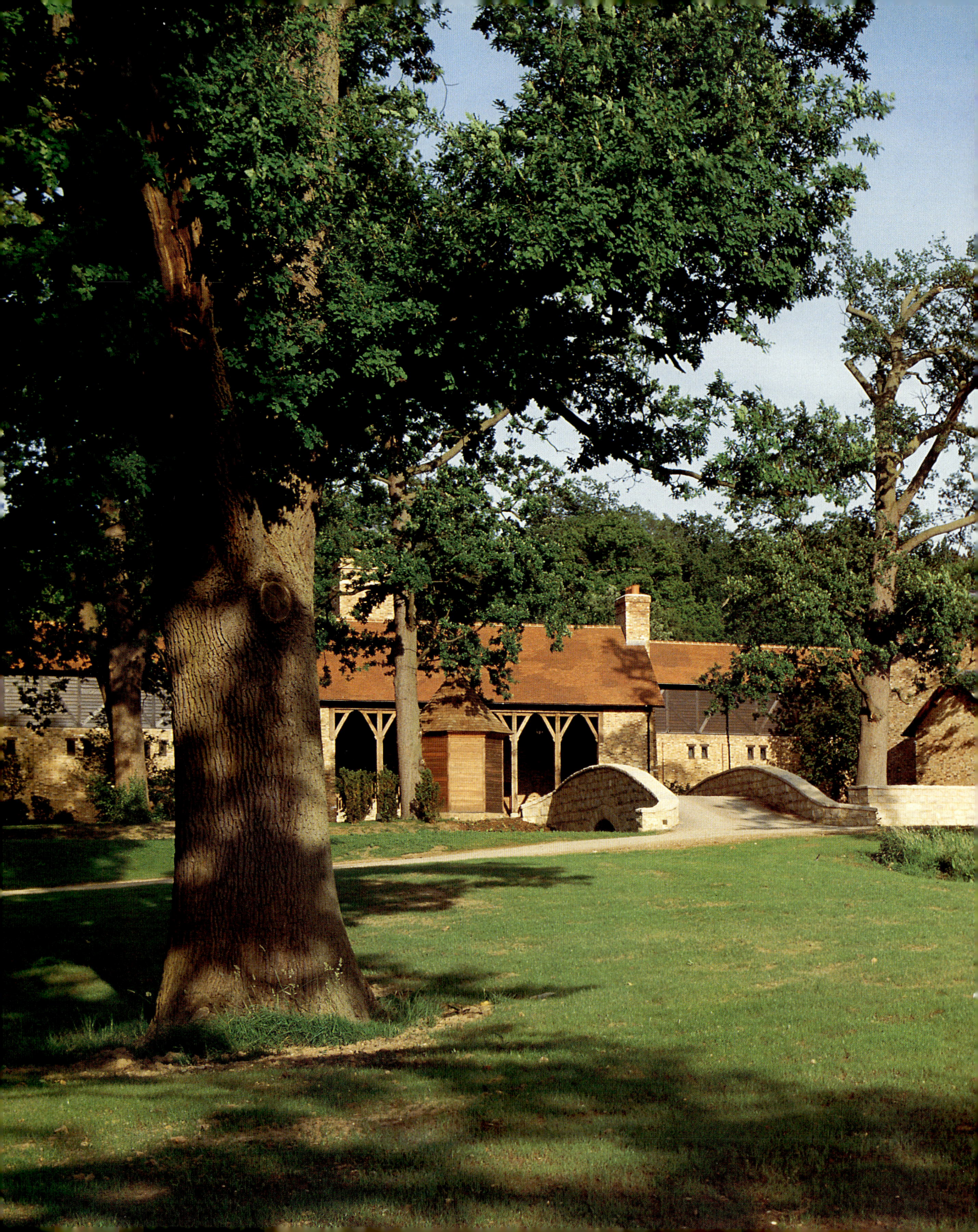

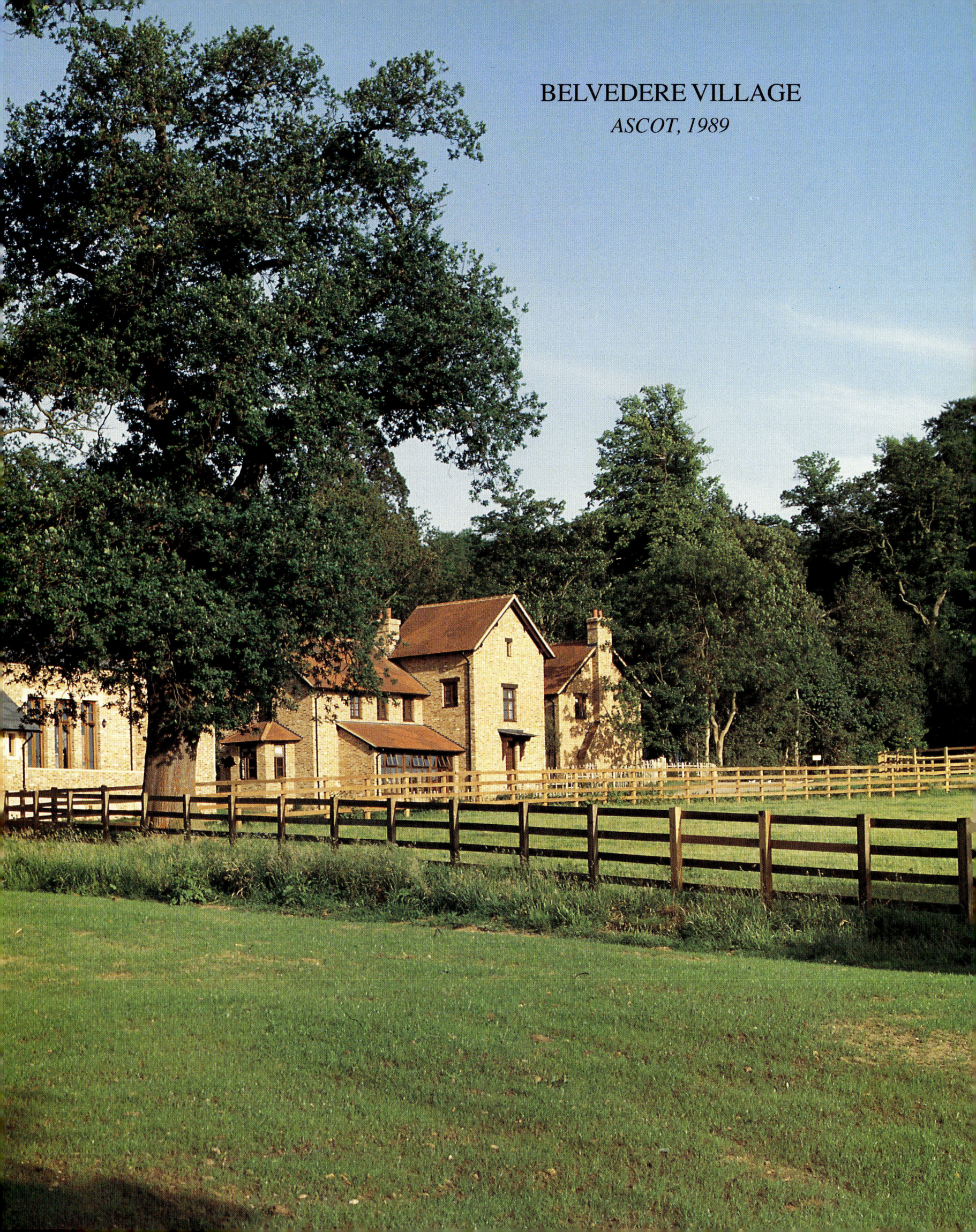

BELVEDERE VILLAGE
ASCOT, 1989

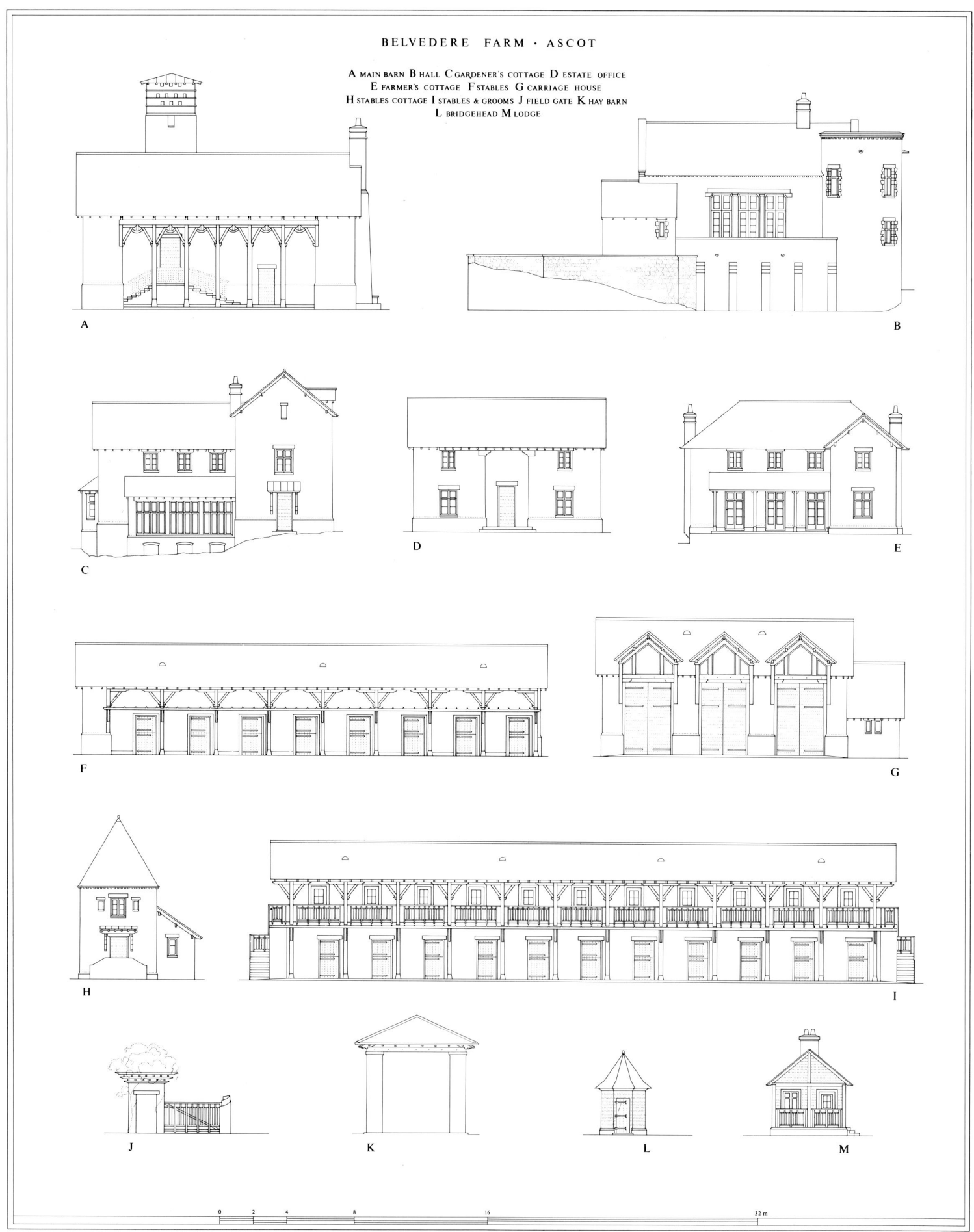

*Nowadays
we have become accustomed to the idea that our buildings and towns express the 'spirit of the age'.
But architecture has grown up with man, not merely with the circumstances of an age.
Our buildings and towns are not the monopoly of one particular period
but arise with man and endure with human nature. Consider the beauty of the English village. It is
wedded to the countryside and to the simplicity of straightforward construction.
Its buildings are pleasurable and at the same time convey a sense of the necessary by
remaining close up to nature for inspiration.*

*This project comprises a number of cottages, farm buildings and stables. It is set in a beautiful
Surrey landscape close to Ascot. This is a village that unfolds around three main spaces: the
farm court, the residential court and the stable yard. These courts provide spatial unity and
containment for the various aspects of the brief. They are of dissimilar type and scale but they
connect to form a chain of interrelated spaces. The buildings around them are in a constant
dialogue with each other so that, together with the landscape, they create a sense of place
establishing open vistas, perspective views or dramatic closures.*

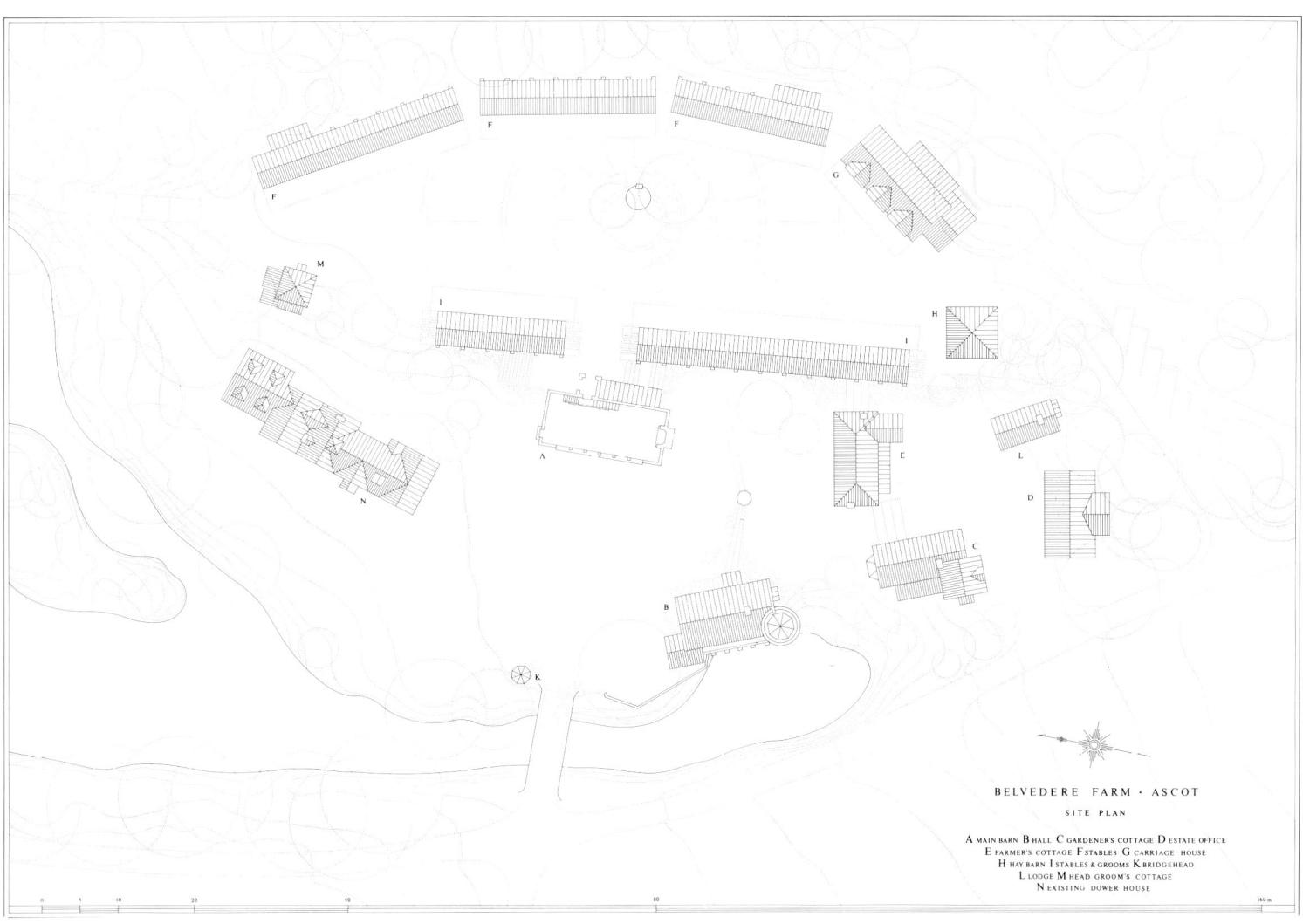

BELVEDERE FARM · ASCOT
SITE PLAN

A MAIN BARN B HALL C GARDENER'S COTTAGE D ESTATE OFFICE
E FARMER'S COTTAGE F STABLES G CARRIAGE HOUSE
H HAY BARN I STABLES & GROOMS K BRIDGEHEAD
L LODGE M HEAD GROOM'S COTTAGE
N EXISTING DOWER HOUSE

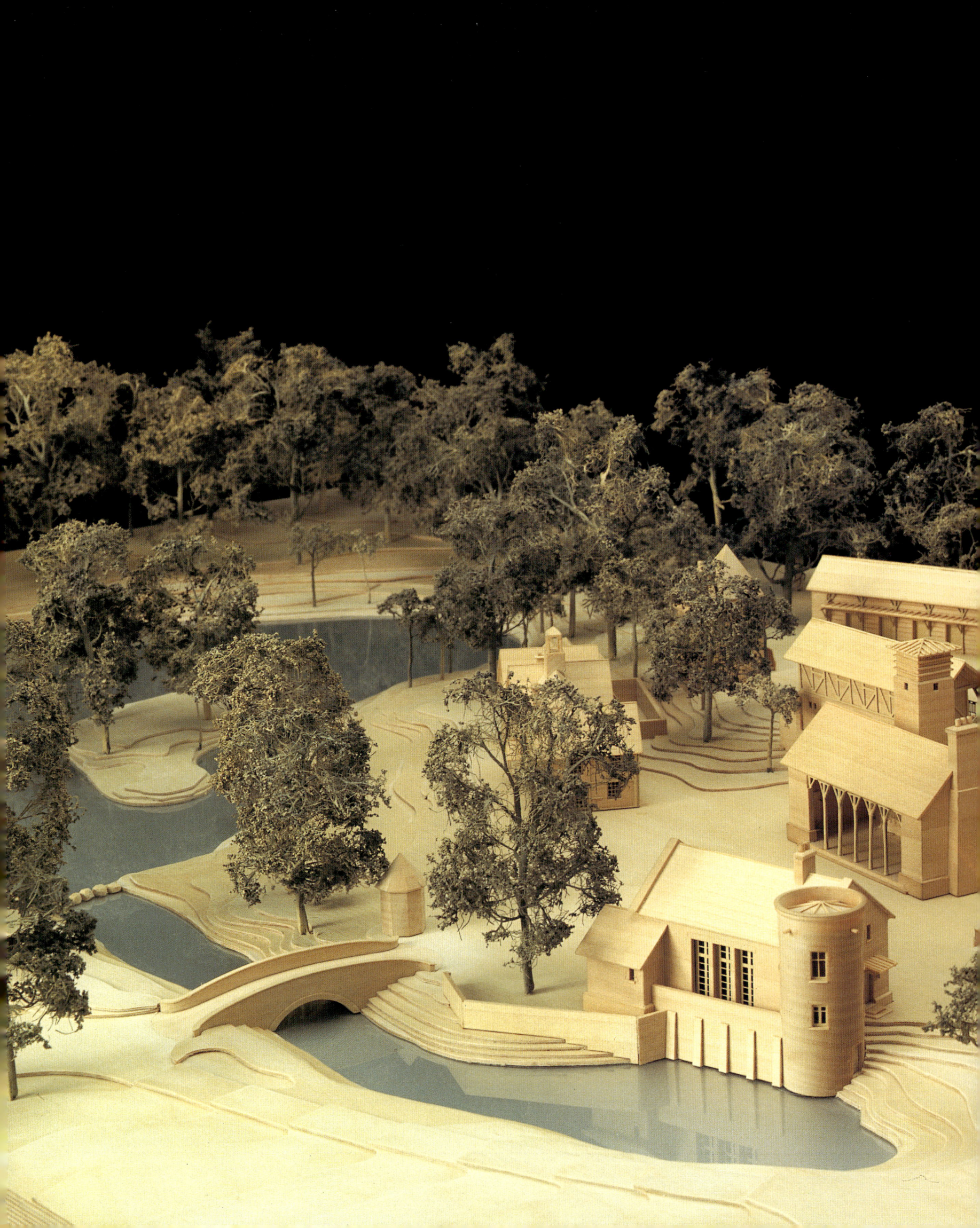

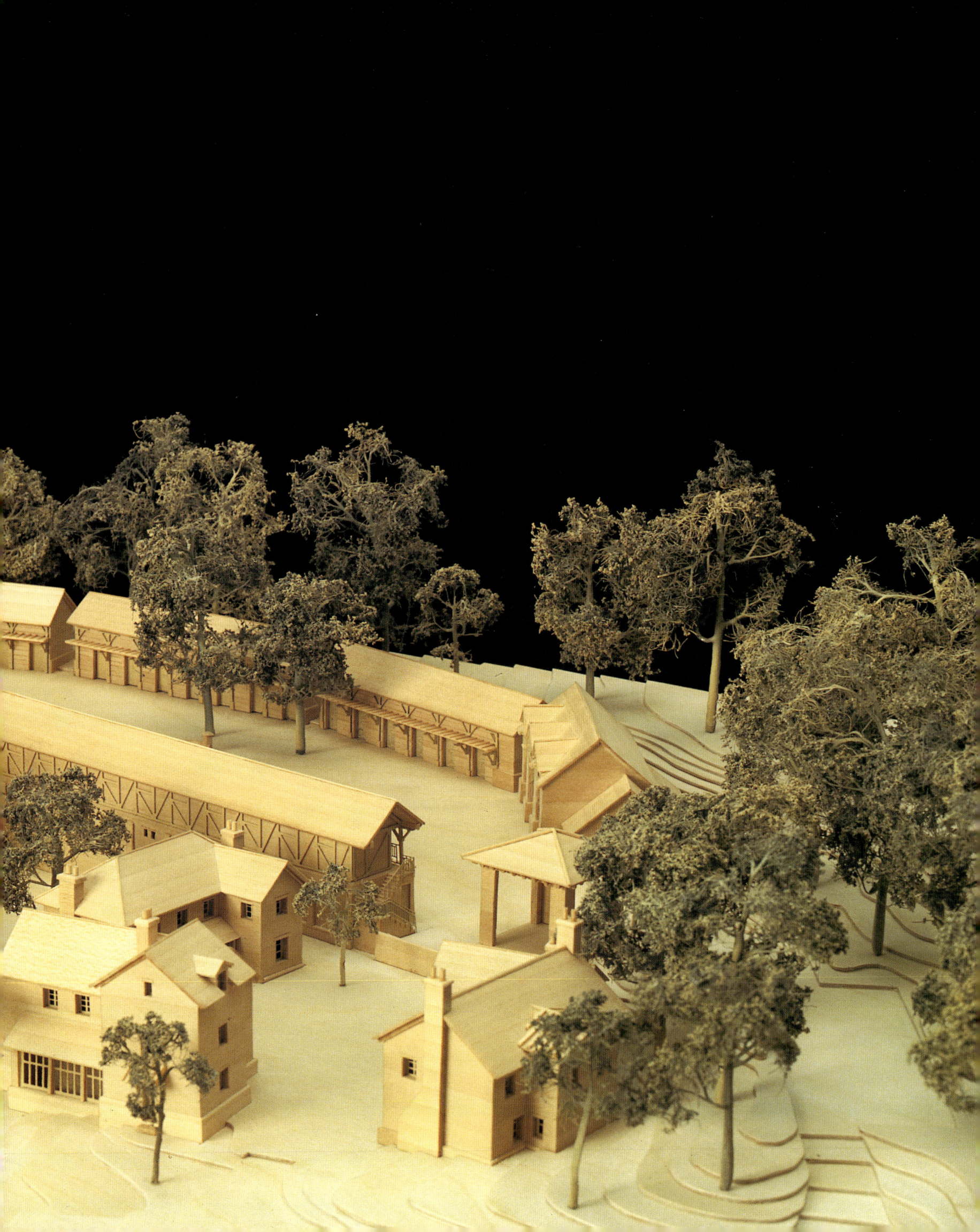

MAIN BARN AND HALL

We have extended the existing pond to form a boundary that separates the Farm Court from the lane and the land beyond. The court is reached across a new stone bridge that springs from an ancient crossroads and gently arches between the mature oaks to a timber bridgehead.

Facing the bridgehead is the Main Barn with its line of timber posts sitting on York stone bases. The barn, with its great oak roof and monumental fireplace is an open structure intended for a variety of public functions. A dovecote tower marks the urban ensemble of the whole village and shows the way to the route up towards the stable court.

Opposite the barn and overlooking the pond stands the Hall. Raised on a plinth above the court and supported by buttressed walls to the west, the Hall displays its hierarchical importance not by size but by the refinement of its details and materials. The building is organised in an additive manner around a central hall. Its oak roof and fireplace are variations on the theme encountered in the Main Barn and from the balcony overlooking the pond distant views of the open landscape can be enjoyed.

The Farm Court is bounded by these two buildings together with the Farmer's Cottage and Stables as well as the existing fifteenth-century Dower House. It has the urbanity of a village square and at its centre there is an ancient well which, together with the subtle change of levels and the newly planted lime trees, provides a focus to the court and gives it an intimate scale.

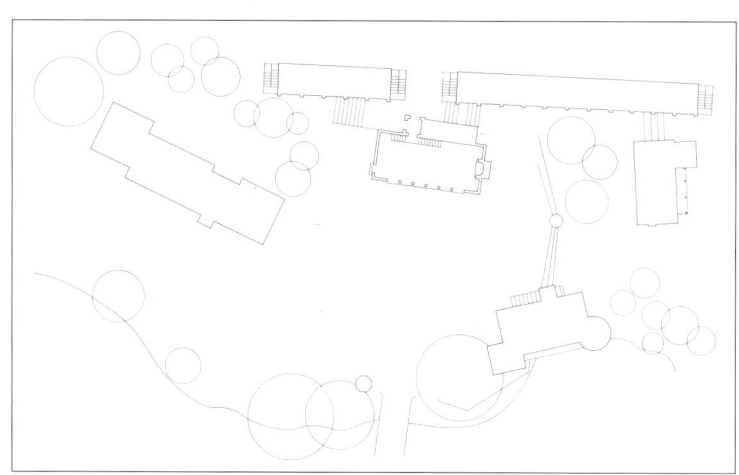

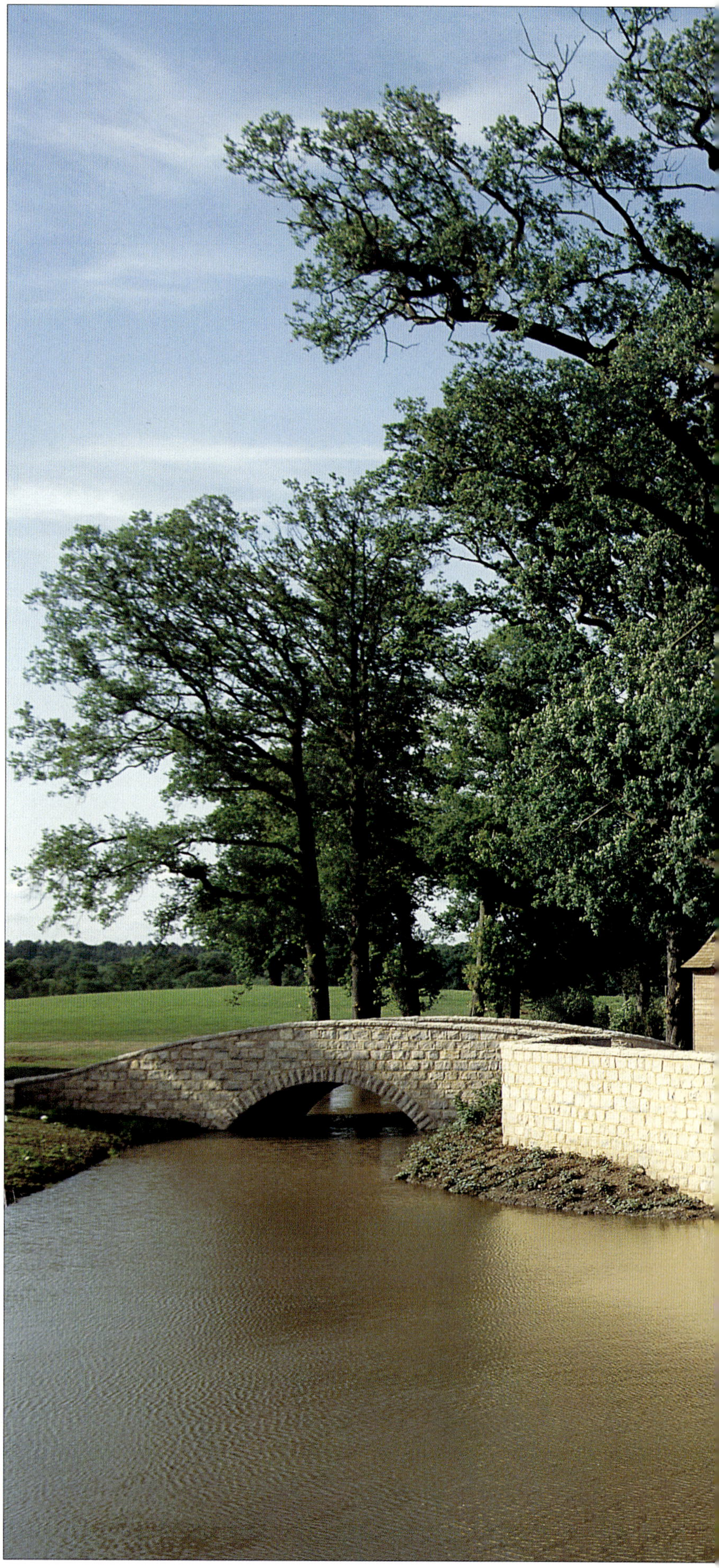

SITE PLAN AND VIEW OF MAIN BARN AND HALL

MAIN BARN AND HALL

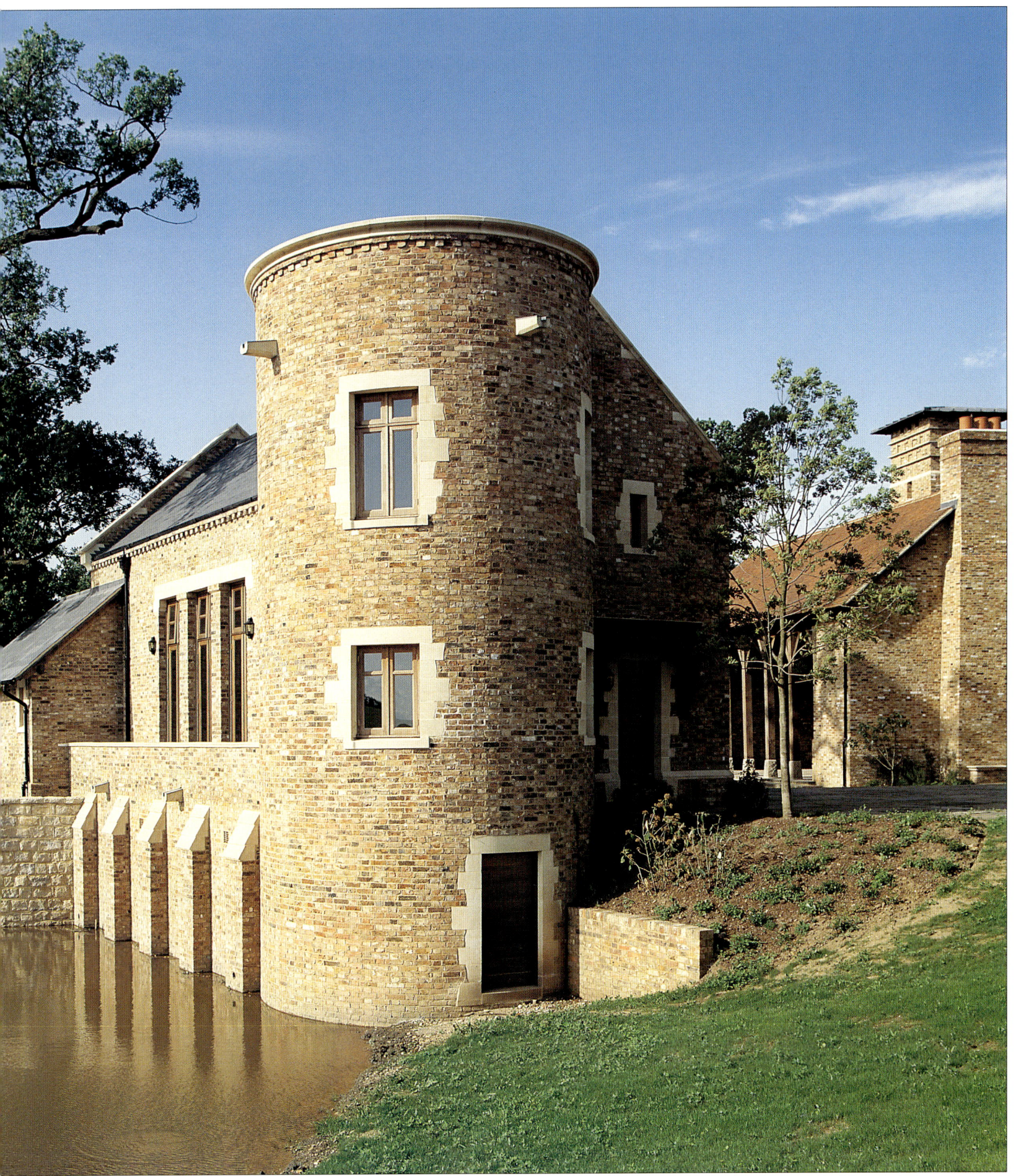

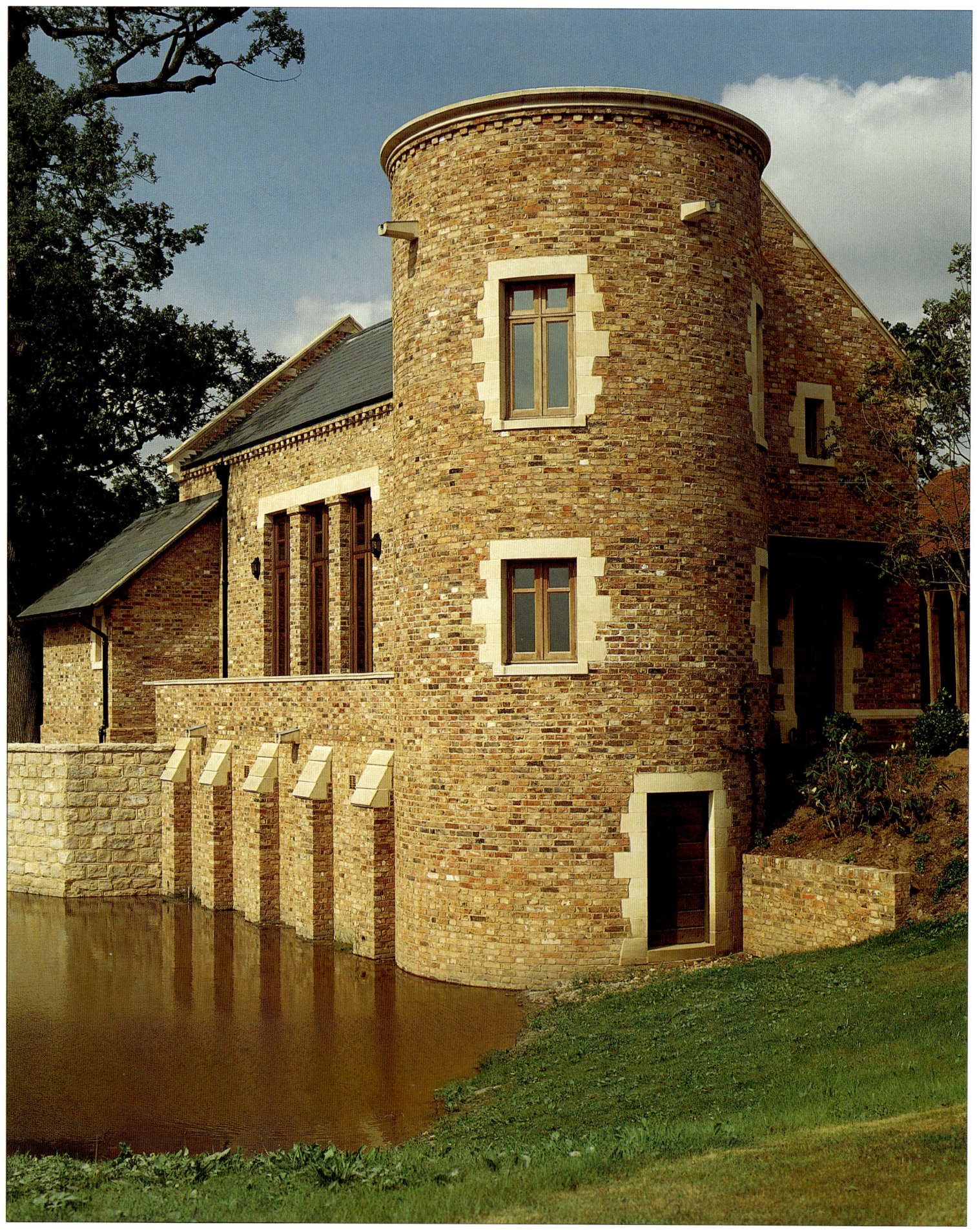

VIEW OF THE HALL FROM THE SOUTH-WEST

MAIN BARN AND HALL

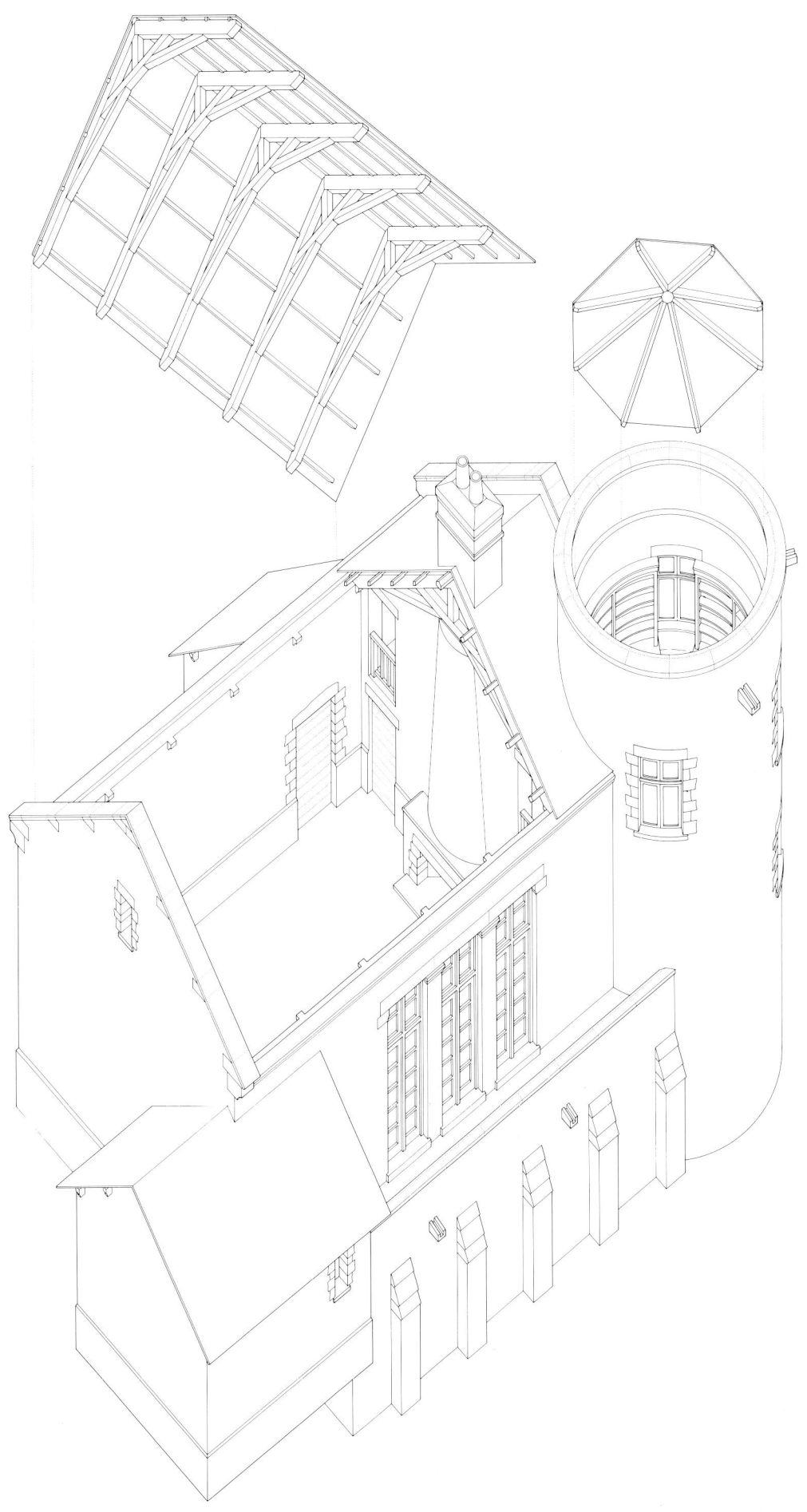

AXONOMETRIC OF THE HALL

DEMETRI PORPHYRIOS

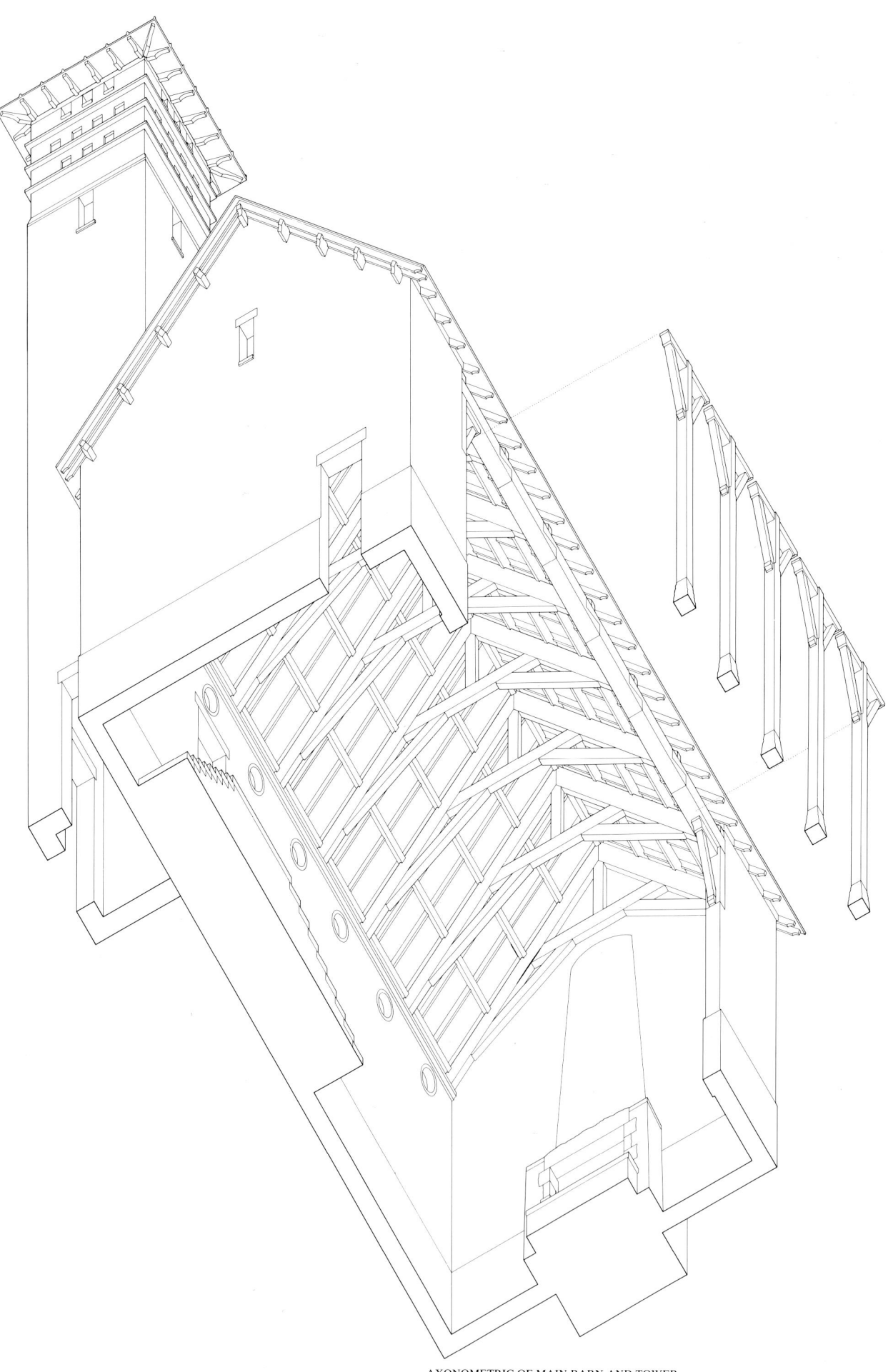

AXONOMETRIC OF MAIN BARN AND TOWER

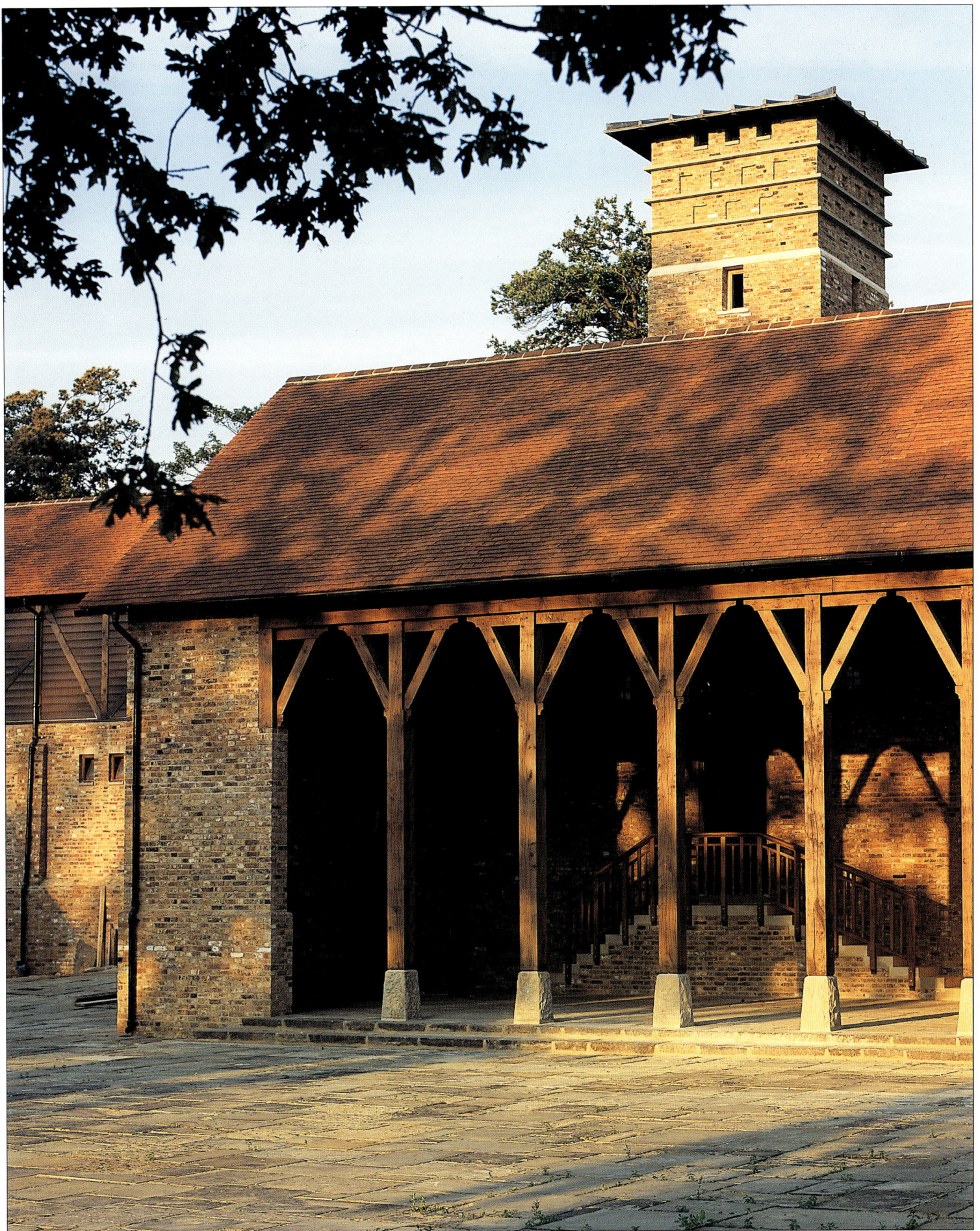

VIEW OF MAIN BARN AND TOWER

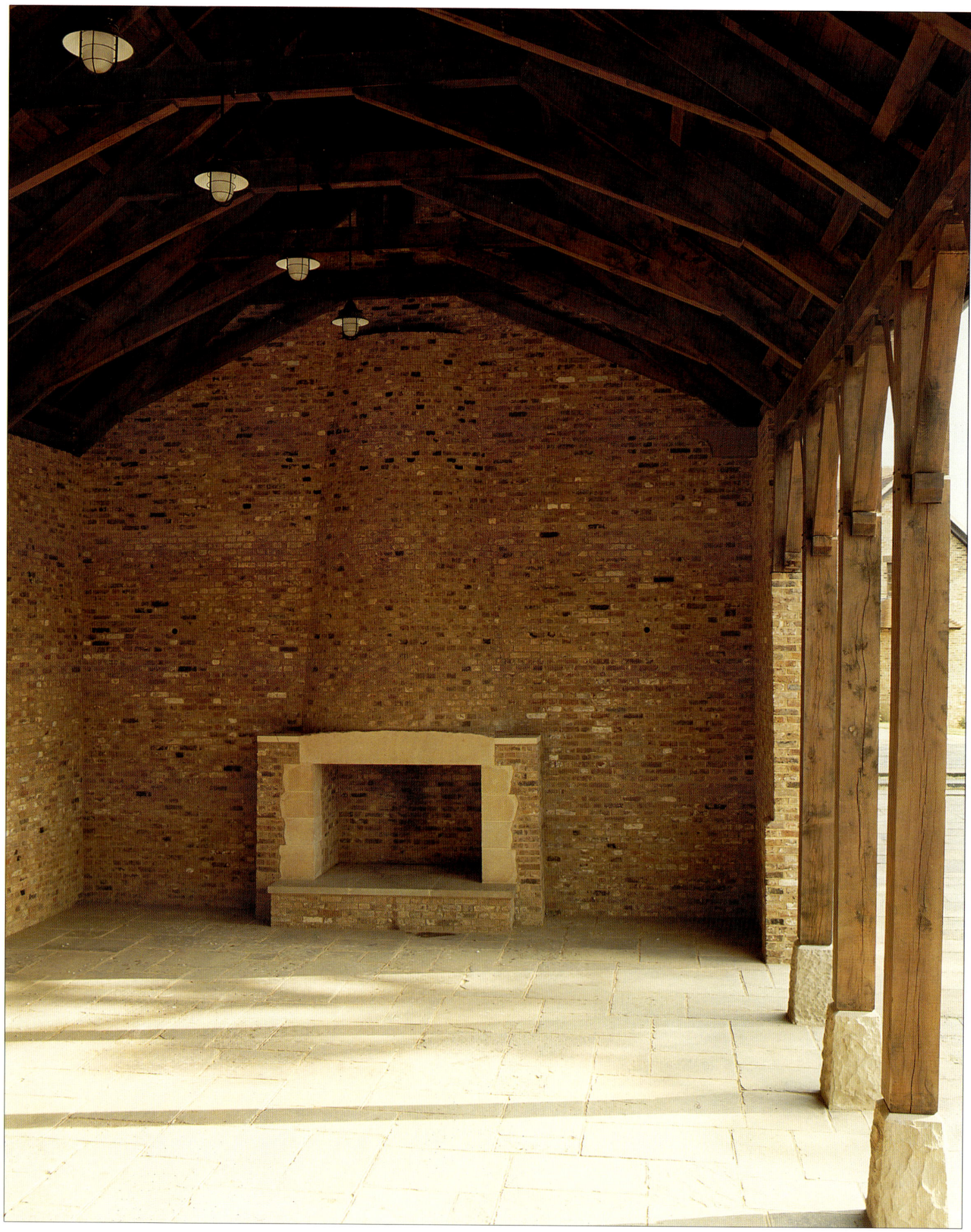

INTERIOR VIEW OF MAIN BARN

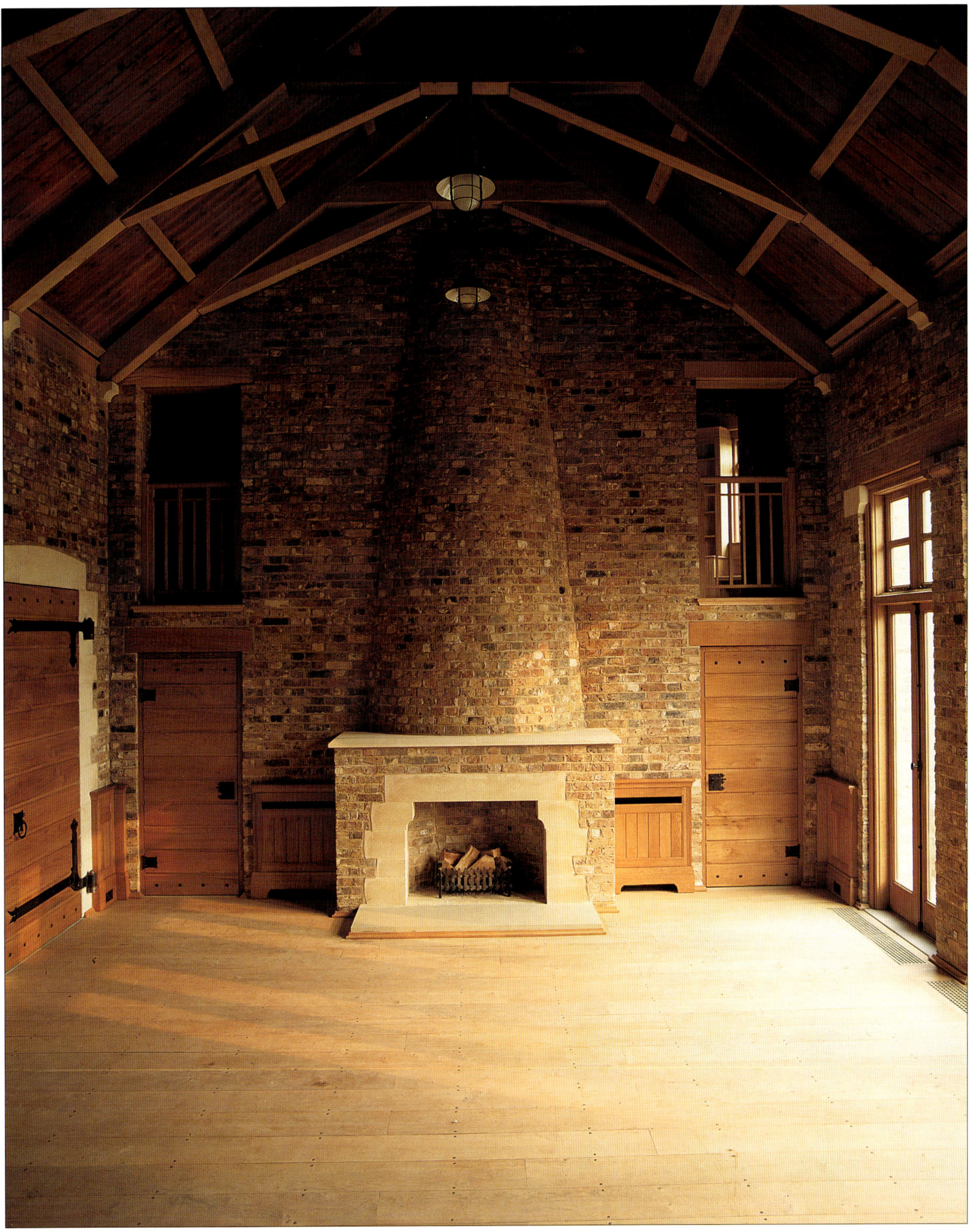

INTERIOR VIEW OF THE HALL

HOUSES AND COTTAGES

A number of cottages together with the estate office are grouped to form the Residential Court. This is connected to the Farm Court by two short flights of steps and it is entered also directly from the lane. The emphasis here is on the informal nature of villages. The different cottages are related in scale and materials while their grouping emphasises the spatial enclosure of the court.

The Estate Office has a double height recessed entrance that is made visible from the Farm Court so as to emphasise its relative importance within the residential court. Between the Farmer's Cottage and the stable block a vista opens up towards the dovecote tower. A slight disalignment between the Main Barn and the stable block helps accentuate the perspective view while modelling the tower in the round.

The Farmer's and Gardener's Cottages as well as the Estate Office are all constructed in a mixture of second-hand red Surrey and yellow London bricks with tiled roofs. The eaves and joinery details are generally similar throughout, although each cottage is given its individual character by the configuration of the plan and its overall massing based on the requirements of the brief. The cottages have an additive character that allows considerable flexibility in their organisation. Indeed during construction many modifications were made to suit the changing requirements of the brief. The Lodge, by contrast, is a single-storey timber structure set into the forested land and its raised porch inflects towards a passage that leads to the stable yard.

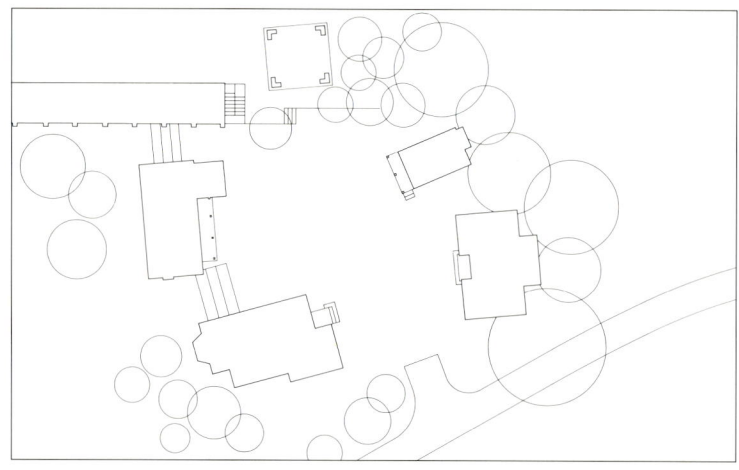

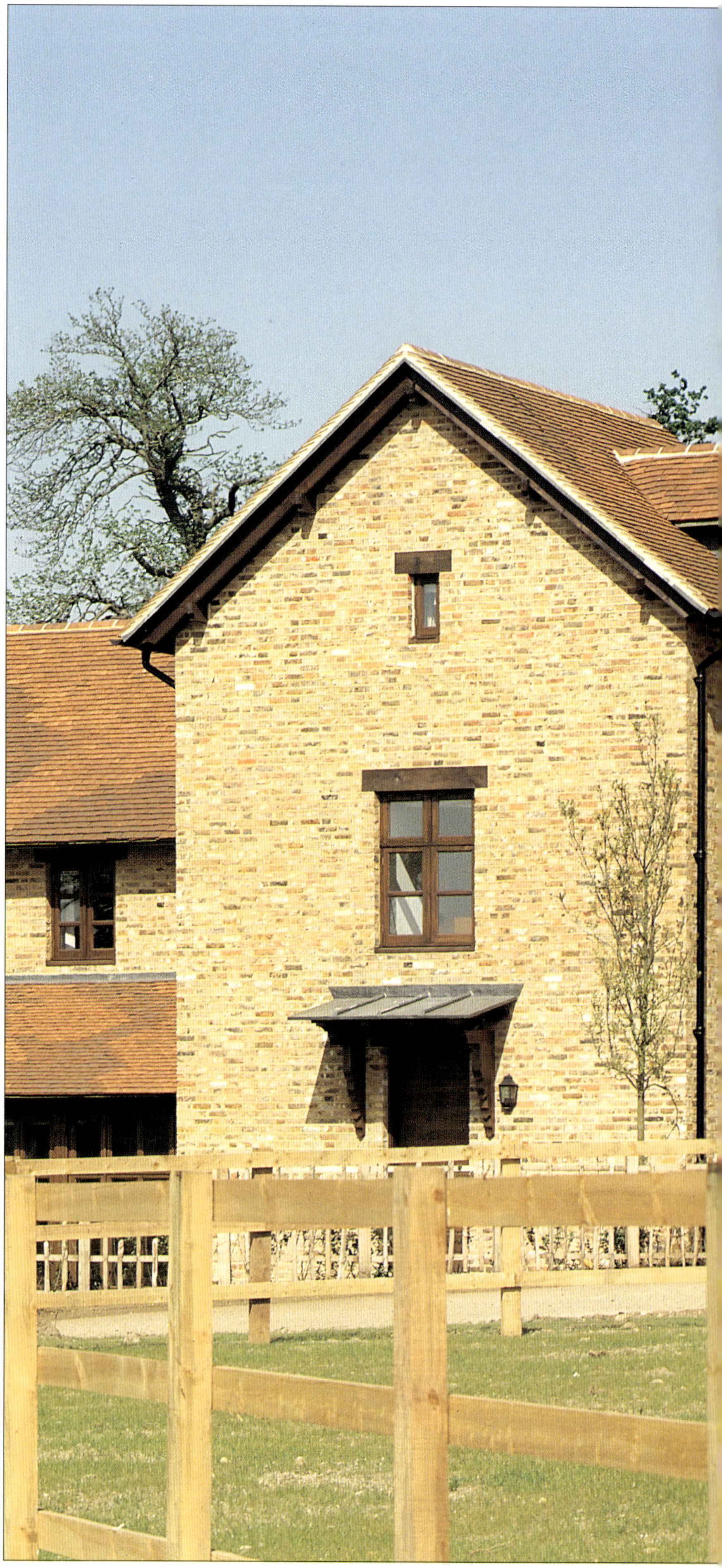

SITE PLAN AND VIEW OF THE RESIDENTIAL COURT

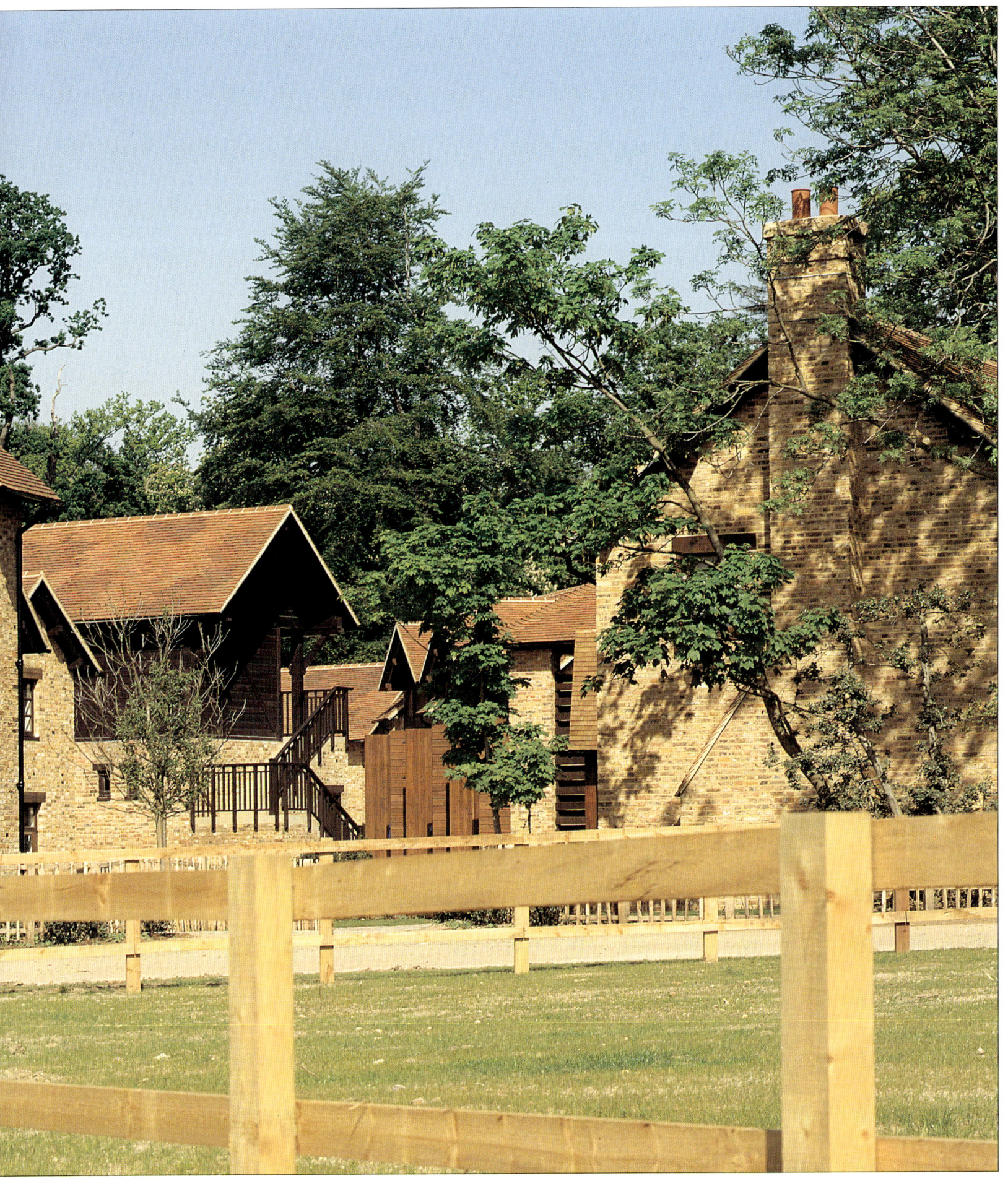

DEMETRI PORPHYRIOS

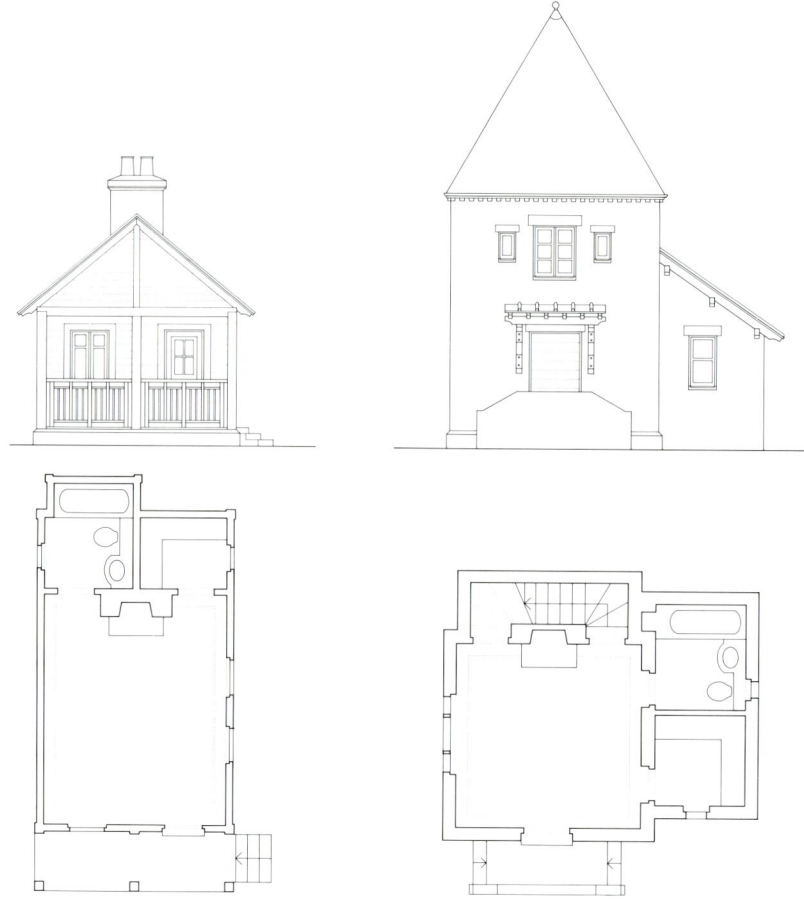

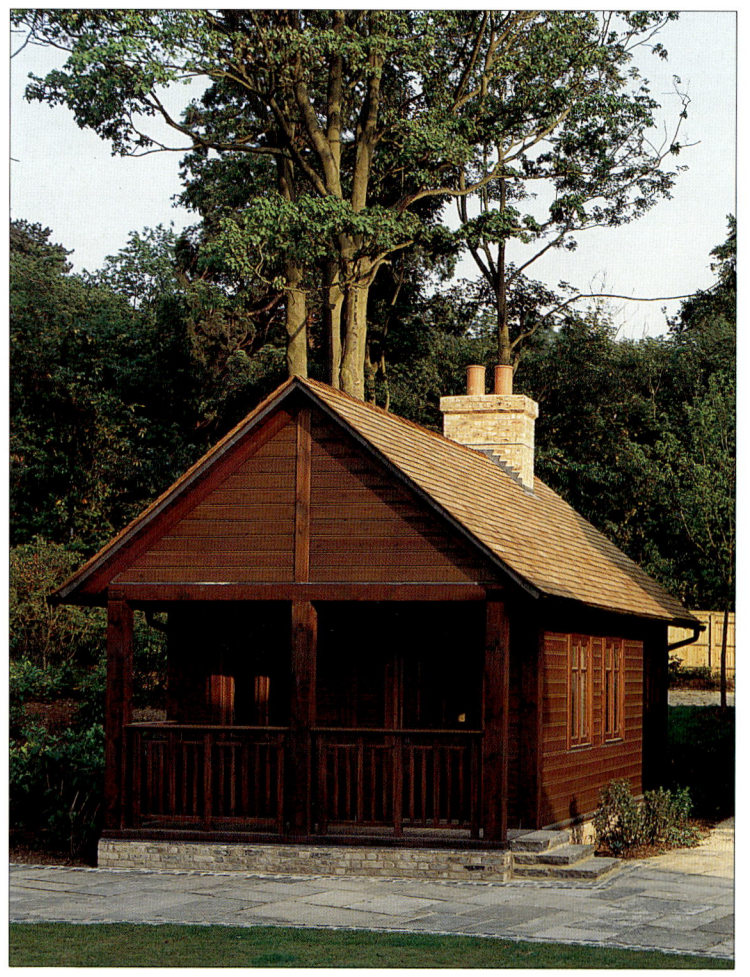
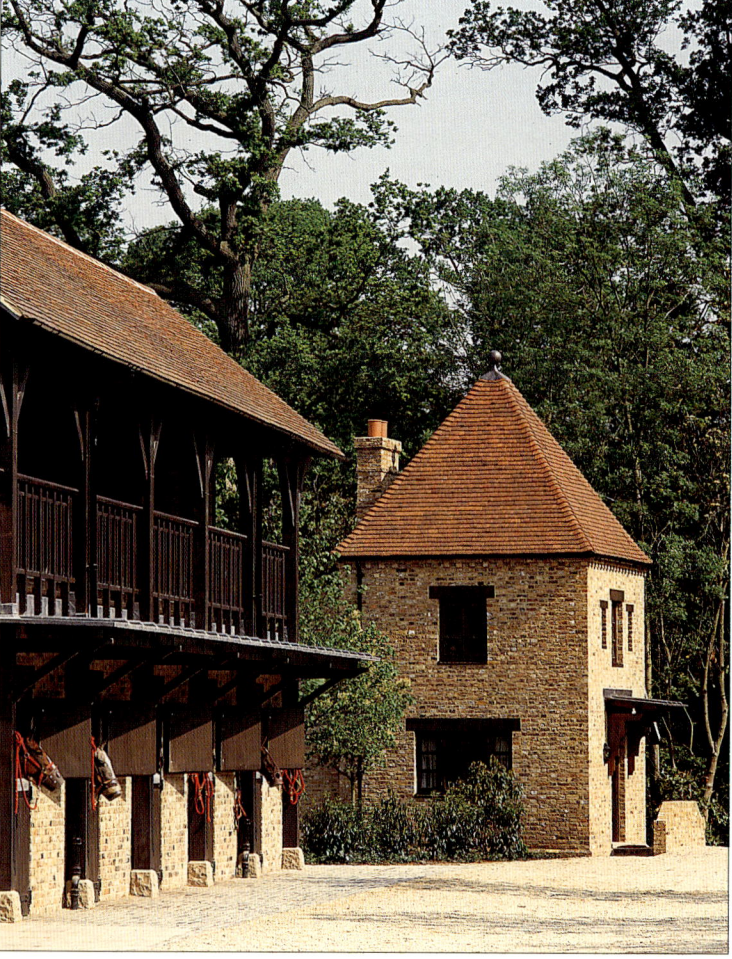

PLANS AND ELEVATIONS (ABOVE) AND VIEWS (BELOW) OF LODGE AND HEAD GROOM'S COTTAGE

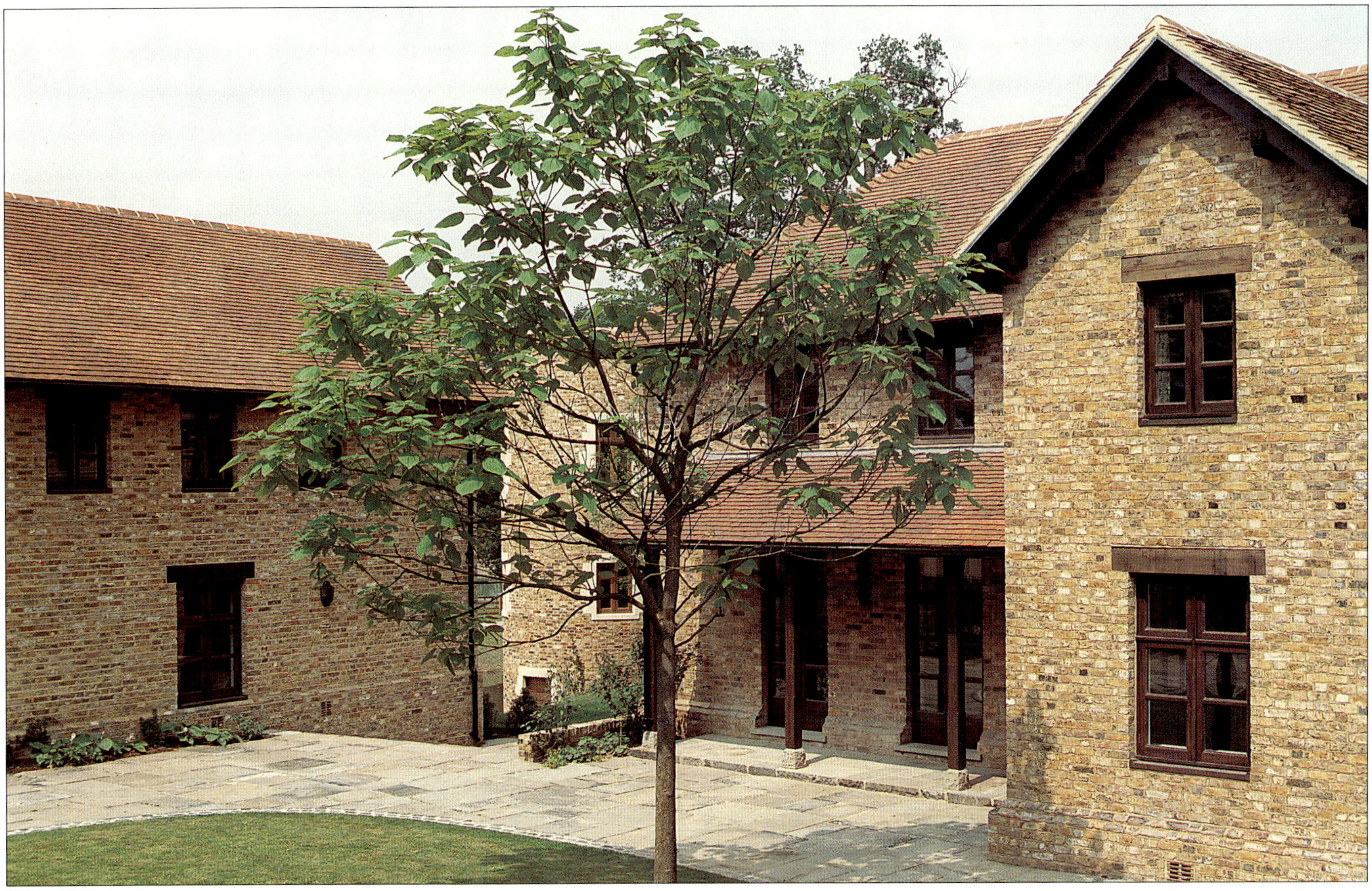

HOUSES AND COTTAGES

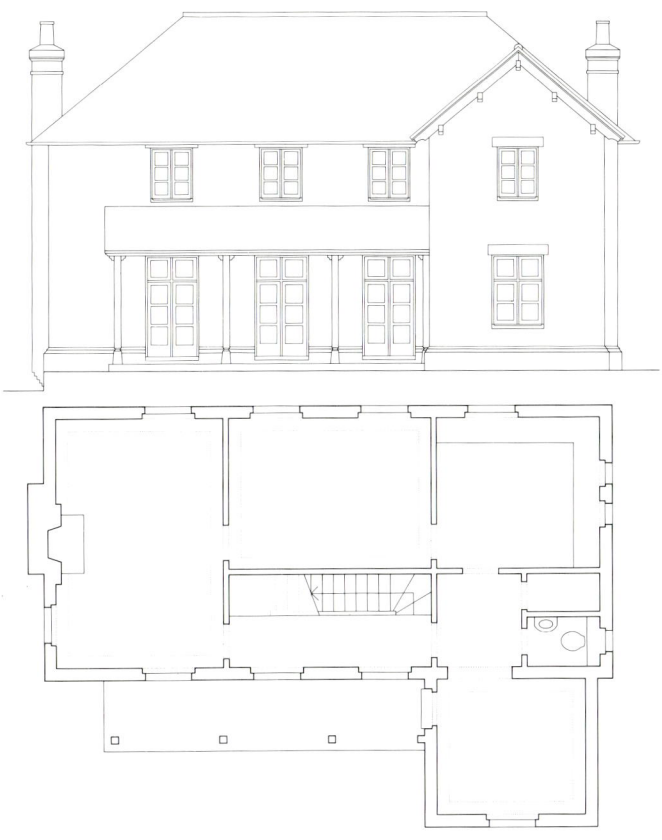

ABOVE: PLAN AND ELEVATION OF FARMER'S COTTAGE; *BELOW*: VIEW OF RESIDENTIAL COURT

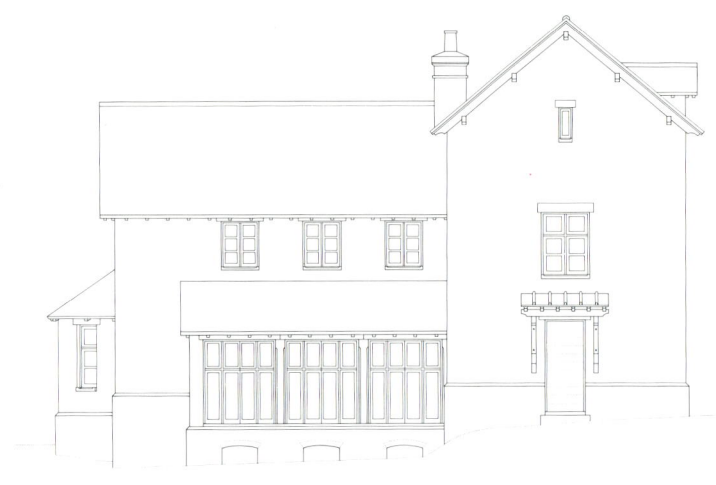

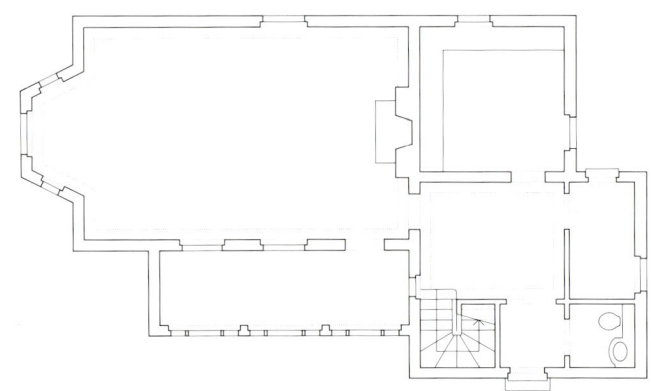

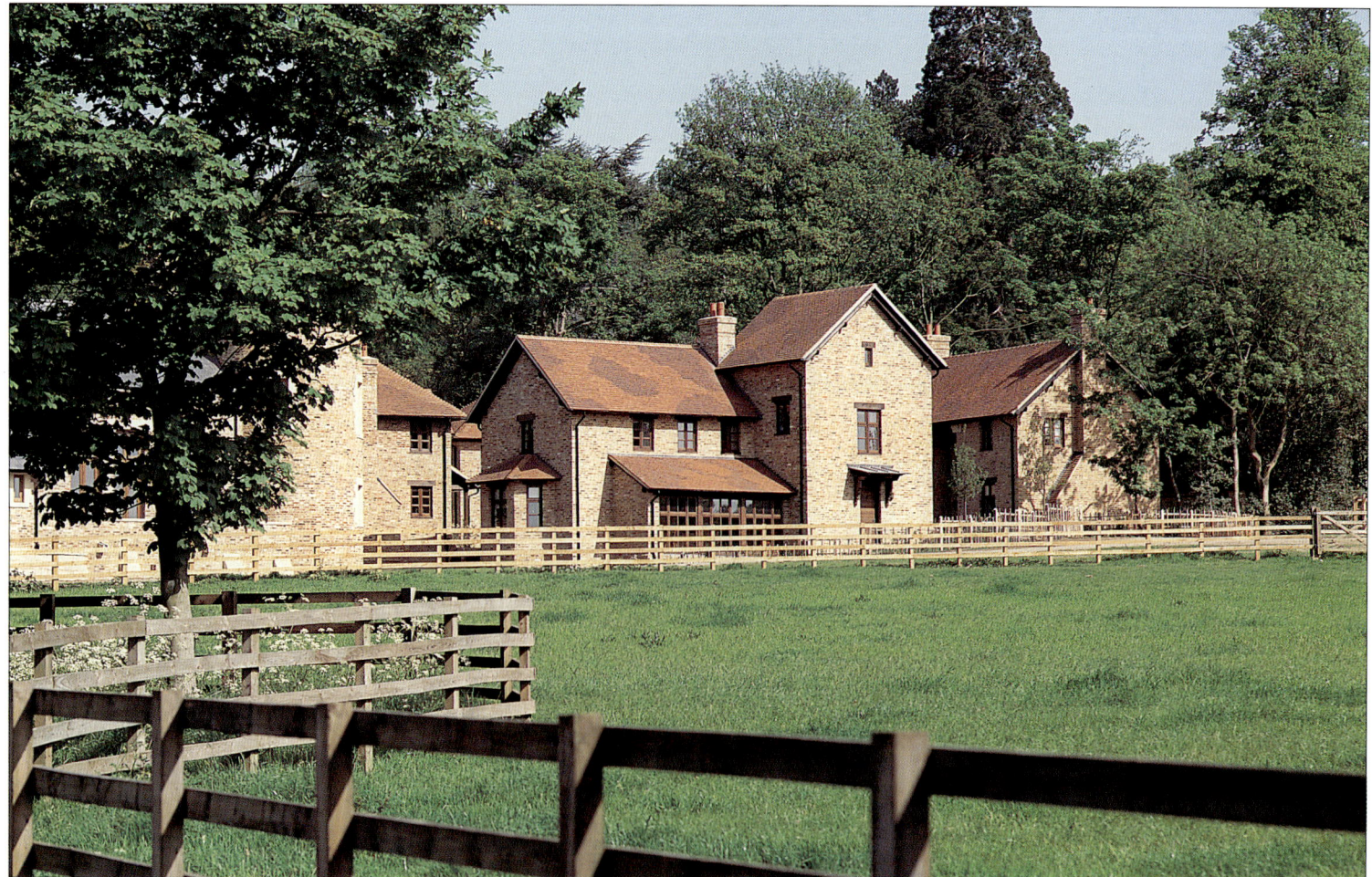

ABOVE: PLAN AND ELEVATION OF GARDENER'S COTTAGE; *BELOW*: VIEW OF GARDENER'S COTTAGE FROM THE PADDOCKS

HOUSES AND COTTAGES

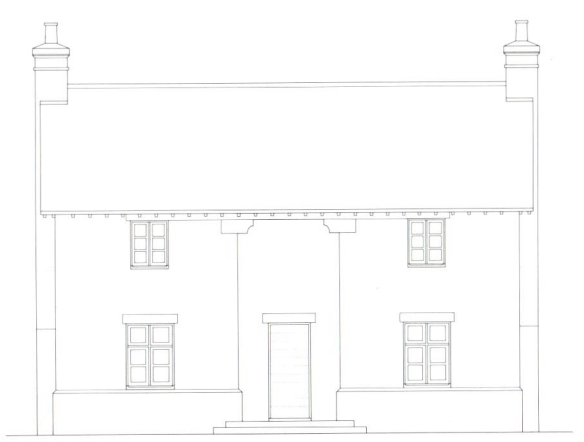

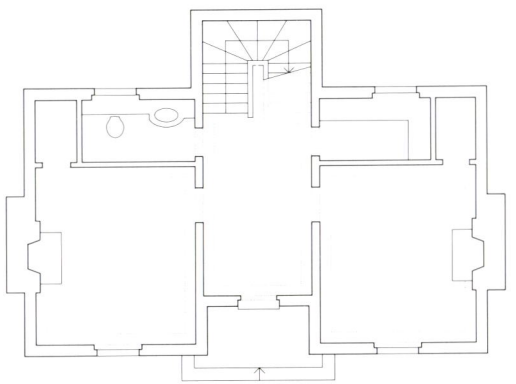

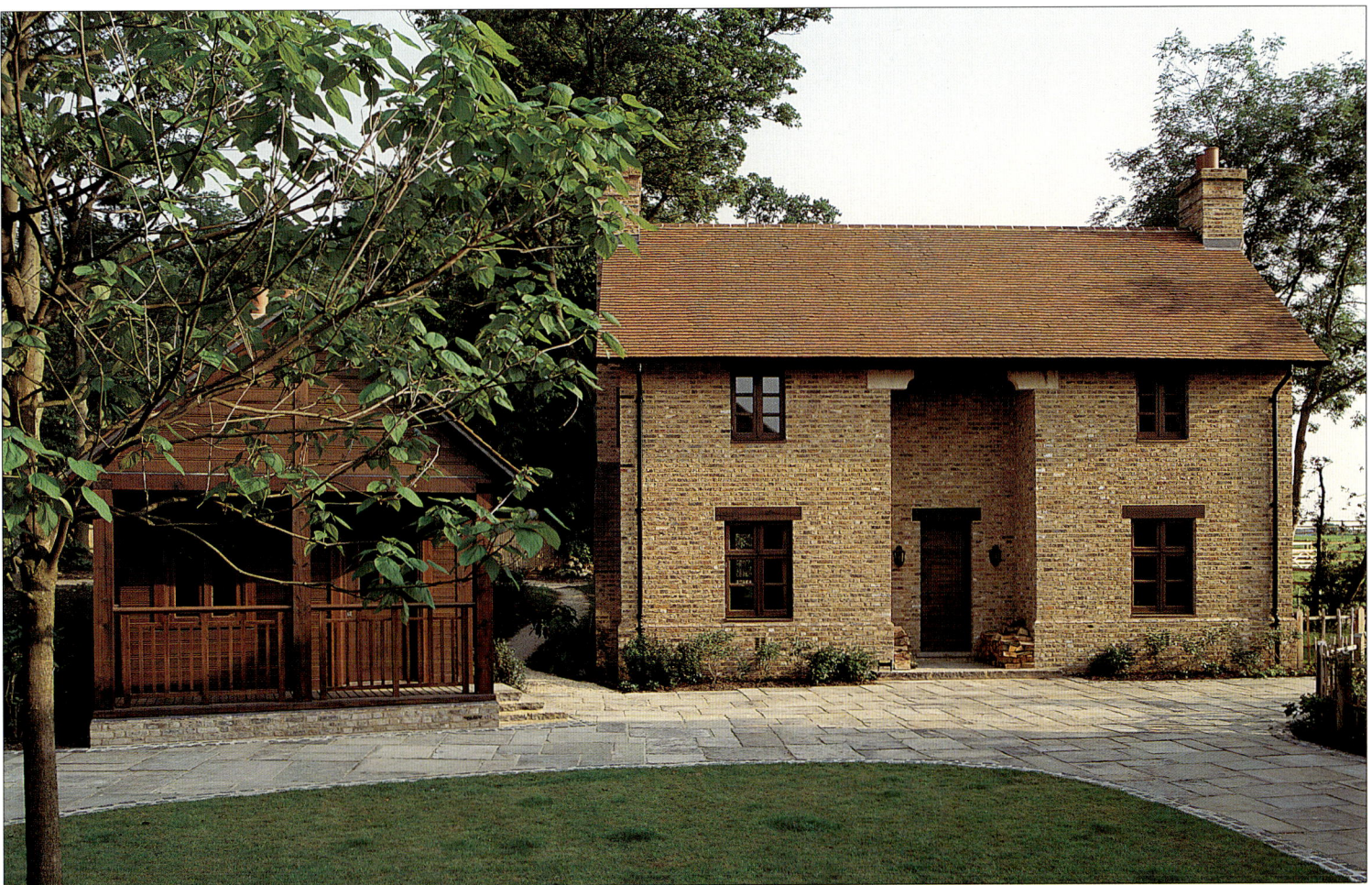

ABOVE: PLAN AND ELEVATION OF ESTATE OFFICE; *BELOW*: VIEW OF THE ESTATE OFFICE AND LODGE

35

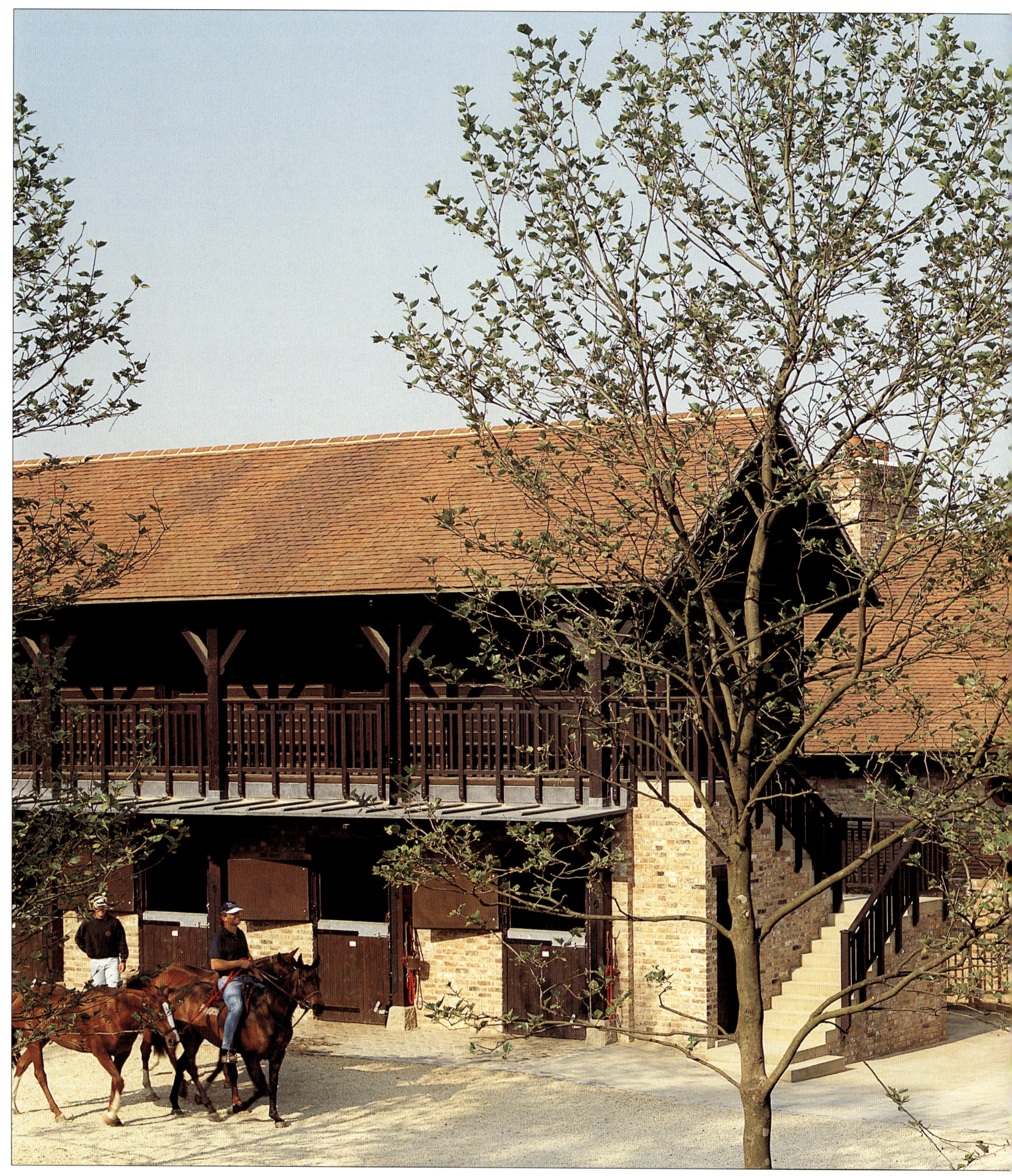

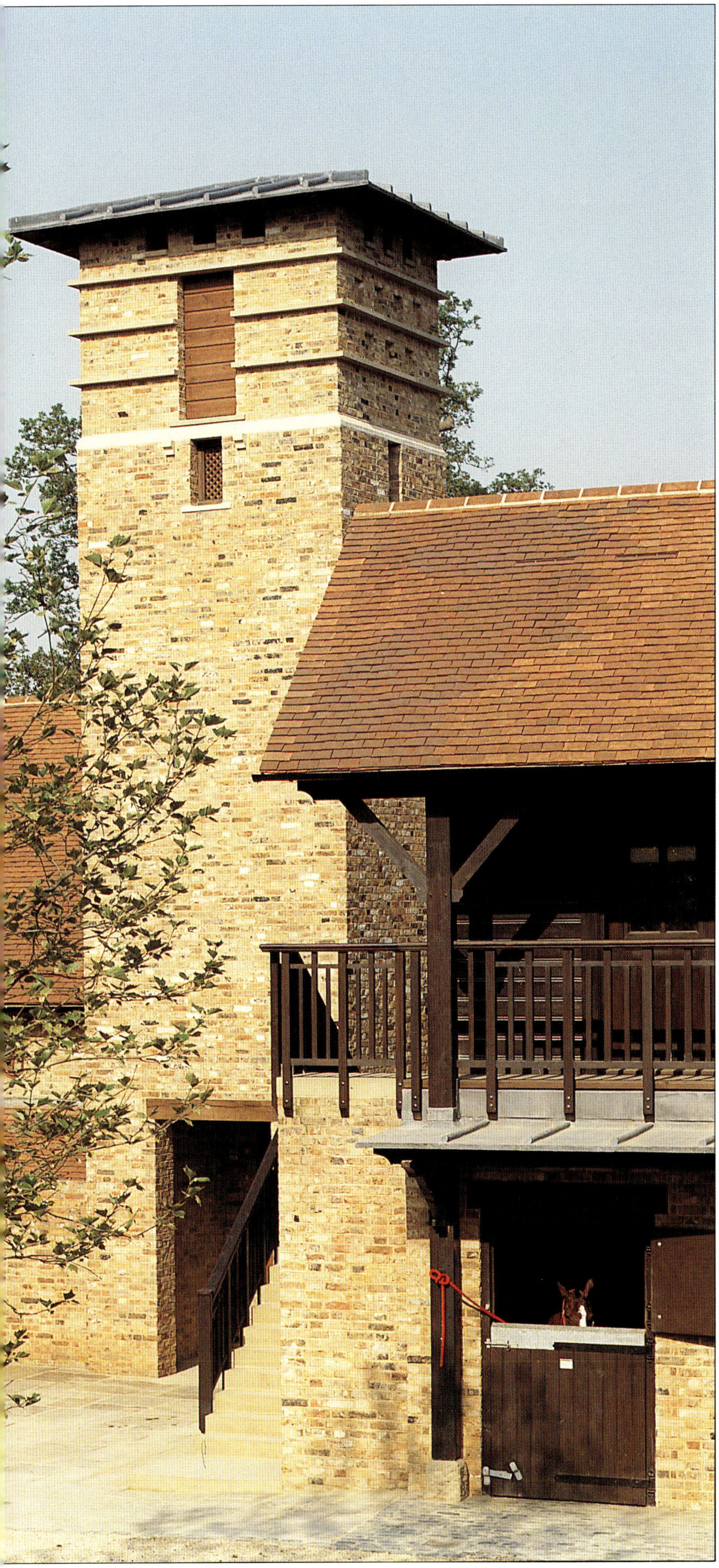

STABLE YARD

The Stable Yard is situated to the east close to the forested area. It is formed by a number of buildings which are frontally arranged each with a cobbled apron in front. At the centre it has a granite water trough with a canopy of mature trees. From here one can see the dovecote tower emerging through an opening formed by the two-storey stables.

Most of the buildings in the Yard are stables designed on a regular bay system. Some are single storey whilst others have accommodation for the grooms above. Eaves, canopies, posts, brackets and all joinery details are generally similar but their composition varies to meet the exigencies both of site and purpose. All brickwork is in second-hand red Surrey and yellow London stocks. Variations in the mix and colour of bricks give individual character to buildings. All timberwork is in stained softwood and all roofs are in mixed red clay tiles with extensive use of lead sheeting for the canopies. The grooms' accommodation is a timber-framed structure with a continuous balcony sitting over the brick stables below.

The Carriage House is an example of a further development of the stable type. It comprises a large hall with various appendages for tack rooms and stores to the rear and at the front it features three large gabled doors. Above each door slatted timber screens light the hall which has a trussed roof, timber panelled walls to dado height and a cobbled floor. The Head Groom's Cottage is essentially a small tower with ancillary rooms clinging around it while the Hay Barn is a single but monumental tetrapylon.

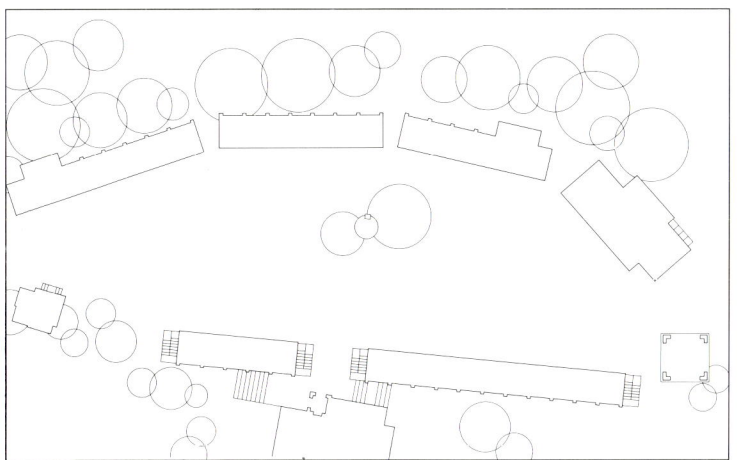

SITE PLAN AND VIEW OF STABLE YARD

DEMETRI PORPHYRIOS

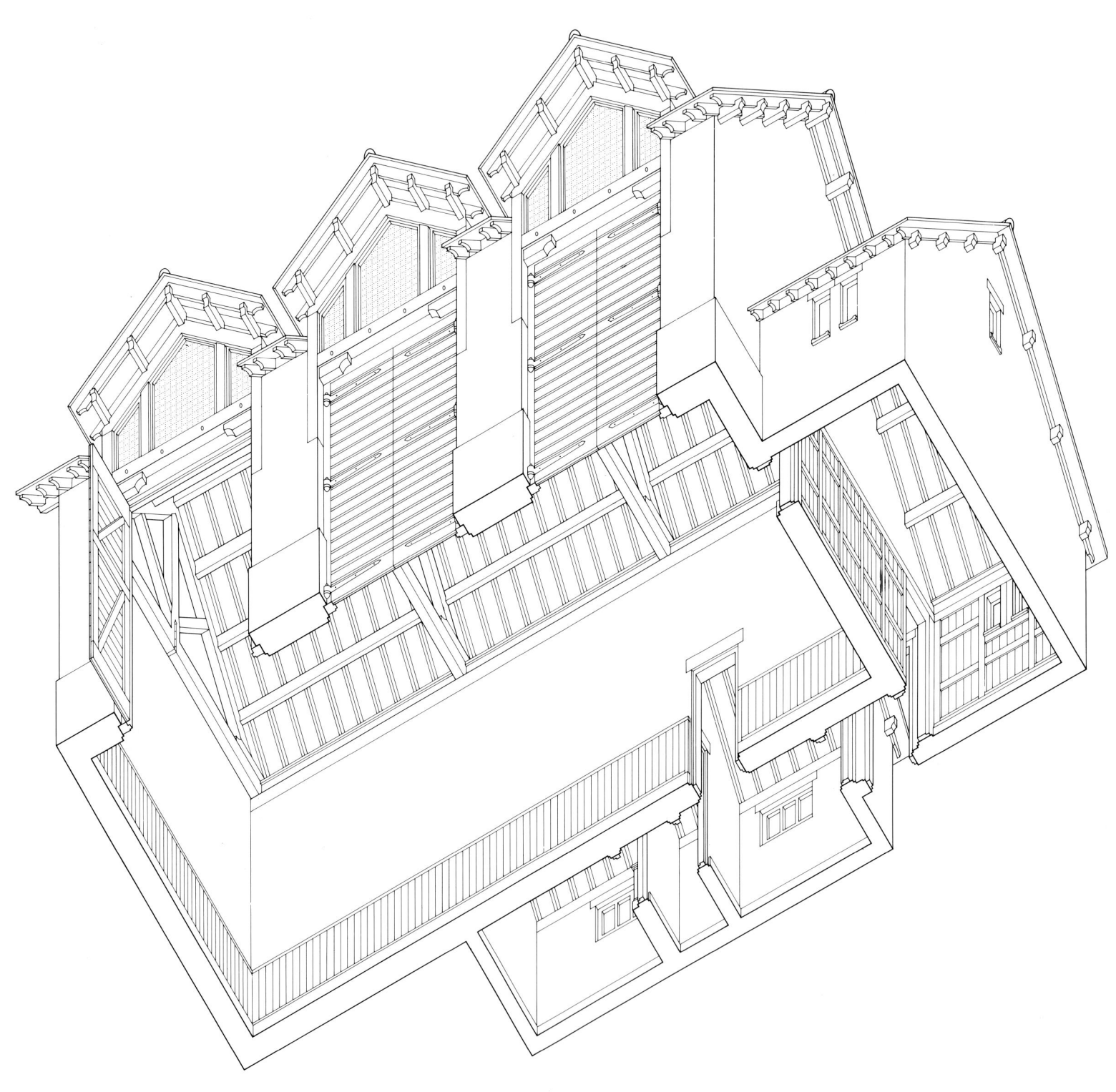

AXONOMETRIC OF CARRIAGE HOUSE

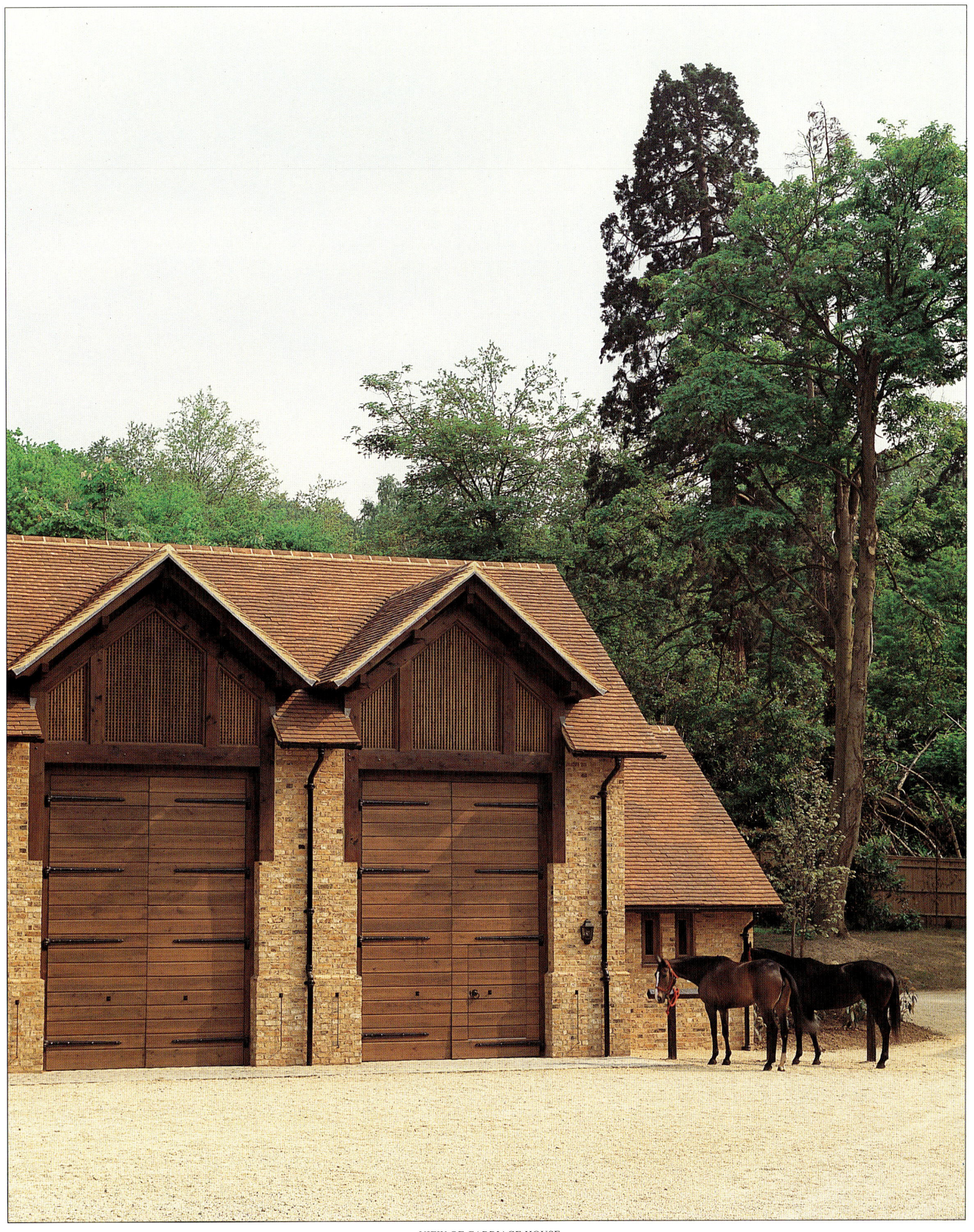

VIEW OF CARRIAGE HOUSE

DEMETRI PORPHYRIOS

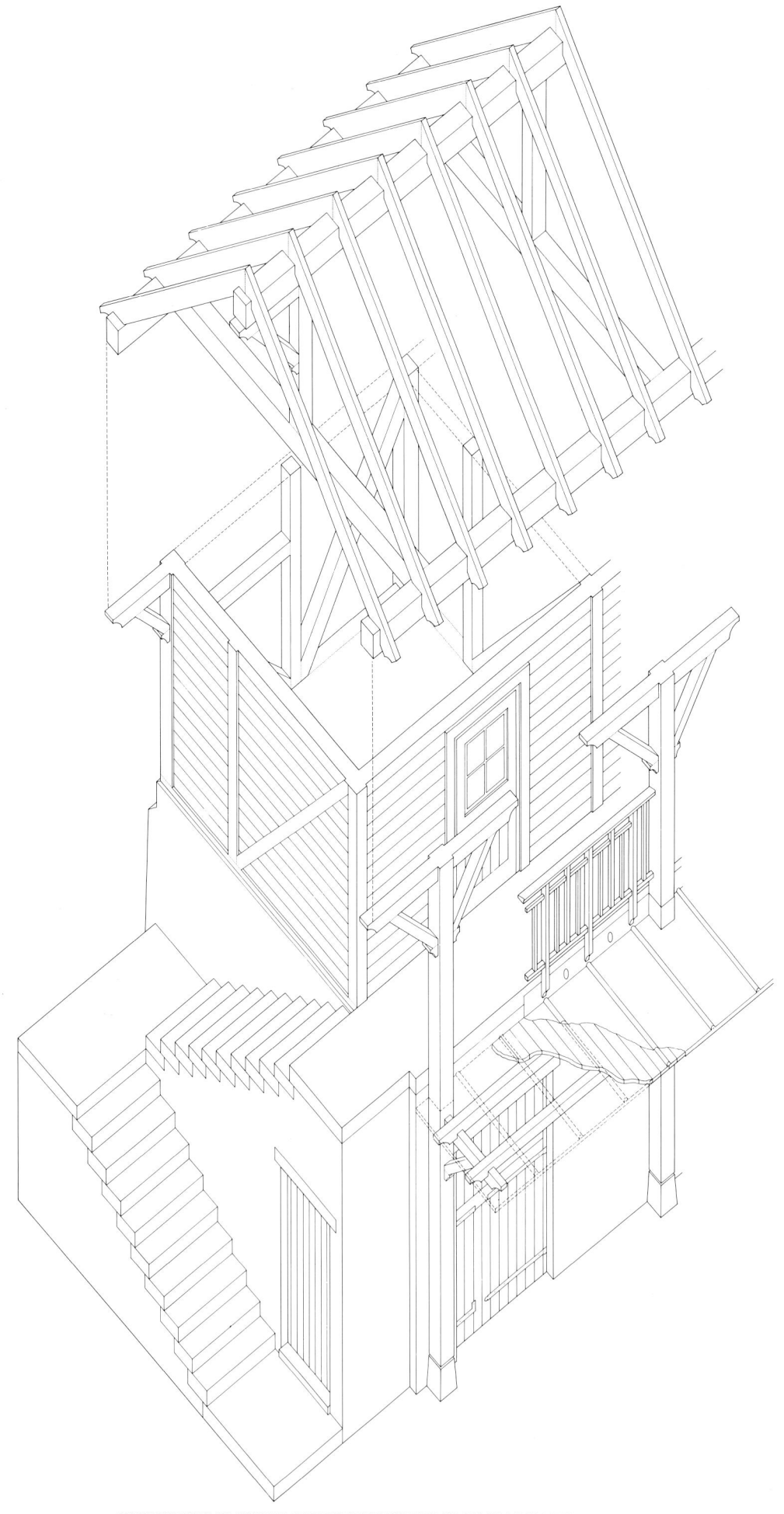

AXONOMETRIC OF TYPICAL BAY OF STABLES WITH GROOMS' ACCOMMODATION ABOVE

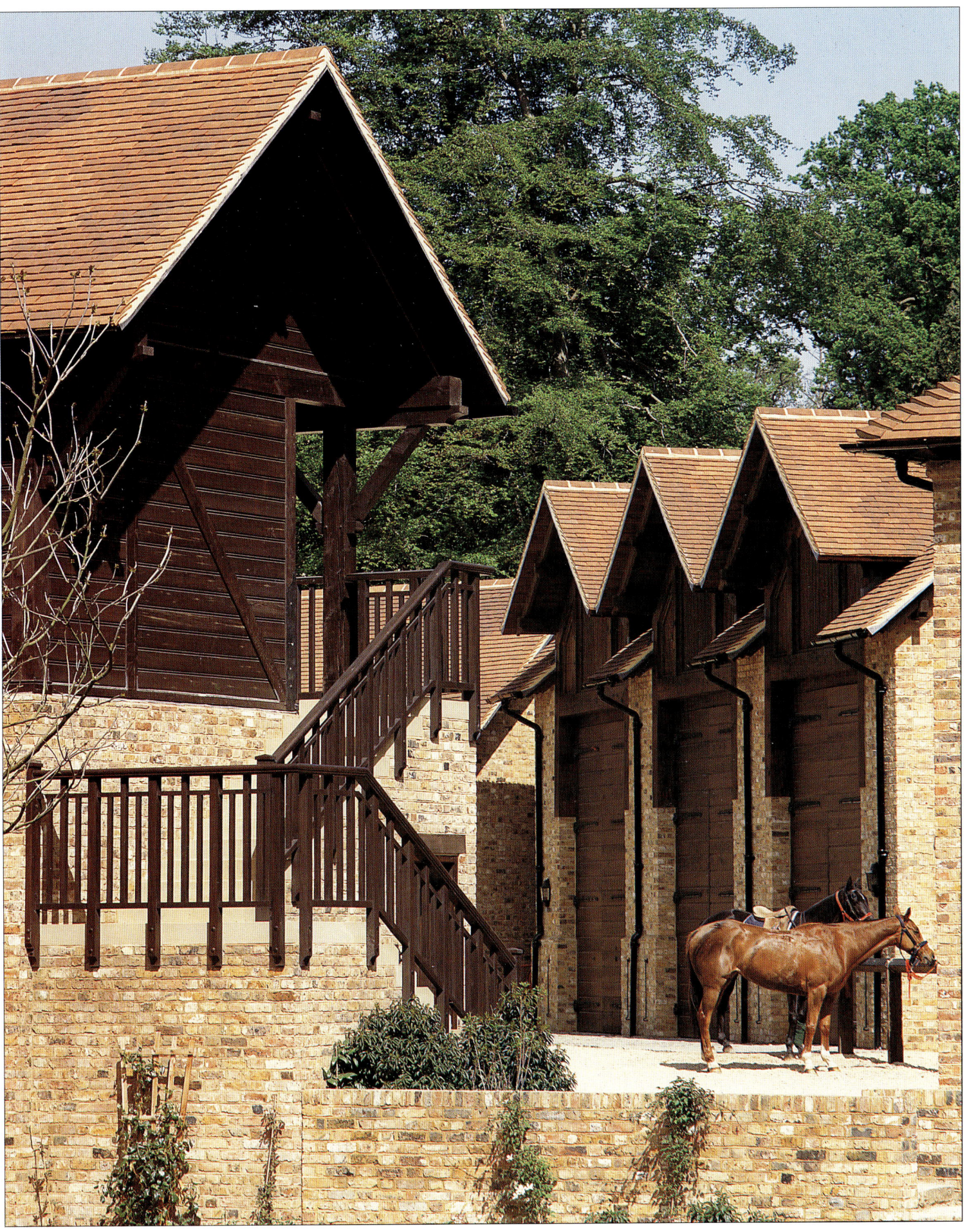
VIEW OF STABLES WITH GROOMS' ACCOMMODATION ABOVE AND THE CARRIAGE HOUSE BEYOND

DEMETRI PORPHYRIOS

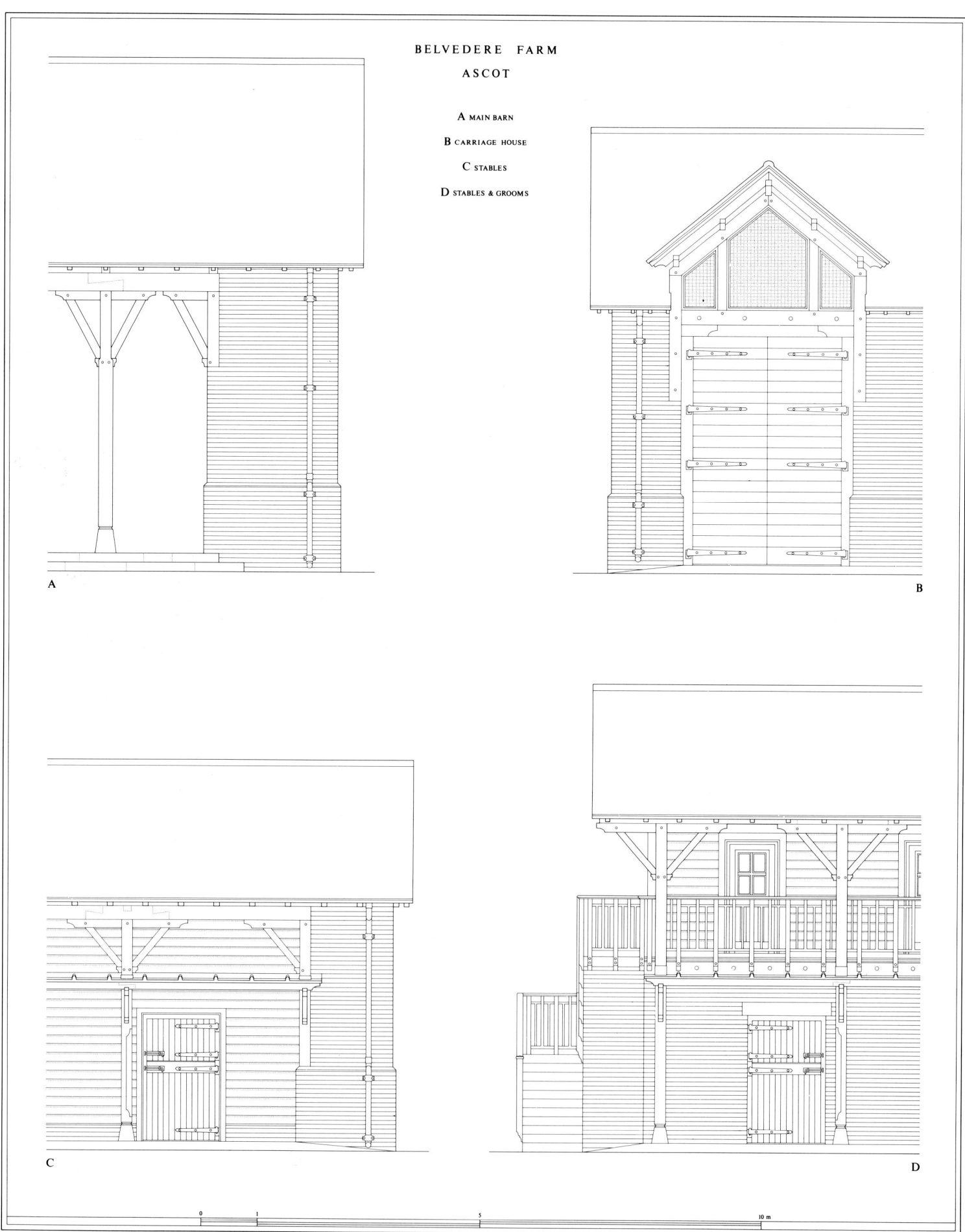

COMPARATIVE PART ELEVATIONS OF FARM AND STABLE BUILDINGS

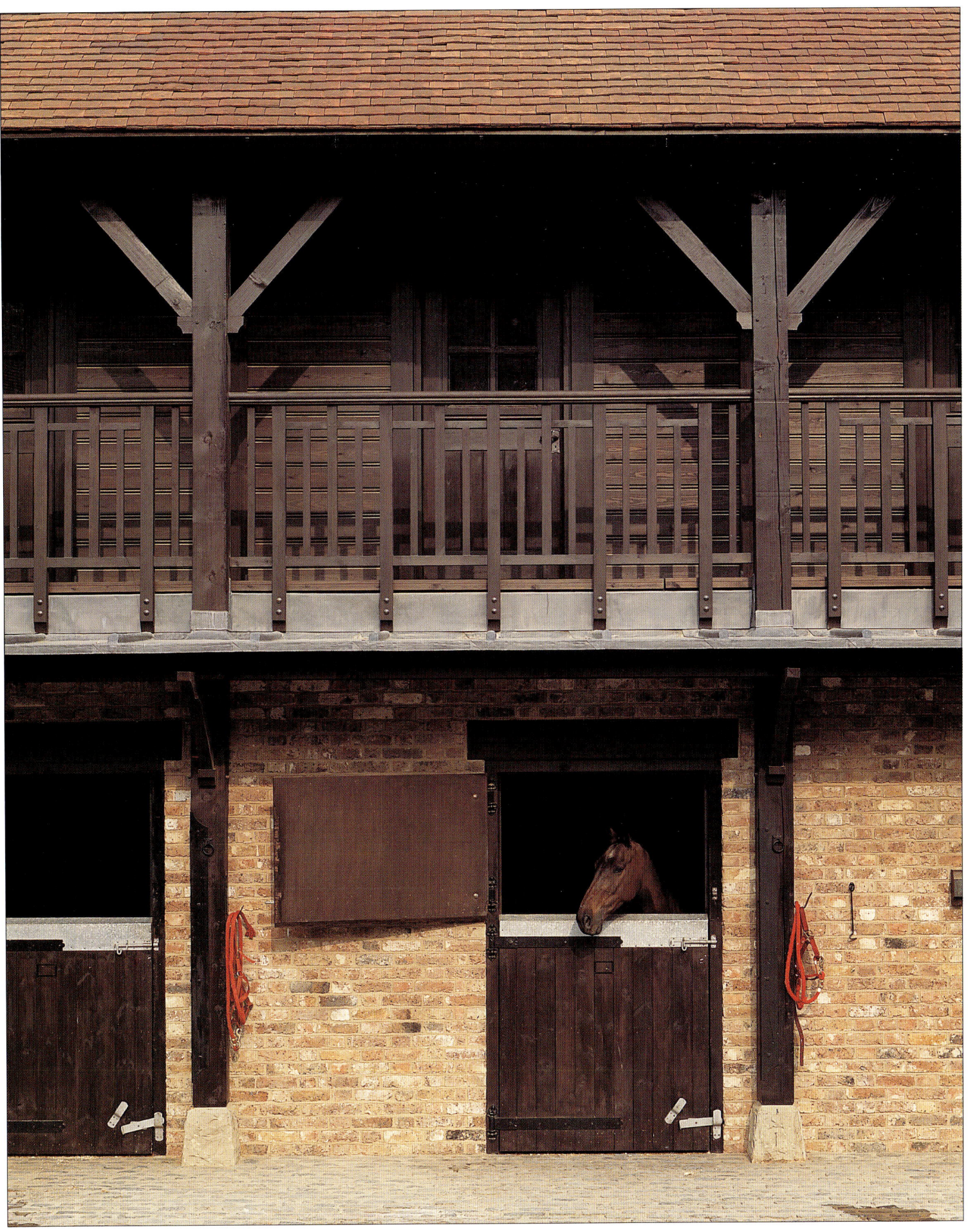

DETAIL VIEW OF STABLES WITH GROOMS' ACCOMMODATION ABOVE

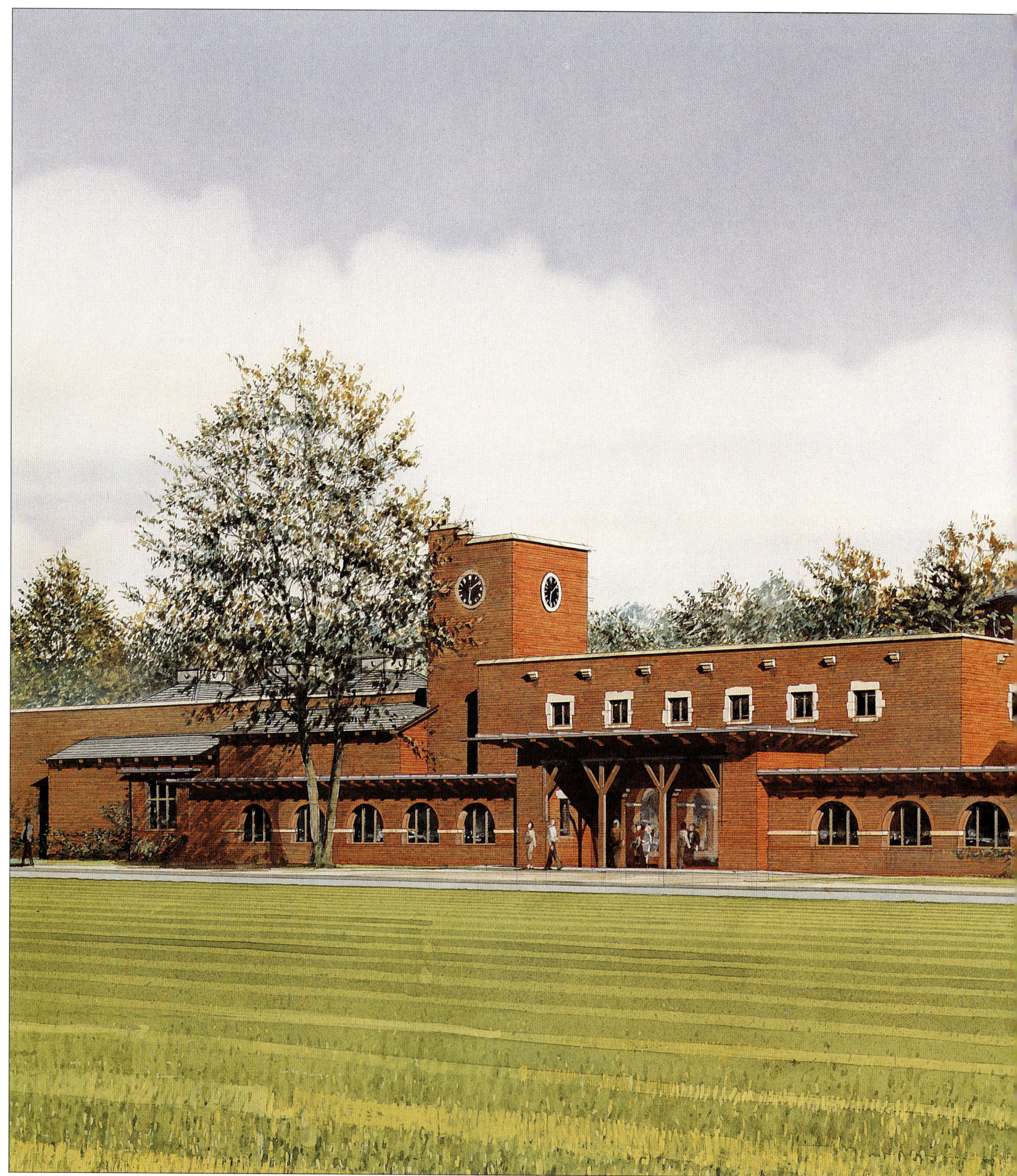

PERSPECTIVE VIEW FROM THE FIELDS

RURAL HISTORY CENTRE
READING UNIVERSITY, 1992

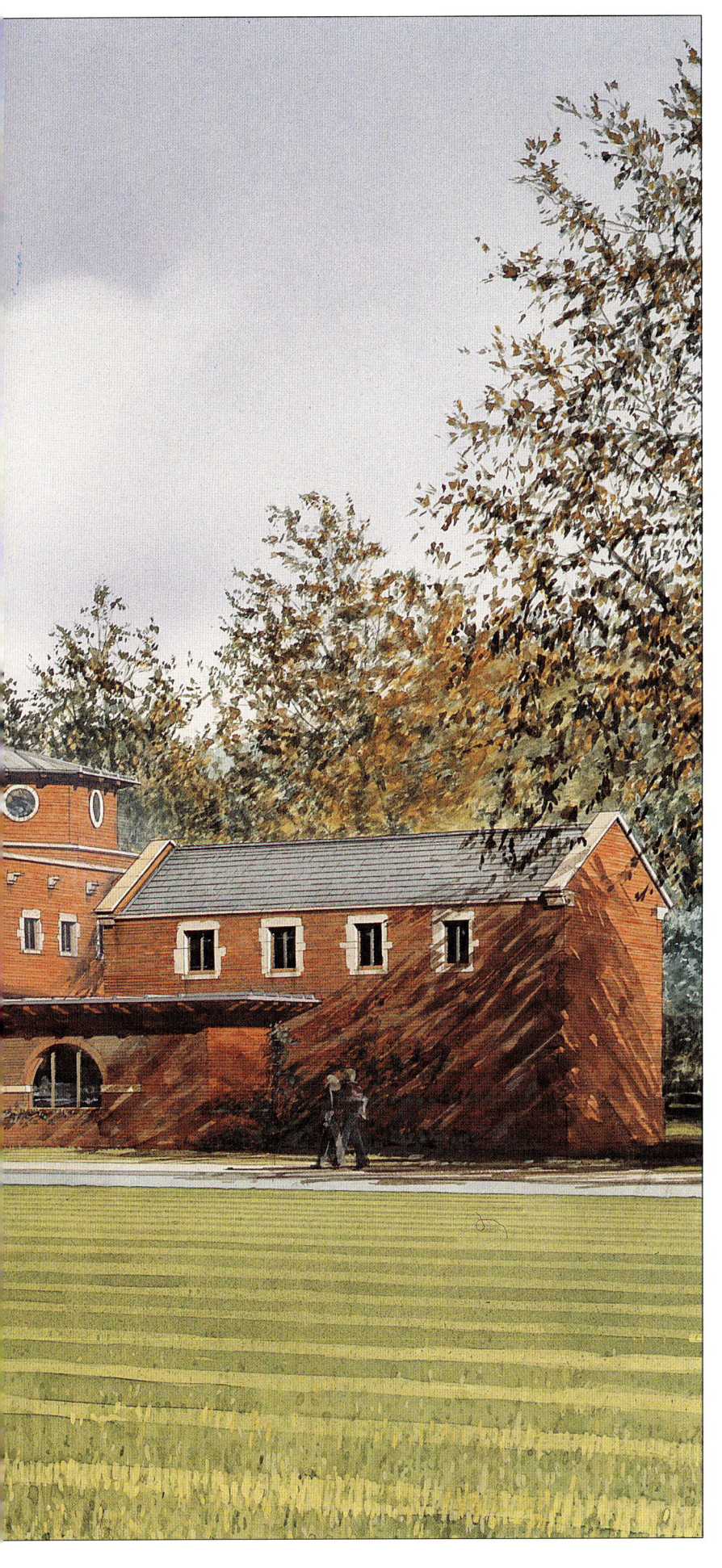

The need for a permanent building to house the Rural History Centre has long been recognised by the University. A limited competition was held and this is the winning scheme.

The new building is located along Chancellors Way, at the main entrance to the University campus. The great expanse of the adjacent playing fields and the backdrop of the mature woodland are characteristic features of the site. We have broken up the massing of the building so that full advantage is taken of the foreshortened as well as the distant views the site offers.

The main entrance is marked by a timber-roofed portico with flanking wings on either side. Upon entry one arrives at the very heart of the building: an open-air court surrounded by a five metre wide arcade. The various activities of the brief are organised around this central arcaded court. Instead of daedalic corridors, the plan brings together all necessary circulation for the building and turns it into a place of unique character.

The lecture hall and seminar rooms are located close to the main entrance. The offices and study rooms for the academic staff are on the first floor overlooking the central court. All archival stores and reserve collections are on the ground floor.

To the south of the central court and on axis with the main entrance is the Library. This is an octagonal room with a lofty reading room in the centre, support services in the ambulatory and open access shelving in the gallery above.

The exhibition gallery to the east of the central court is a great hall marked by a series of brick columns in the centre and engaged pilasters along the perimeter walls; all supporting a roof comprising a number of truncated pyramids with skylit tops. An increased draught effect is created by a system of wind induced extraction which is enhanced by the shape of the pyramidal roofs in a manner similar to the traditional principle of passive ventilation found in oast houses.

The building is constructed in load bearing walls with red facing bricks externally. Copings, corbels, window and door surrounds and band courses are all in natural stone. Roofs are in timber and are finished in natural slates or lead.

Our reference point has been the brick architecture common in the Reading area and more generally the traditional materials of which the greatest part of this country is made.

DEMETRI PORPHYRIOS

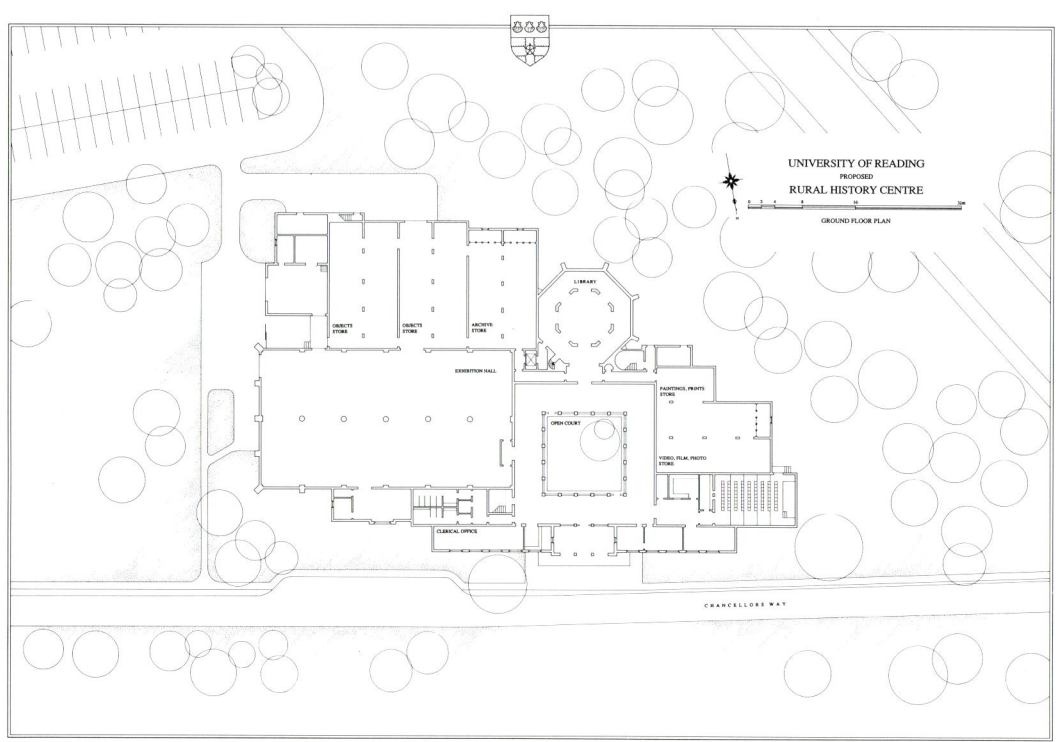

GROUND-FLOOR PLAN

NORTH ELEVATION FACING THE FIELDS

RURAL HISTORY CENTRE

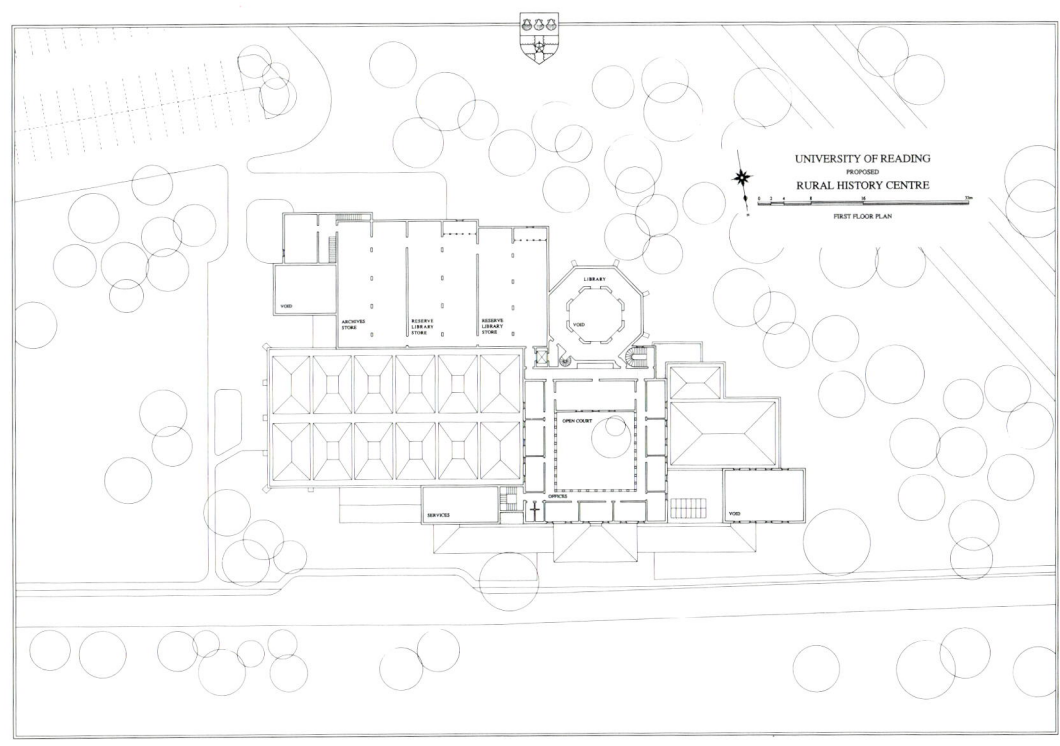

FIRST-FLOOR PLAN

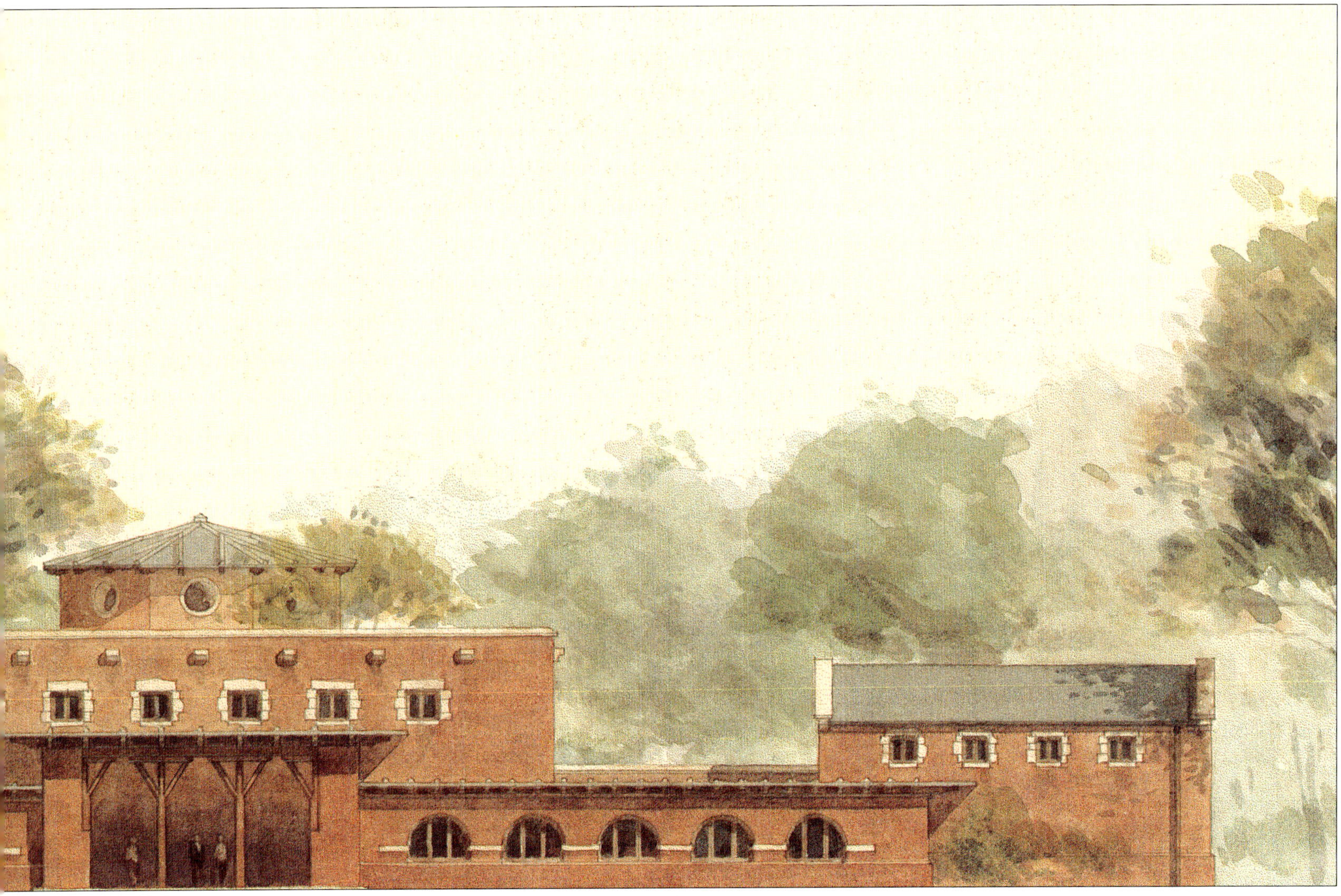

DEMETRI PORPHYRIOS

PERSPECTIVE VIEW OF EXHIBITION HALL

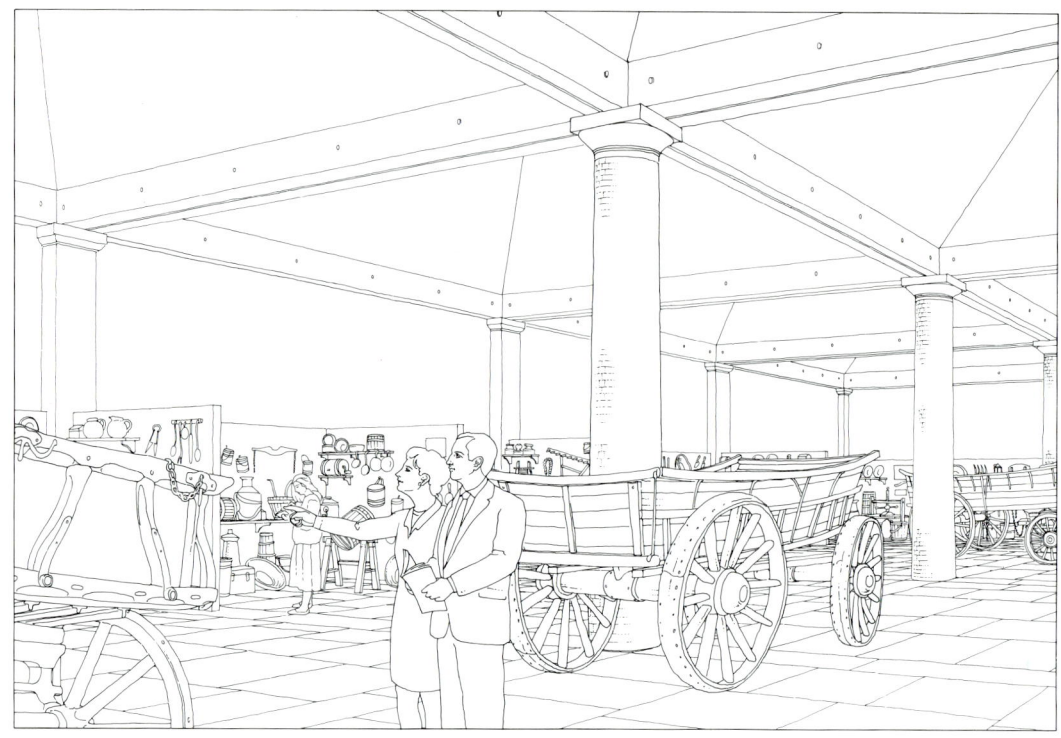

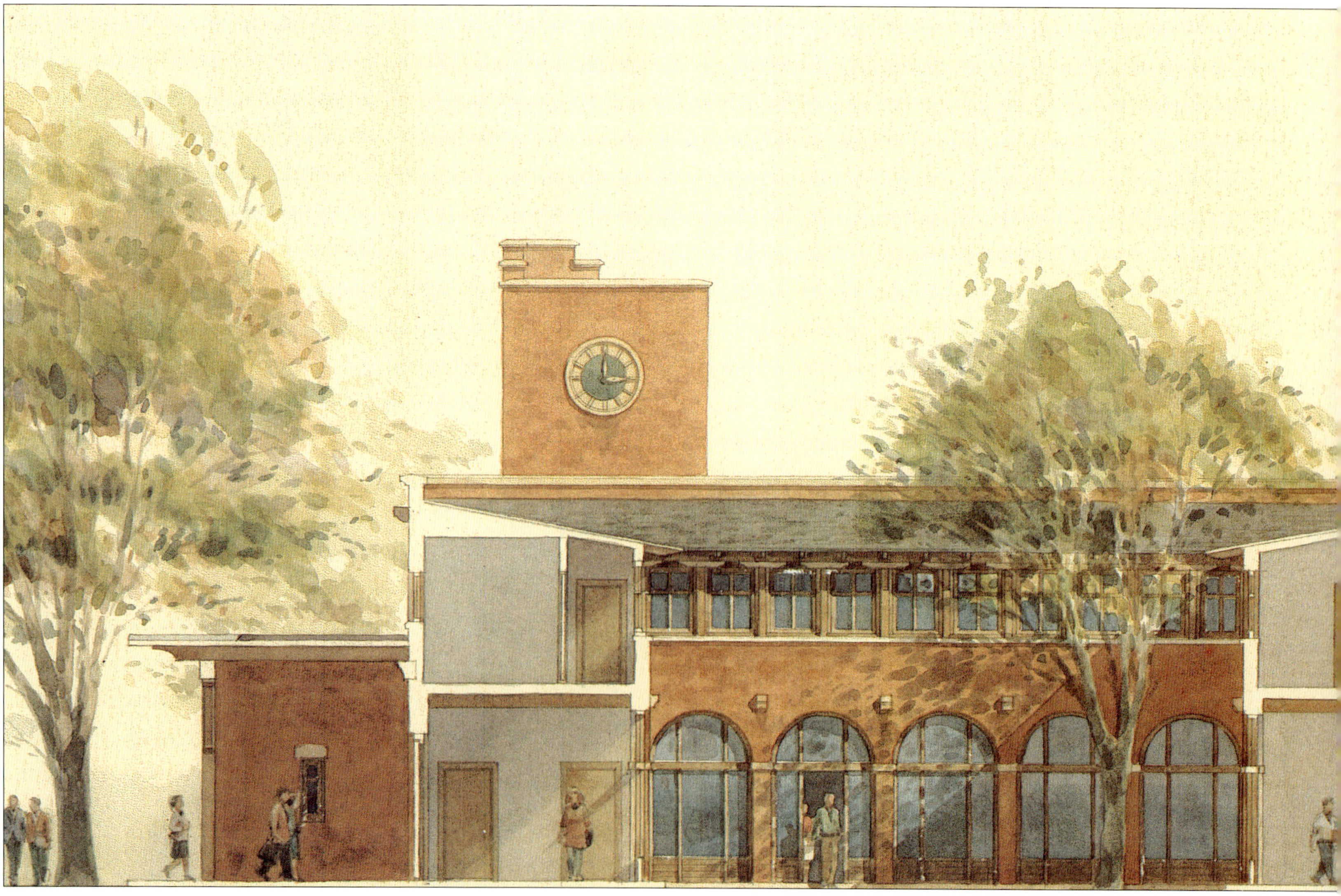

SECTION THROUGH OPEN COURT AND LIBRARY

RURAL HISTORY CENTRE

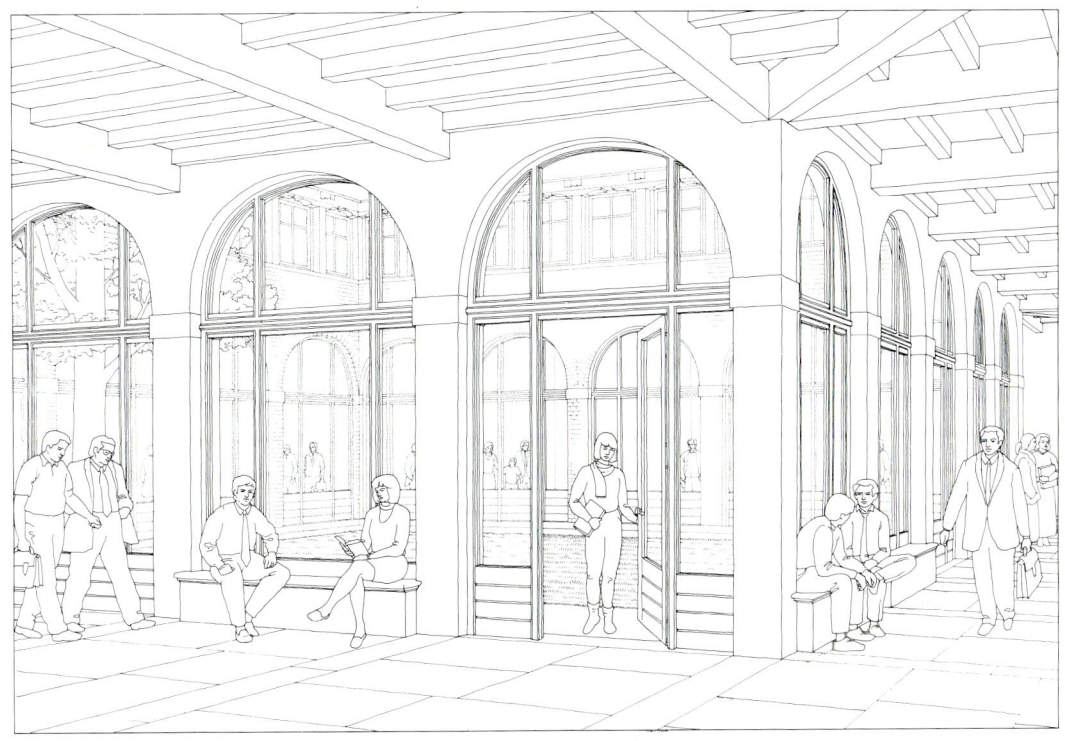

PERSPECTIVE VIEW OF FOYER AND OPEN COURT

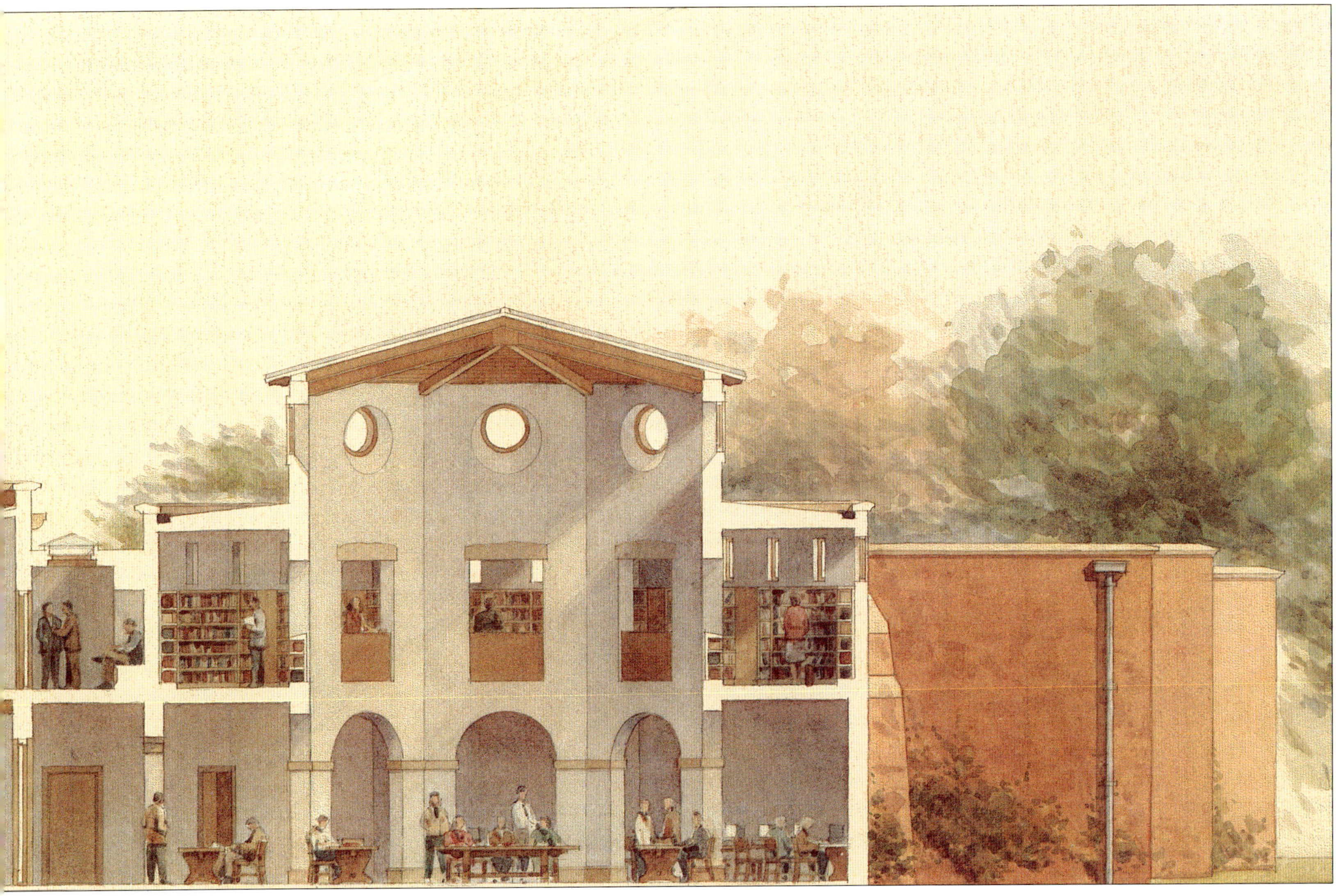

DEMETRI PORPHYRIOS

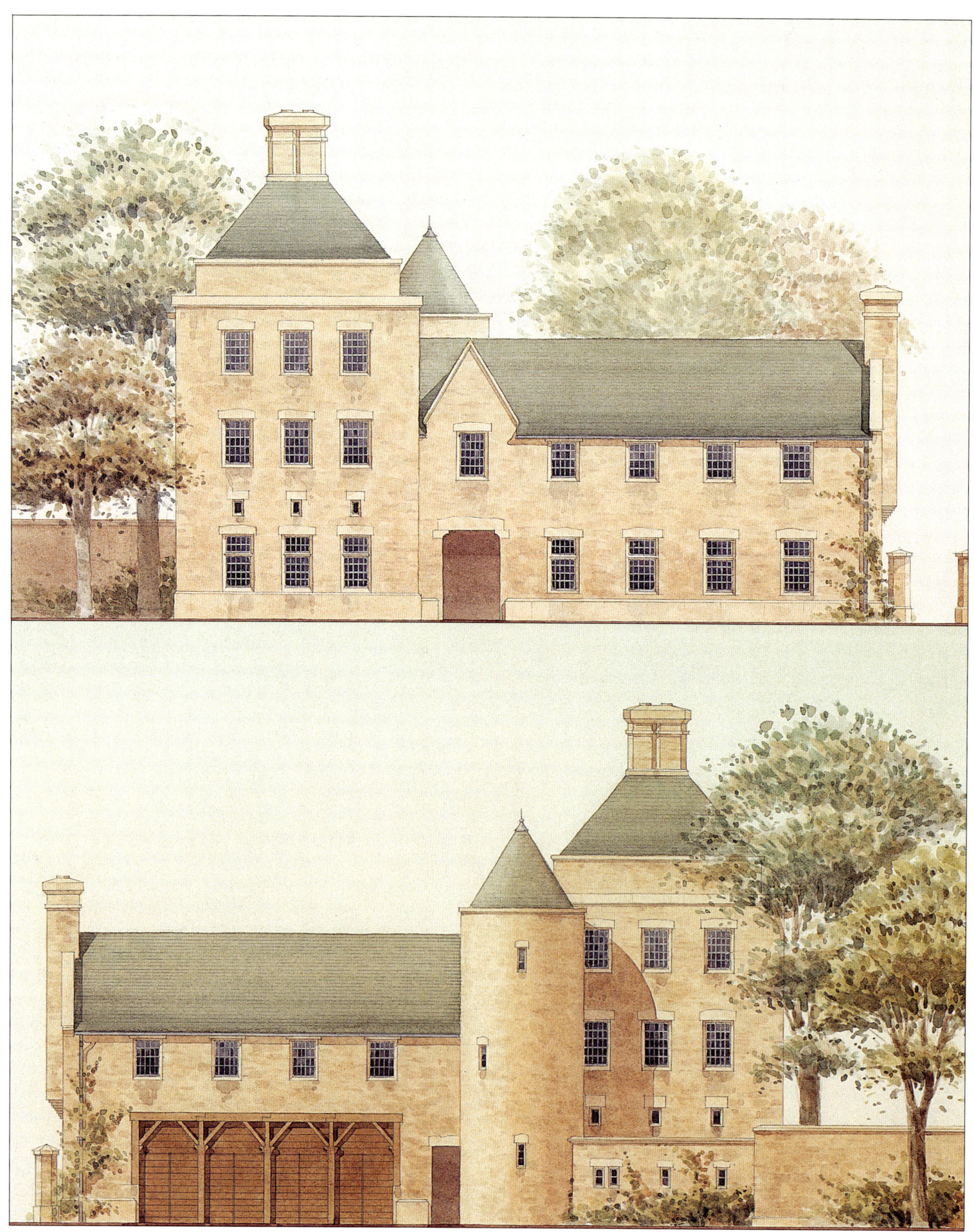

ABOVE: FRONT (WEST) ELEVATION; *BELOW*: REAR (EAST) ELEVATION

WORKSHOPS AND OFFICES IN POUNDBURY
DORCHESTER, 1991

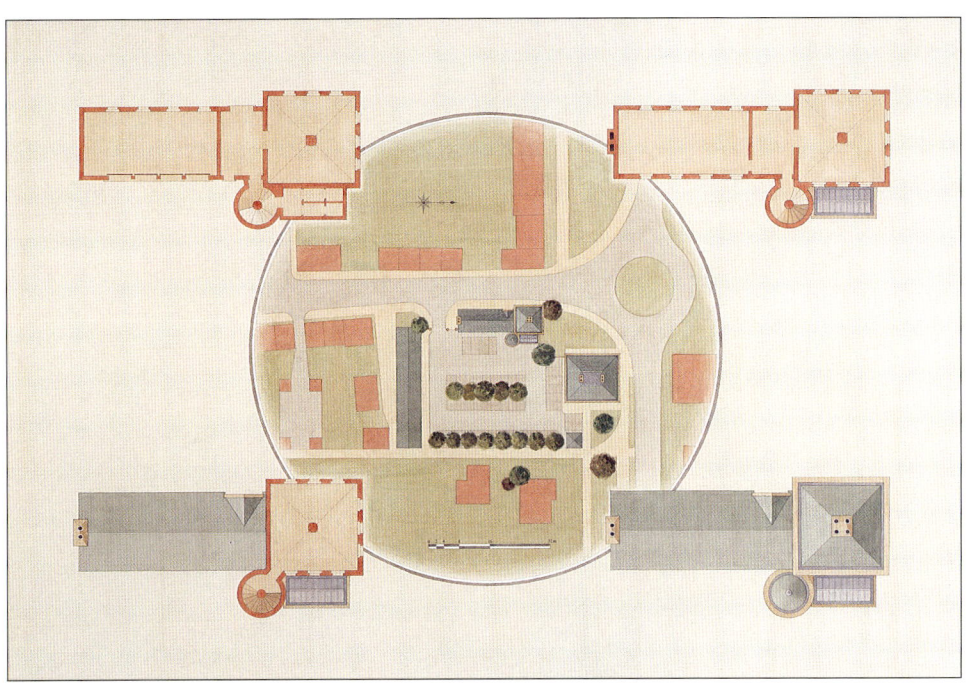

SITE AND FLOOR PLANS

This project is part of the first phase of the Poundbury development in Dorchester undertaken by the Duchy of Cornwall. The overall master plan combines housing, workplaces as well as social and public facilities in the form of a traditional town.

We were asked to provide office accommodation and a number of light industrial workshops. The boundaries of the site together with a code for the use of local materials were established by the masterplan. The buildings are located at one of the most prominent approaches into the new development and, together with the buildings across the street, they act as a gateway into the town.

There is a distinct rural character to the area and our scheme makes use of local stone and slates. Bearing in mind the non-residential use of the buildings we looked for prototypes in the coach houses and inn houses which are typically found in the area. Entered through a covered passage they usually bring together two or more buildings in a rather informal but highly agreeable manner.

In our scheme the main entrance to the offices is through a vaulted passage which at the same time connects the street with the court at the rear. The workshops are entered directly from the court. A separate three-storey building houses the offices. In addition to its perimeter bearing walls this building has a central pier which doubles both as structure and mechanical duct. The two buildings are connected by the staircase tower. Further workshops define the boundaries of the site.

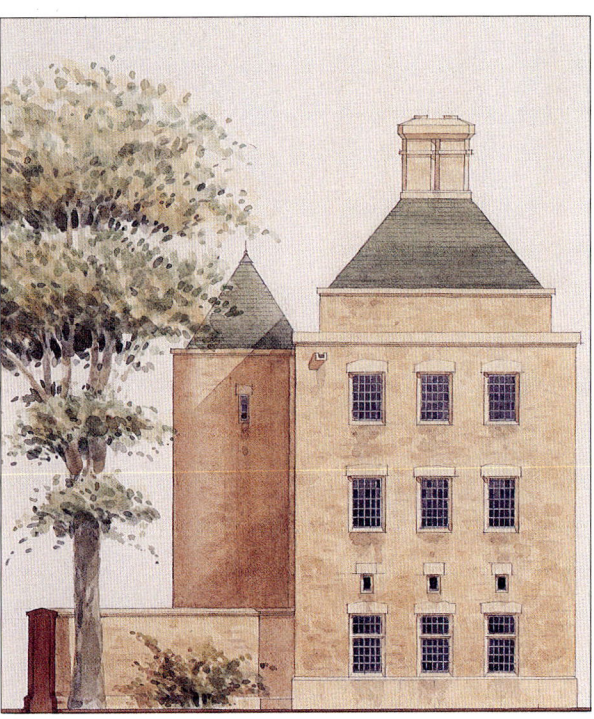

The buildings are constructed in load bearing masonry walls with ashlar stone or range walling externally. They have rough cut stone lintels for openings and local stone slates for the roofs.

This is an architecture that derives from the constructional logic of its natural materials and where the building fabric improves with age and weathering. It is an architecture of simple, straightforward, solid, durable and beautiful buildings.

Working with the local vernacular one constantly marvels at the way by which complex problems are addressed with an ingenious simplicity. Vernacular building has manifold duties to perform but it allows no pure artifice to interfere with the law of sound construction and practical provision.

NORTH ELEVATION

INLAND REVENUE OFFICES
NOTTINGHAM, 1991

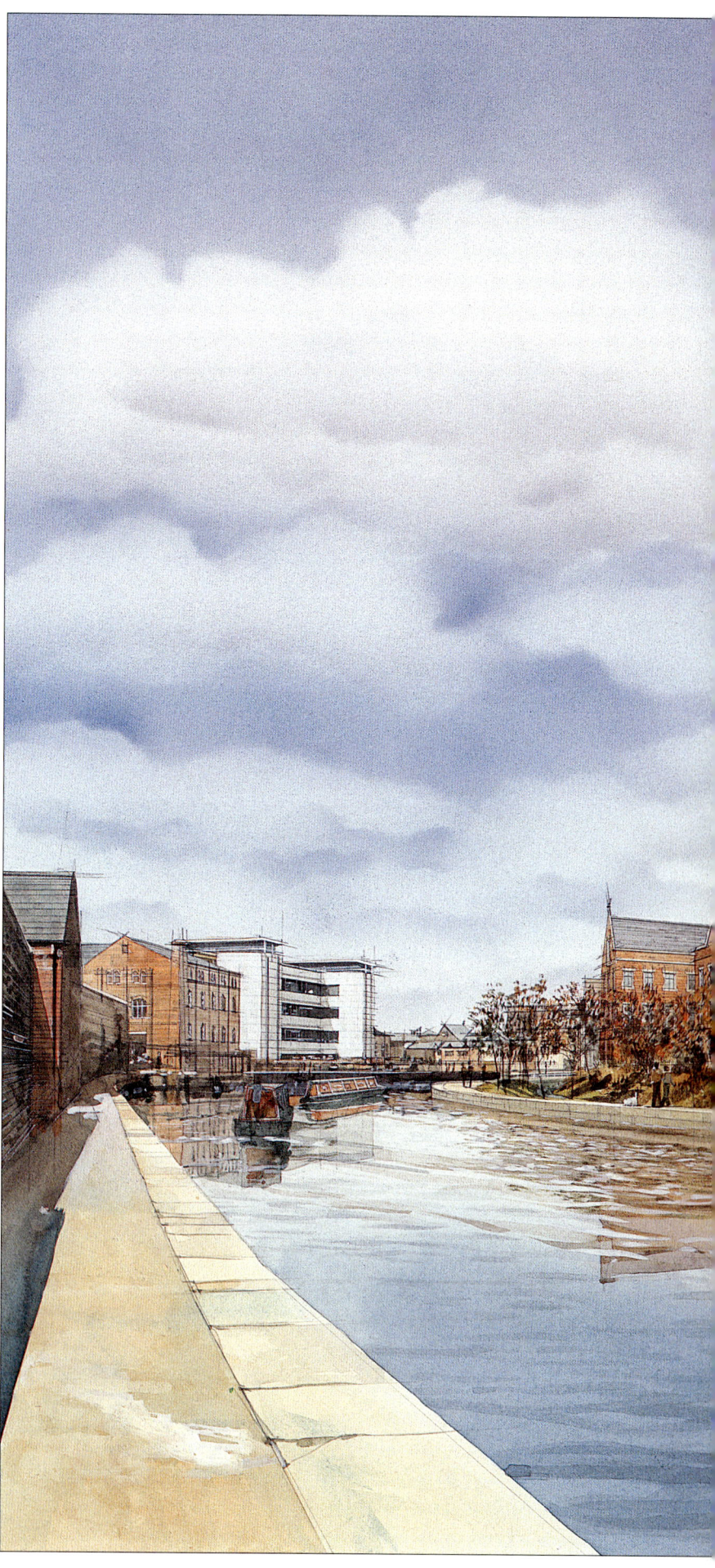

We were one of the six finalists in a national competition for the design of the new headquarters of the Inland Revenue in Nottingham. The derelict site is located between the railway tracks and the canal at the foot of Nottingham Castle. The site is so typical of what has happened along the immediate perimeter of historic centres. These areas have suffered physically from industrial development in the post-war period and they have disintegrated into dumping grounds or 'industrial parks'. Our scheme, therefore, stands both as a generic and a specific proposal.

Another consideration also comes immediately to mind. The usual practice with single use projects of this size is to build one building or a mega-sprawling machine with everything under one roof, all in the name of managerial efficiency. This attitude has invariably led to confusing and inhuman buildings. Yet projects of this size need not necessarily be oppressive; on the contrary, they deserve to be housed in civil places.

The most civil of all places is the city itself. But since the site could not 'plug into' the city fabric (due to the physical barriers surrounding it), the urban model we adopted is that of the collegiate campus. A small city articulated into a number of buildings, streets and courts.

The brief is broken down into a number of office buildings and common facilities buildings, each with their own identifiable entrance and individuality. The office buildings are organised around a series of courts, all of different size, orientation and character yet interconnected as a series of urban events. The common facilities buildings are free-standing or set into the fabric of the office buildings. In designing the urban framework we placed great emphasis on functional/practical considerations, maximum permeability of the urban fabric, alternative routes, and perspective views as they unfold when one moves through the streets and from one court to another.

Our proposal takes as its model the image of the city and its collective representation. The architecture stems from a tried and tested method of construction that does not rely on make-believe high-tech gadgetry. All buildings are in different complementary tones of red brick with a variety of sandstones. Ultimately, our reference point has been the masonry architecture of which the greatest part of this country is made.

INLAND REVENUE OFFICES

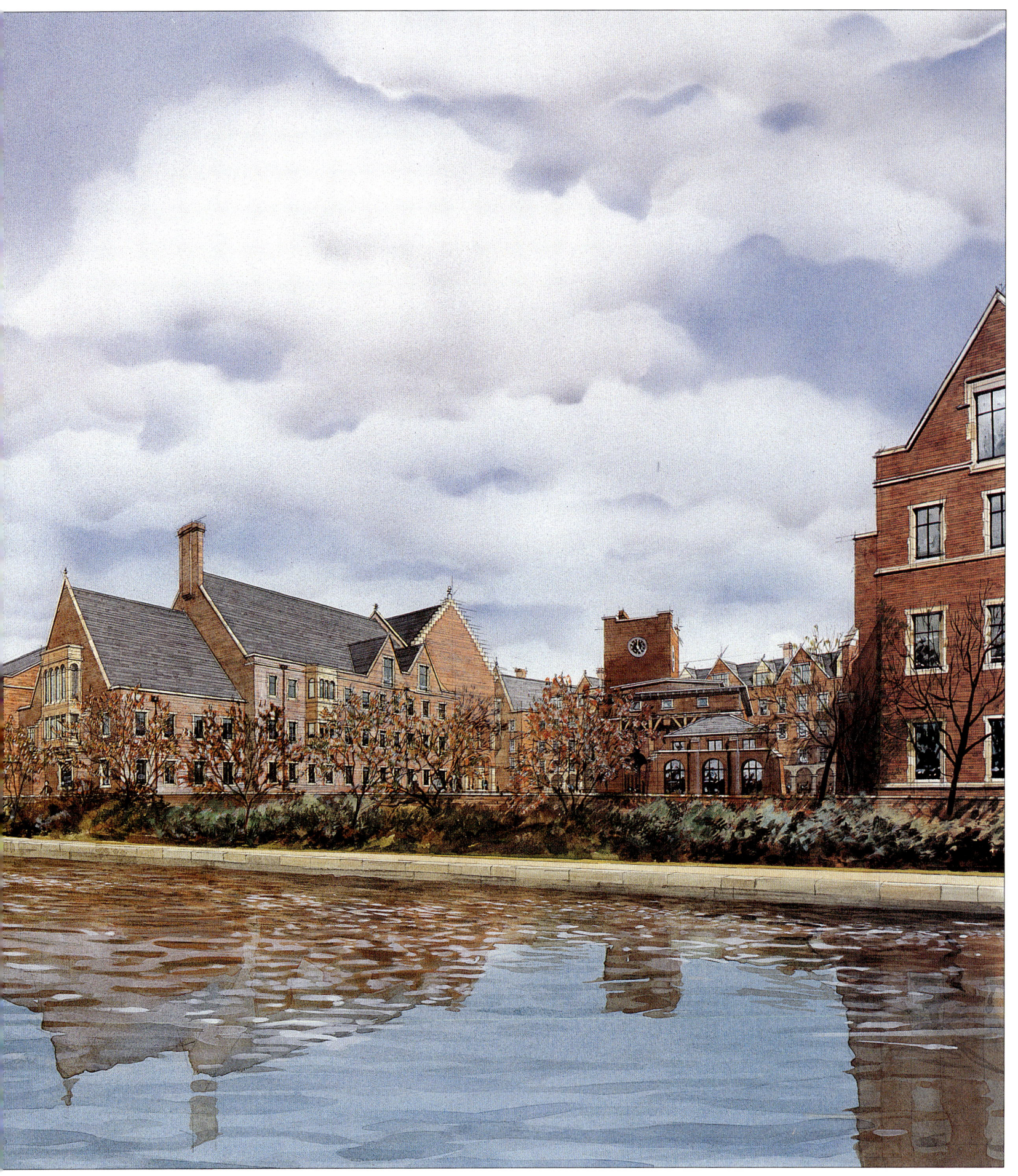

PERSPECTIVE VIEW FROM THE CANAL

DEMETRI PORPHYRIOS

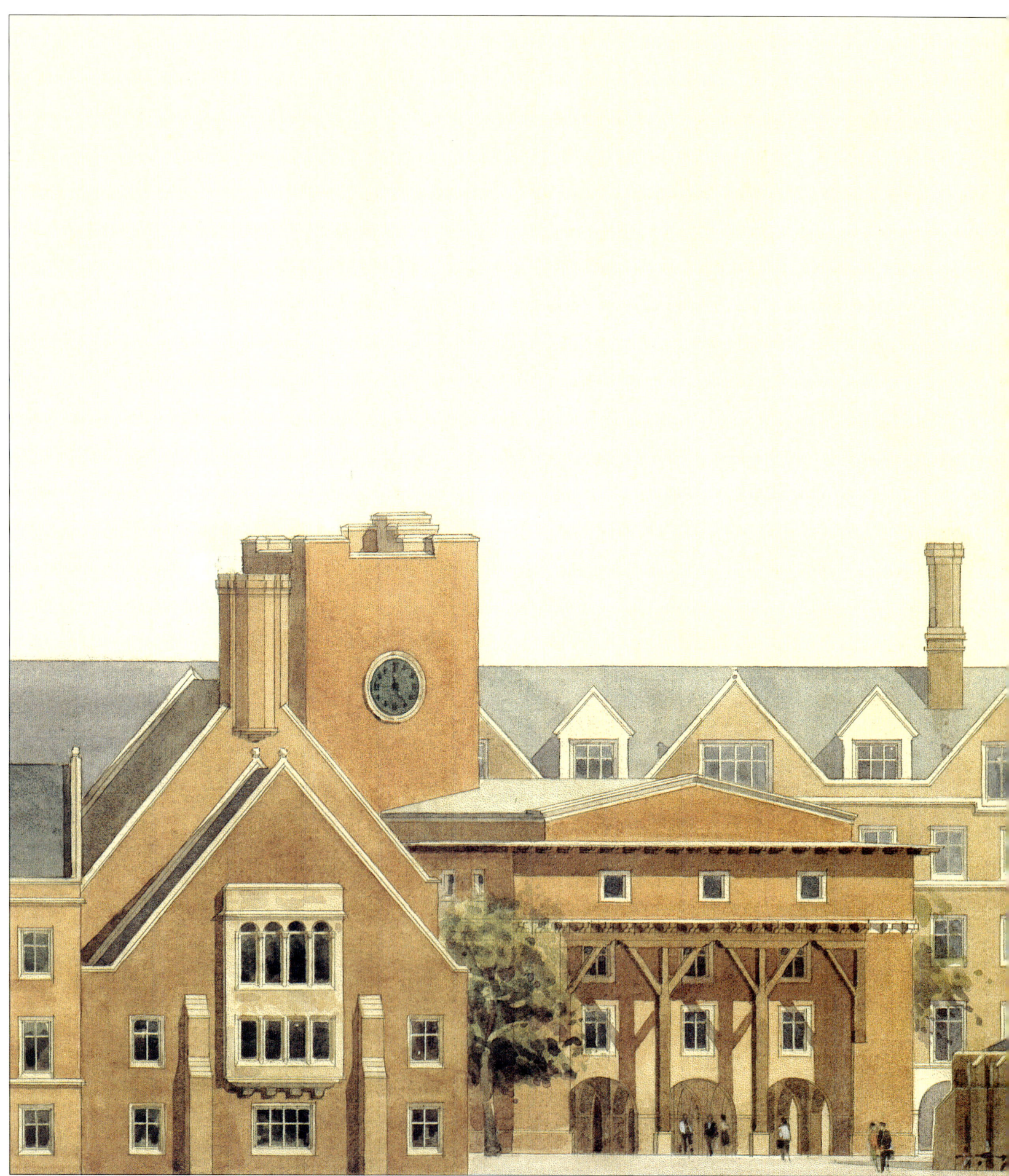

PARTIAL ELEVATION FACING THE CANAL

INLAND REVENUE OFFICES

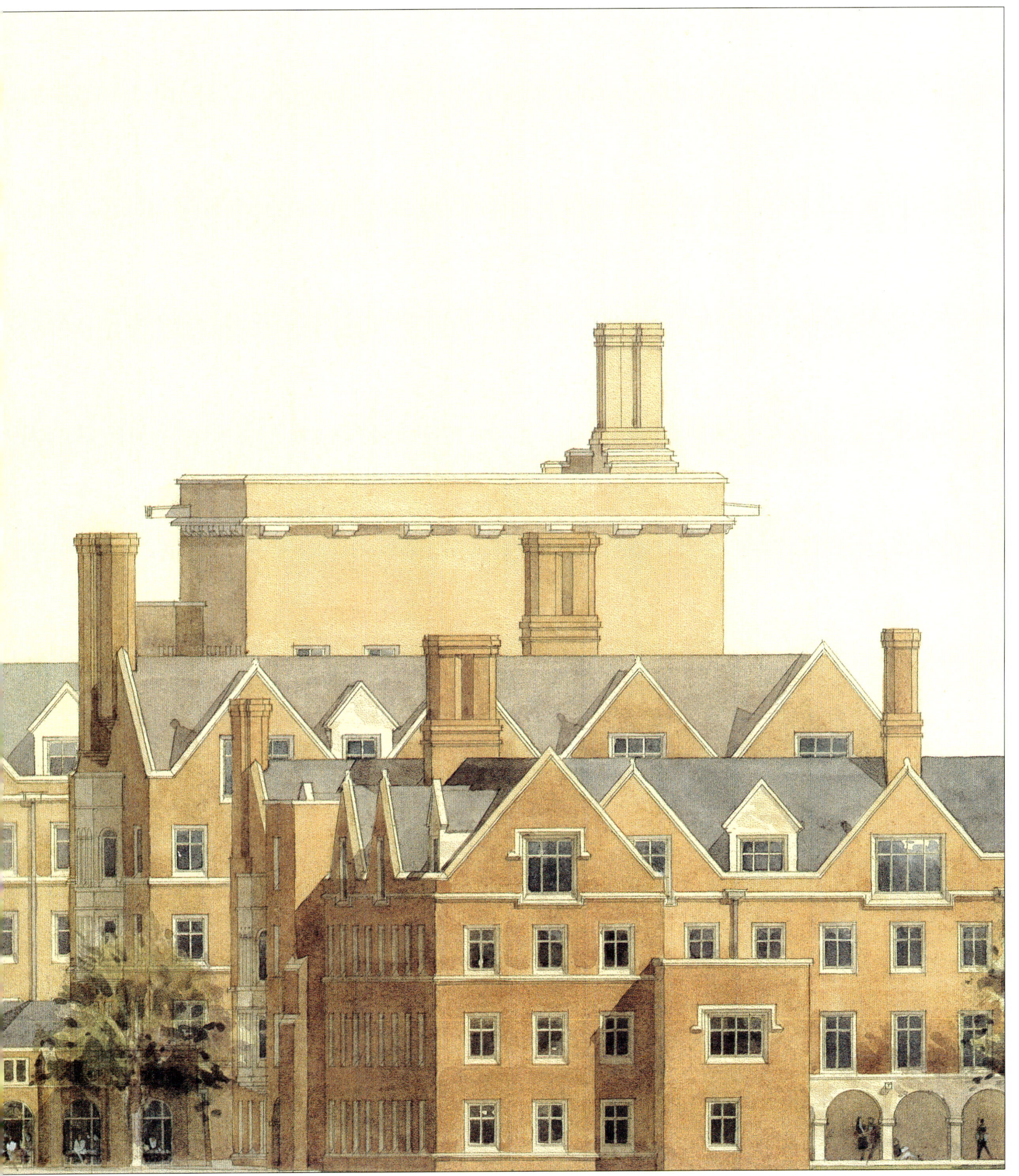

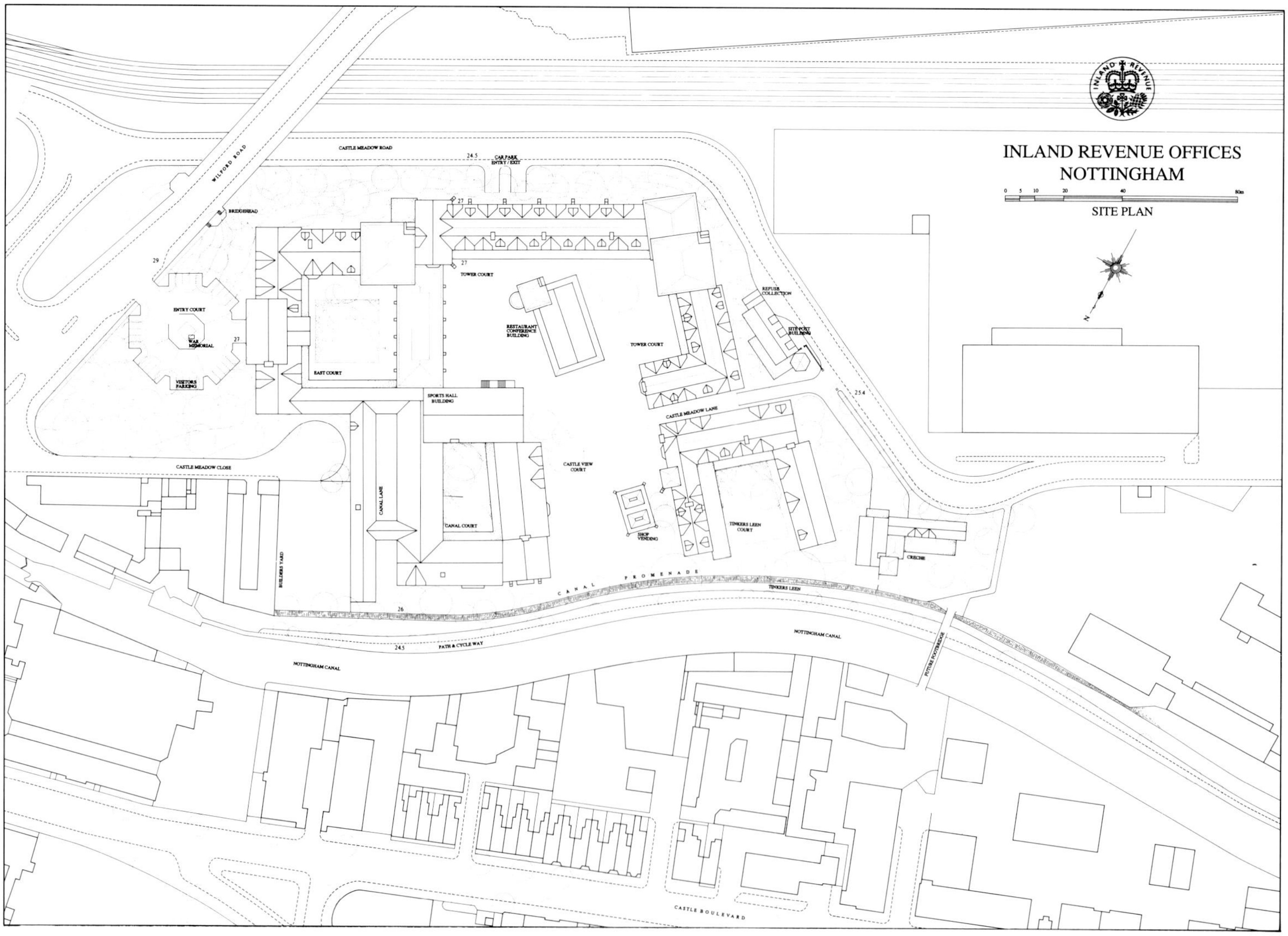

DEMETRI PORPHYRIOS

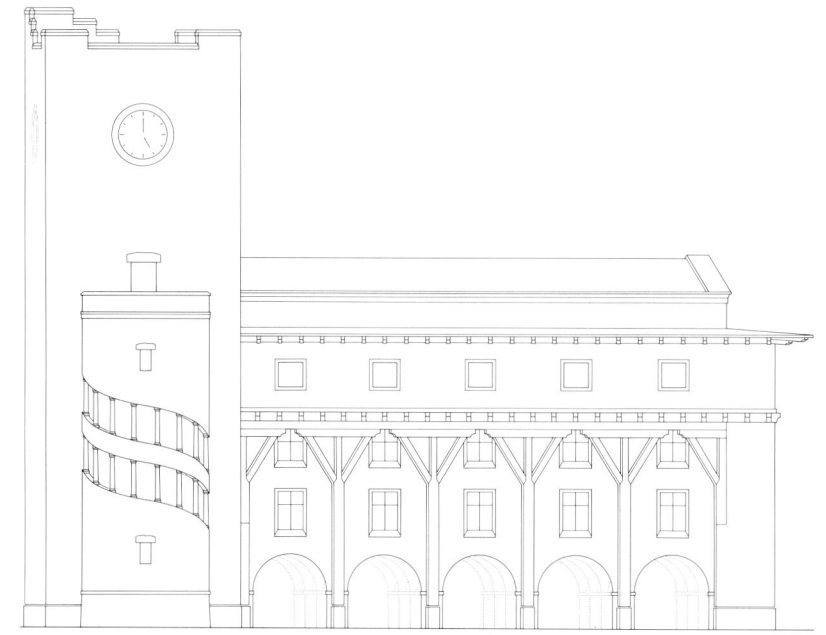

ABOVE: NORTH-EAST ELEVATION OF RESTAURANT AND CONFERENCE BUILDING; *BELOW*: SITE PLAN

INLAND REVENUE OFFICES

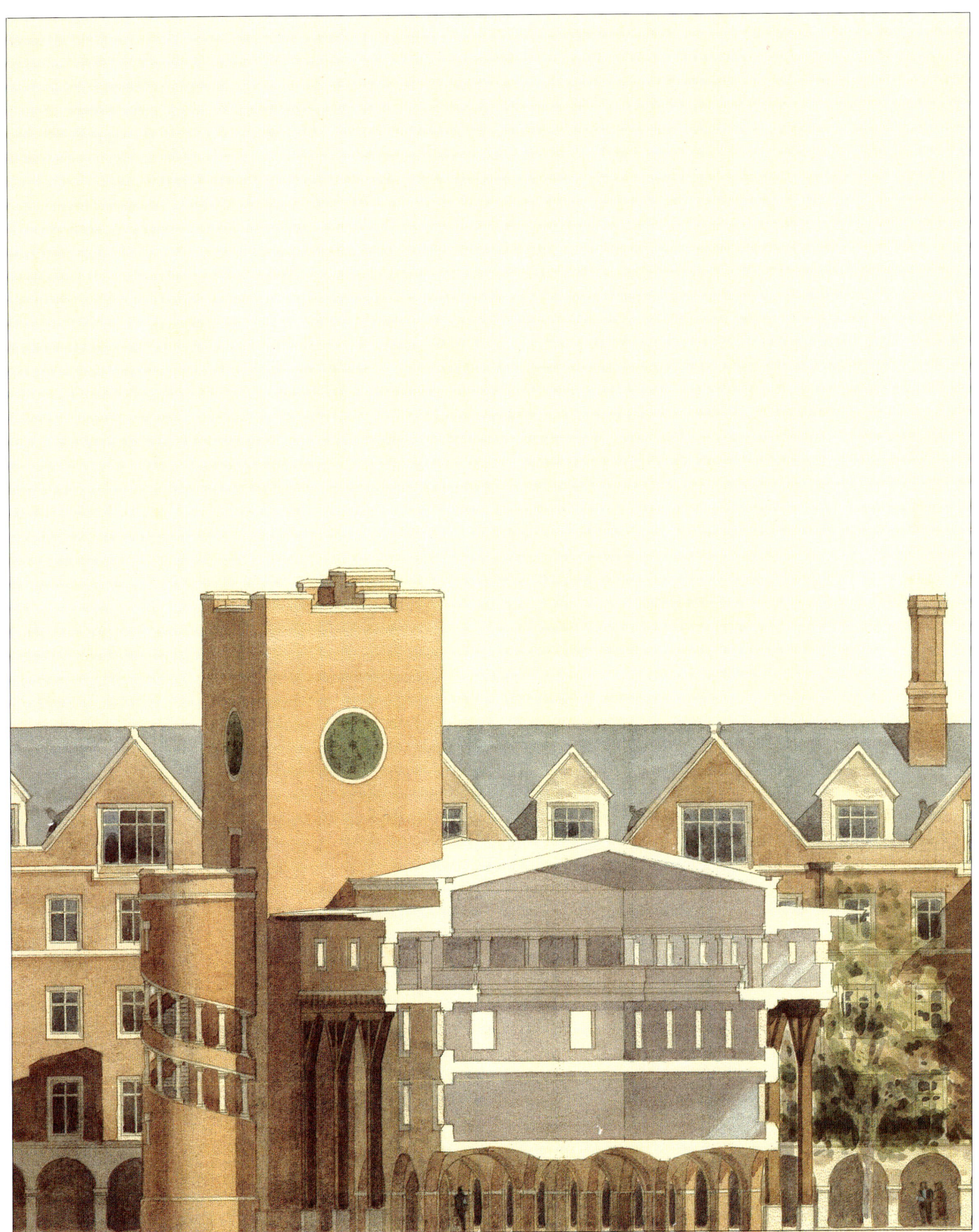

SECTIONAL ELEVATION OF RESTAURANT AND CONFERENCE BUILDING

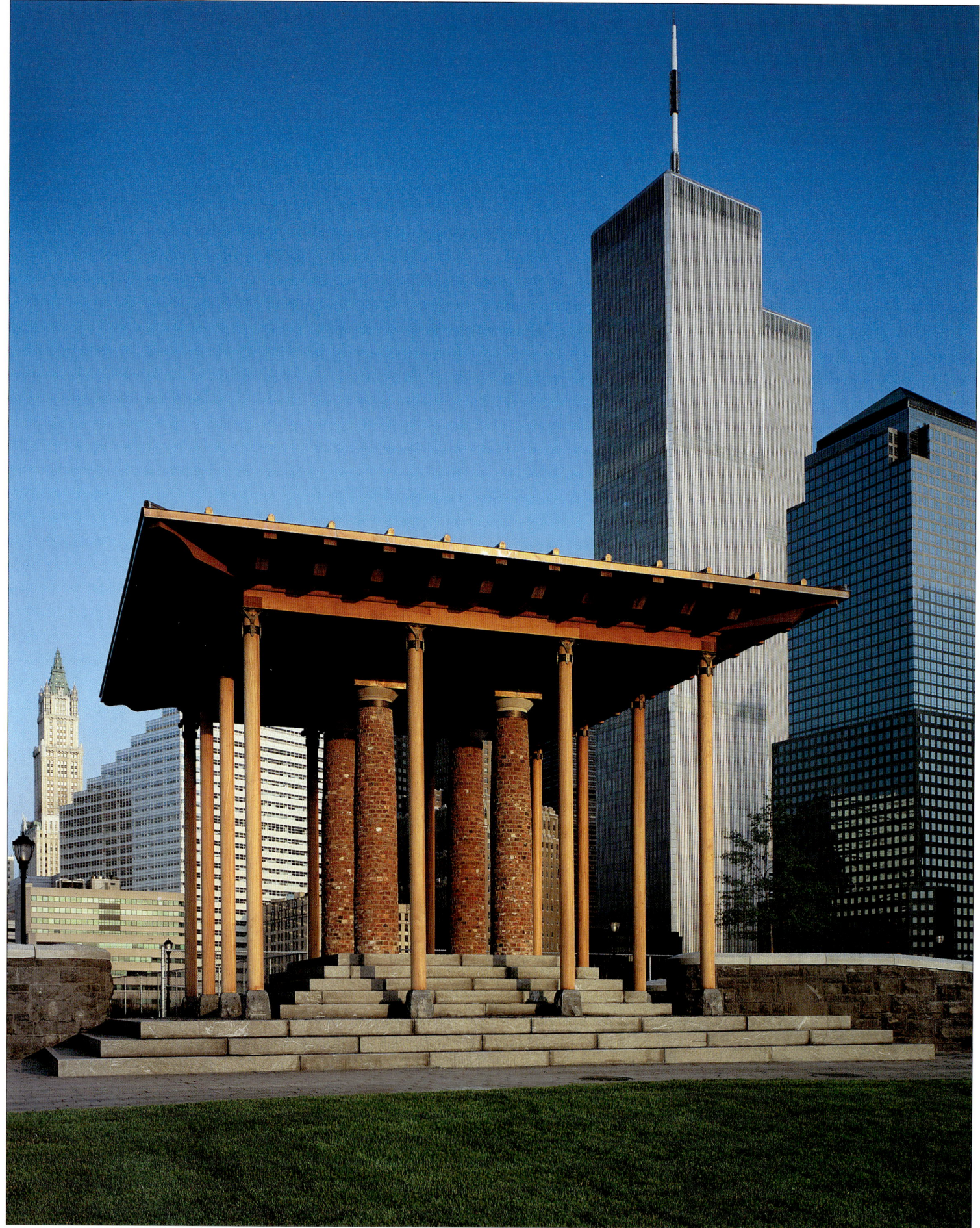

VIEW FROM THE HUDSON RIVER

BATTERY PARK CITY PAVILION
NEW YORK, 1990

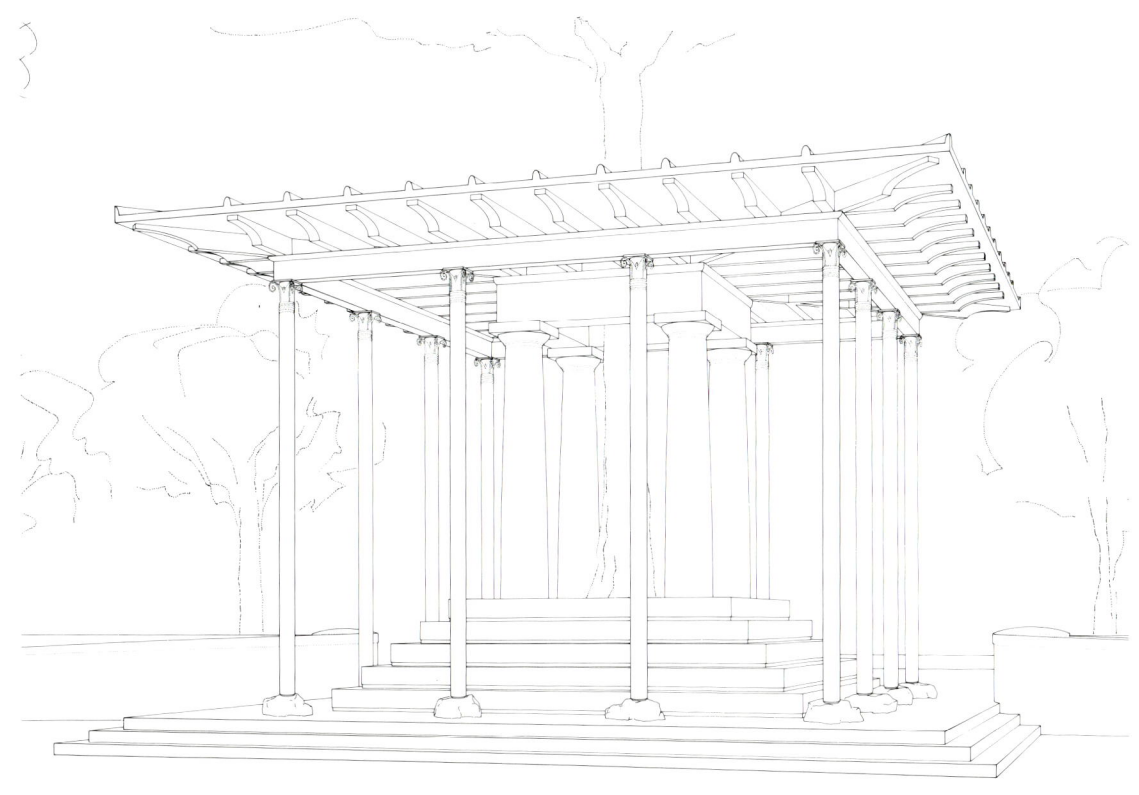

This is the winning design in an invited architectural competition. The pavilion stands at the North Park esplanade in New York's Battery Park City adjacent to the World Financial Centre and the Hudson River.

We were asked to design a belvedere for the park which could also be used as a stage for public events such as music performances. The pavilion takes the form of a stepped mound with a timber peristyle along its perimeter and four brick columns at the centre that mark a covered atrium. The plan and section of the pavilion and the morphology of its constructional elements point clearly to the tectonic nature of architecture.

Along its perimeter, the pavilion has twelve round timber posts: they sit on rough-cut stones and support a perimeter timber lintel which carries the rafters of the roof and its boarding. The roof is covered in copper. The timber posts are surmounted with aeolic capitals. In contrast to the peristyle the four columns of the atrium are in brick with stone doric capitals. Here the language of the shed slowly transforms itself into architecture. This is not, however, a fully developed doric order. The shafts of the columns are in second-hand brickwork, there are no flutings, and the otherwise doric entablature is missing.

The materials are generally teak or mahogany for the timberwork, second-hand red bricks for the doric columns, limestone for the capitals, granite for the bases to the posts and the steps, granite sets for all ground finishes, copper for the roofing, and a special copper and bronze alloy for the aeolic capitals.

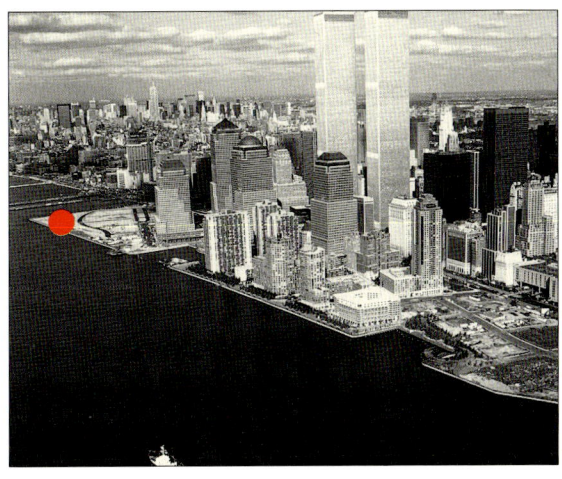

ABOVE: PERSPECTIVE; *BELOW*: LOCATION PHOTOGRAPH

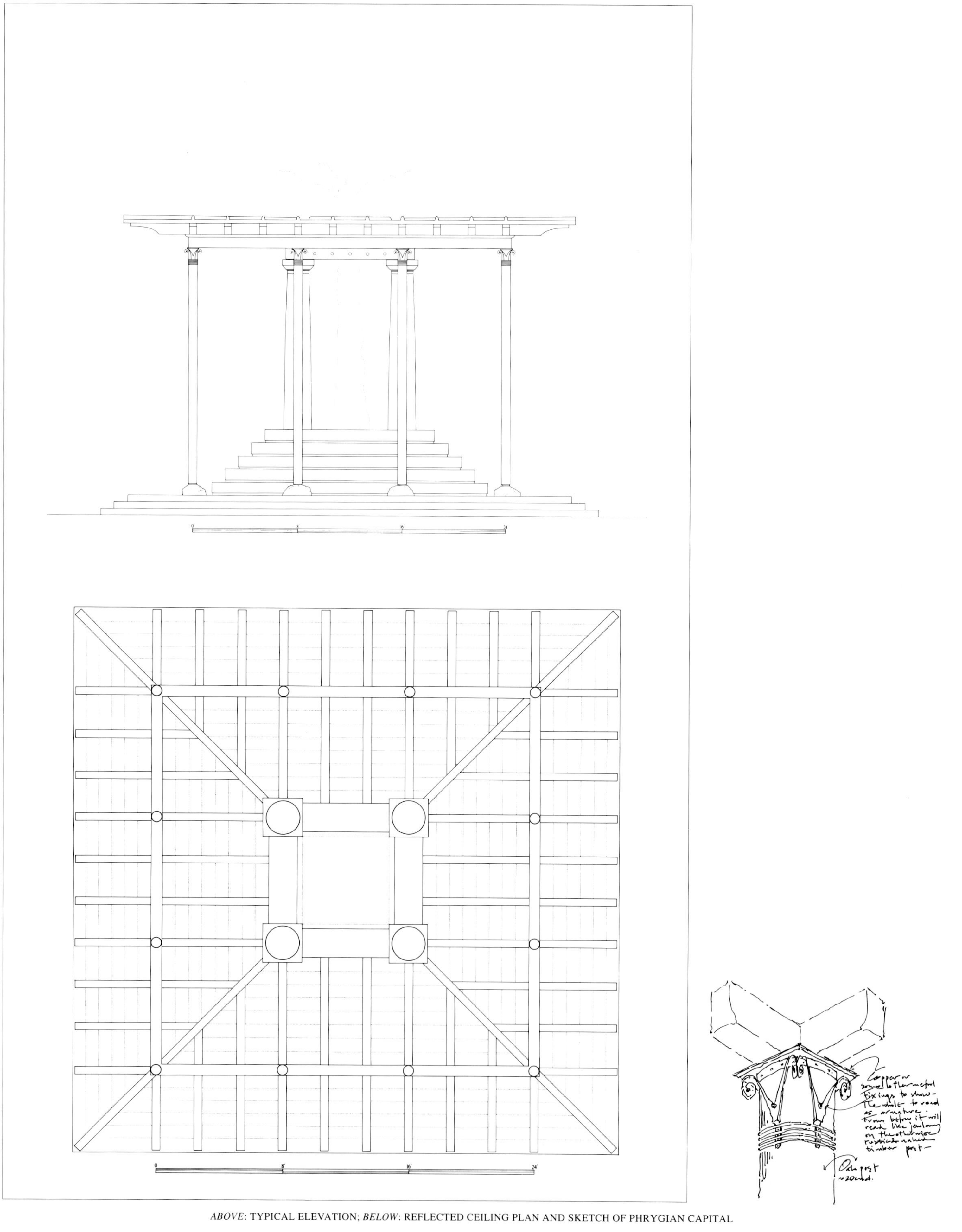

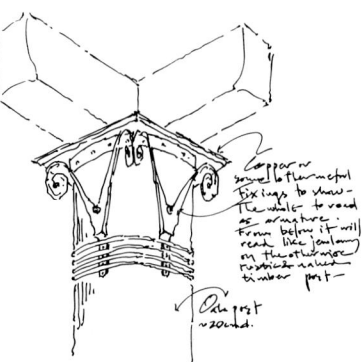

ABOVE: TYPICAL ELEVATION; *BELOW*: REFLECTED CEILING PLAN AND SKETCH OF PHRYGIAN CAPITAL

BATTERY PARK CITY PAVILION

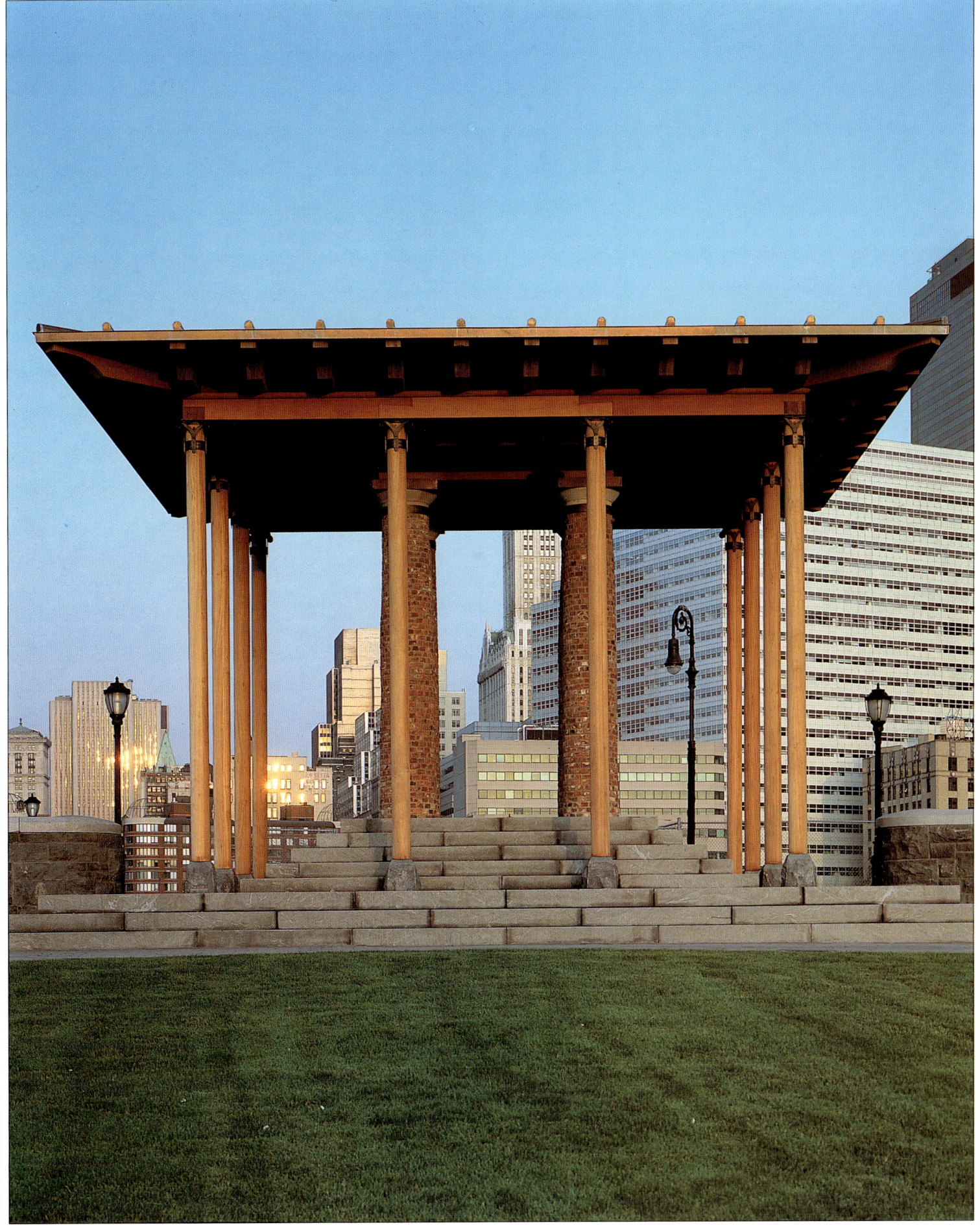

VIEW FROM THE RIVER HUDSON

MAGDALEN COLLEGE
NEW LONGWALL QUADRANGLE OXFORD, 1991

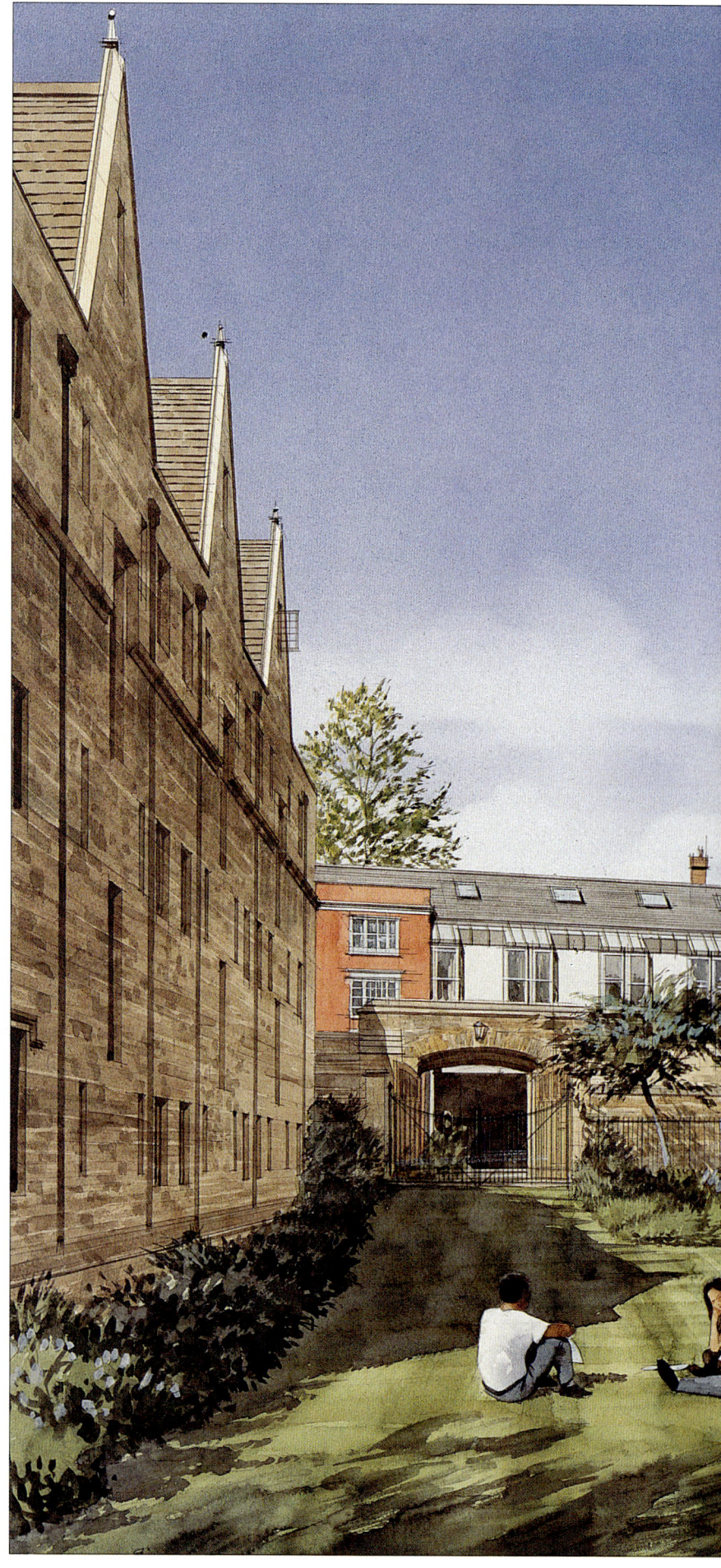

The proposal for a new quadrangle for Magdalen College in Oxford comprises residential accommodation for students and a lecture theatre. The scheme shown here is the winning entry in an invited architectural competition.

Any sensible proposal for the New Longwall Quadrangle cannot disregard the characteristic 'open grain' in the building fabric of Magdalen College. We took the view, therefore, that we must encourage this interplay between solids and voids and, taking into account the requirements of the brief, we proposed a new quadrangle which re-affirms the urban quality of the adjacent quads while opening up to the east towards the deer-park.

The lecture theatre is placed close to the Longwall Gate thus enhancing the area as a place of arrival. It is entered through an octagonal open-air pavilion that leads to a skylit foyer. The theatre proper, a great hall with a raked floor and a trussed oak roof, is a flexible space which features both seating in the round and seating for cinematic projection. The lecture theatre presents itself as an enigmatic camera obscura. Its scale derives from the great round windows that flank its sides between which corbelled volutes are positioned to receive future sculptures.

In siting the residential buildings we broke them down into small units oriented towards the deer park and with maximum views of the Great Tower. The Longwall Range has an arcade appended to its east side while the building next to it steps forward slightly to break the massing of the range when viewed from Longwall Street. Residential accommodation is organised in traditional Oxford sets of two or four rooms per landing.

The buildings are constructed in masonry walls with ashlar stone externally and plaster with lime paint internally. All exposed timber work is in oak. Roofs are generally in stone slates except that of the theatre which is finished in copper.

The contrast between the classical of the theatre and the vernacular of the halls of residence heightens the dialogue between their public and private nature respectively, thus underlining the urban quality of the scheme and its relation to the existing College. This is not an introverted megastructure, but rather a quadrangle where buildings of different character and scale co-exist like members of a family; creating open spaces to be enjoyed by the College community and in harmony with the existing landscape.

MAGDALEN COLLEGE

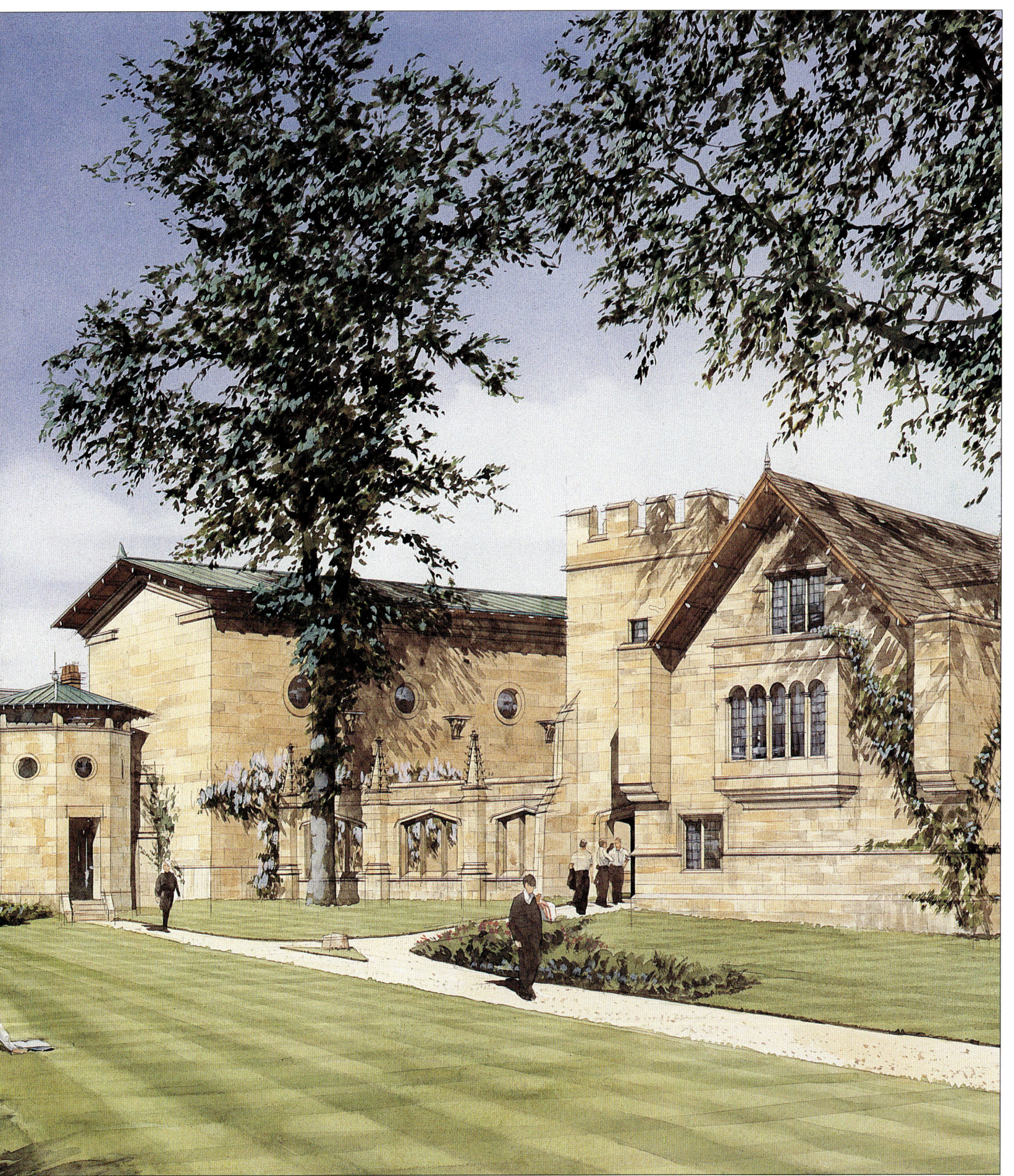

PERSPECTIVE VIEW OF AUDITORIUM AND ENTRANCE TO QUADRANGLE

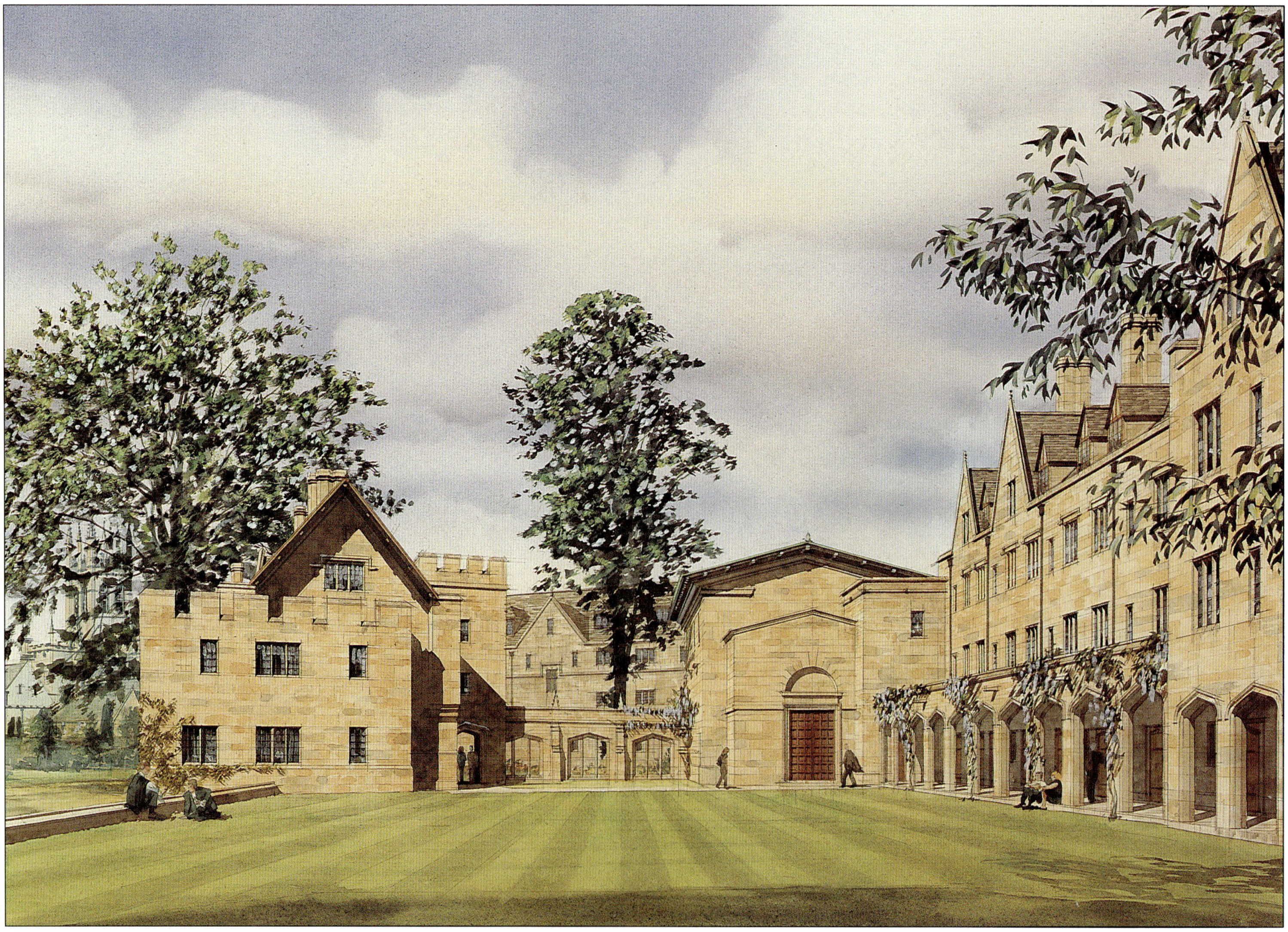

DEMETRI PORPHYRIOS

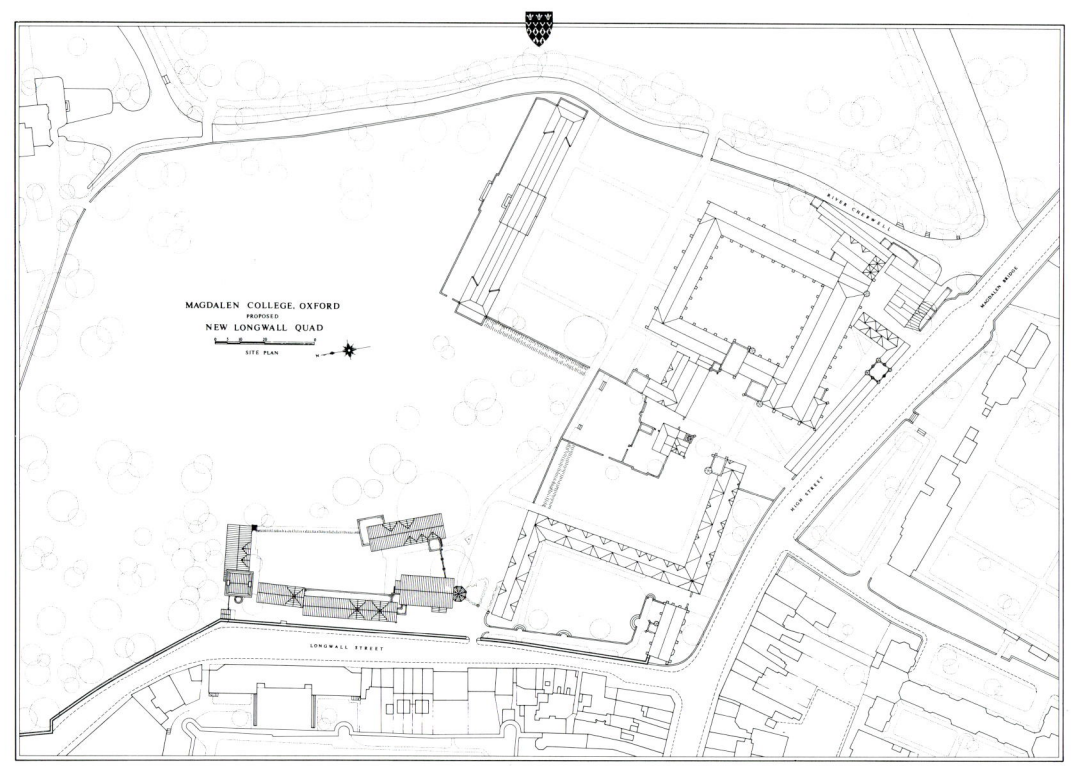

ABOVE: SITE PLAN; *BELOW*: PERSPECTIVE VIEW OF QUADRANGLE

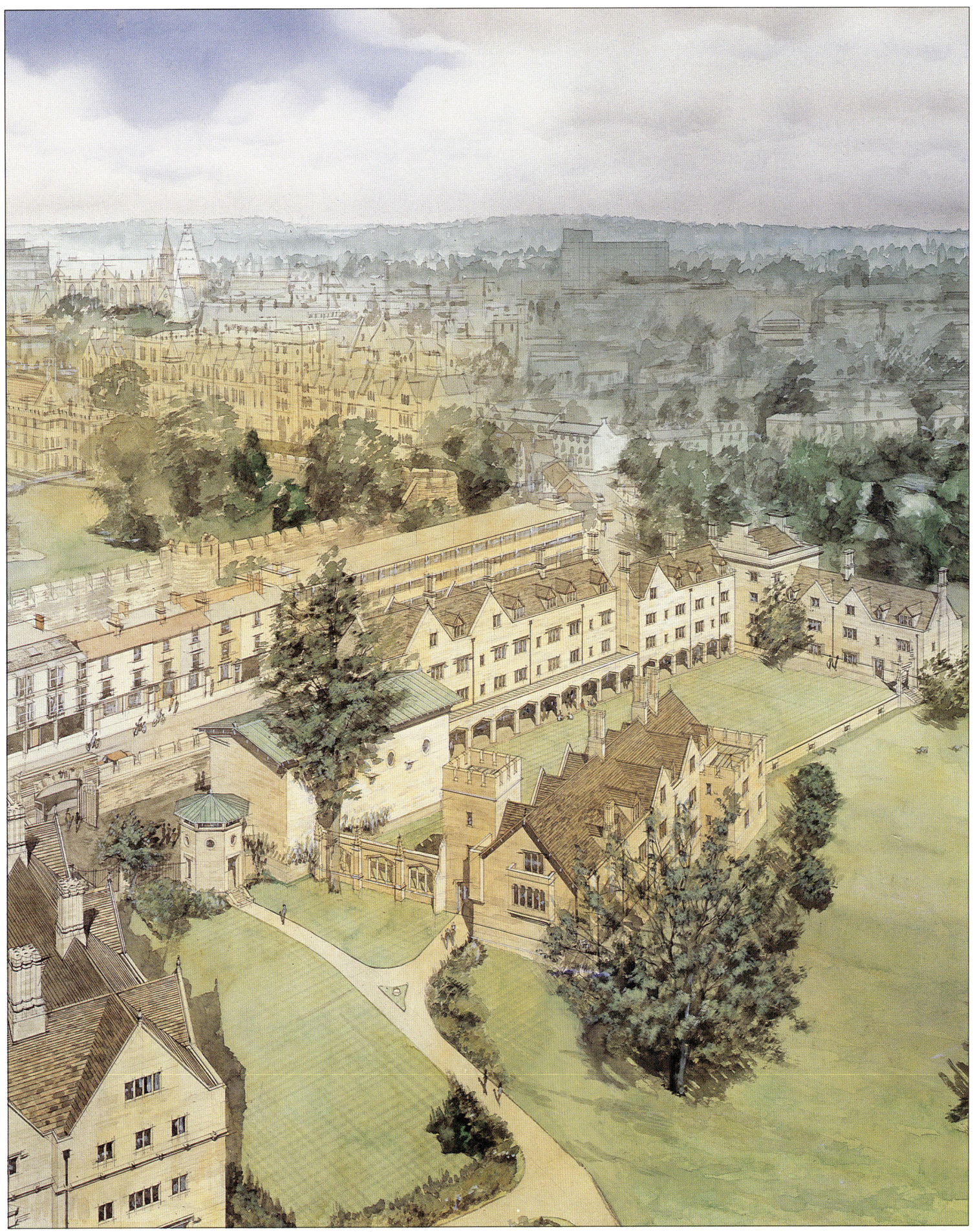

AERIAL PERSPECTIVE VIEW OF QUADRANGLE

DEMETRI PORPHYRIOS

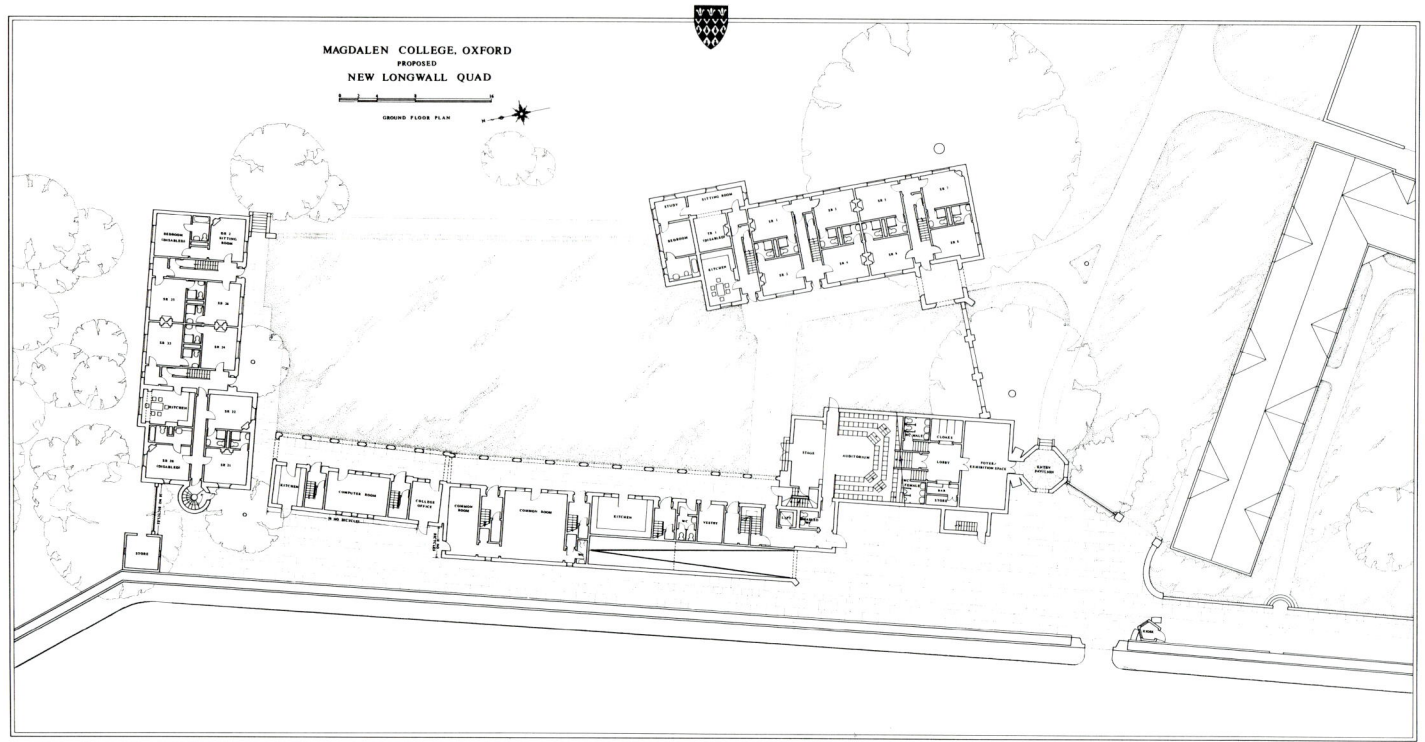

GROUND-FLOOR PLAN

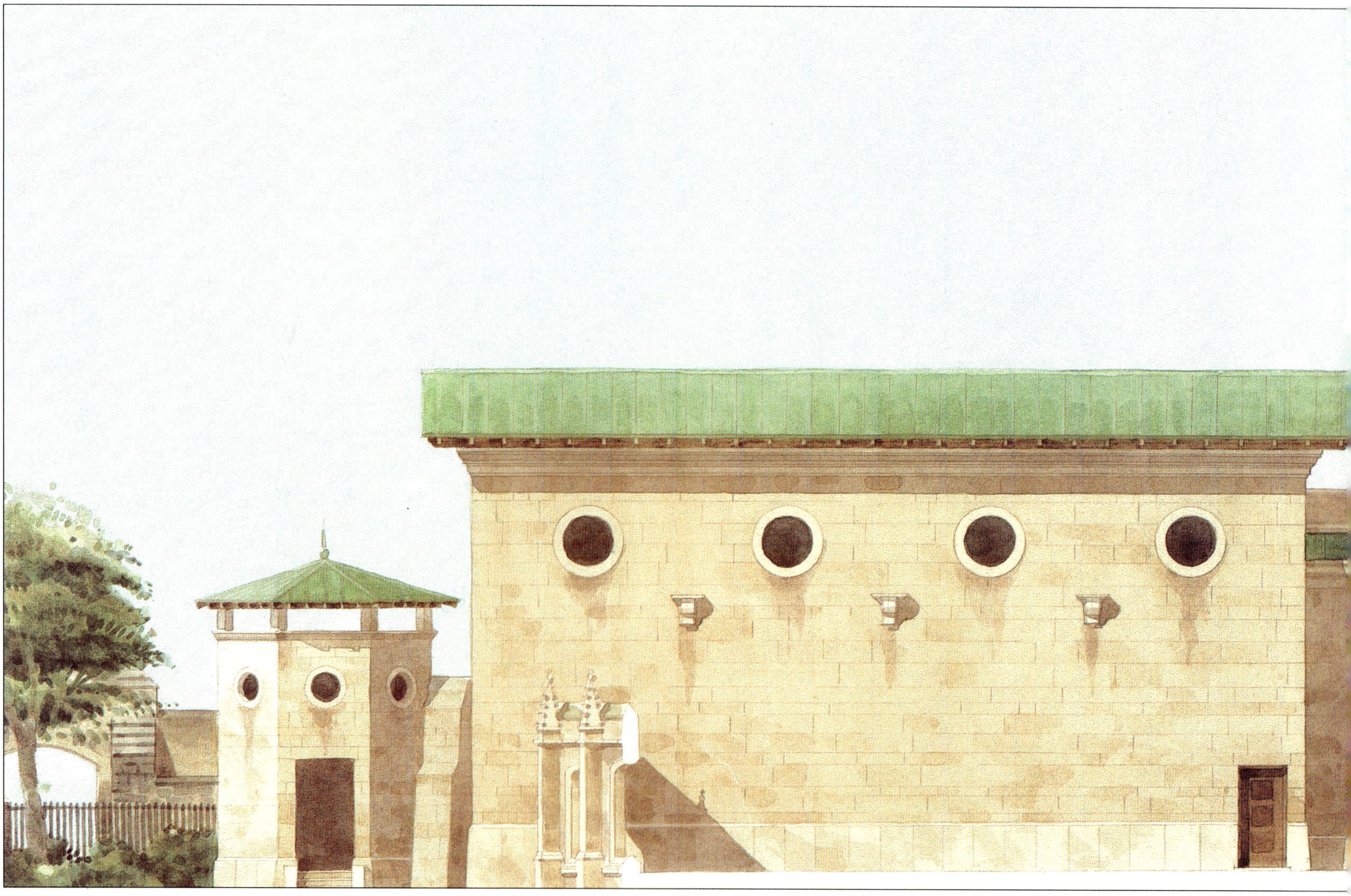

SECTIONAL ELEVATION THROUGH THE QUADRANGLE

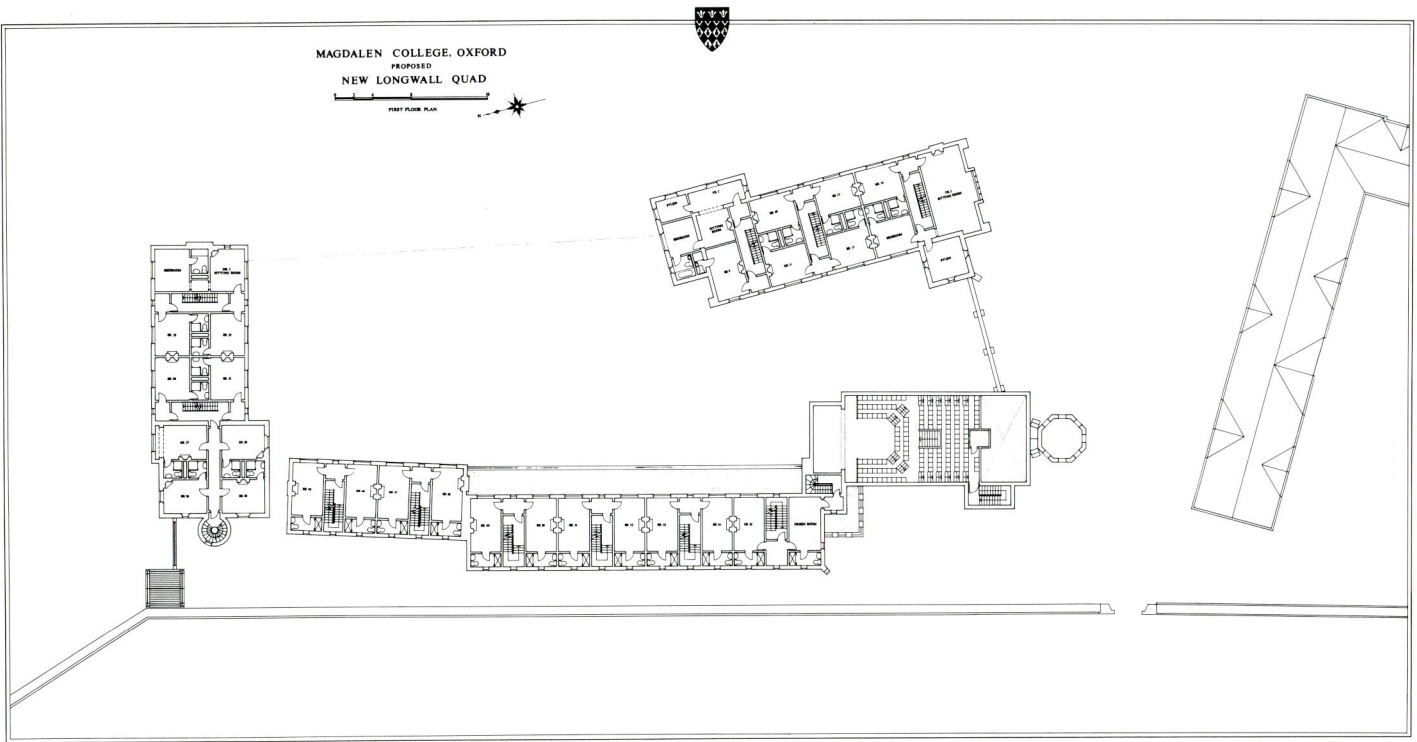

FIRST-FLOOR PLAN

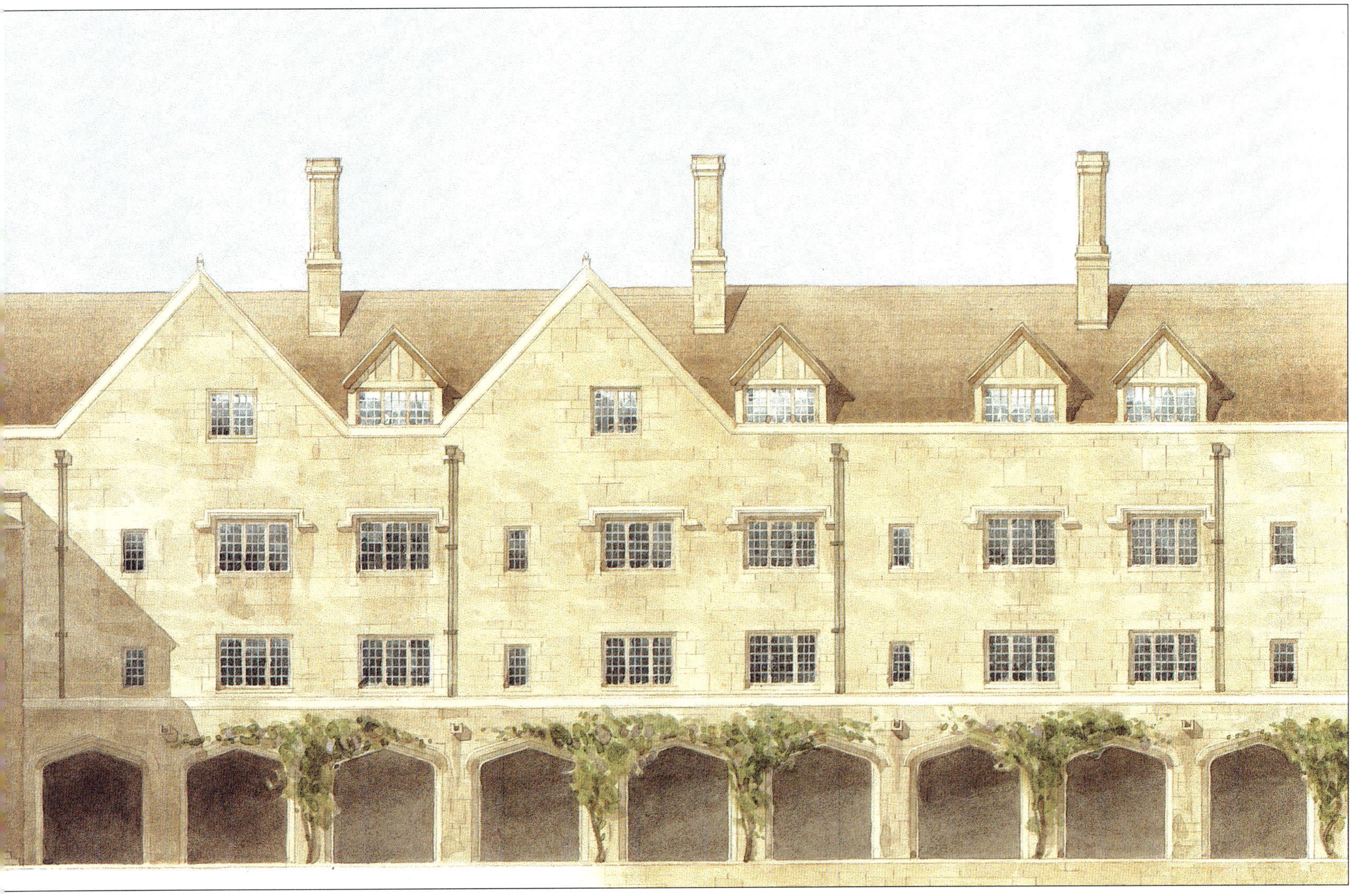

DEMETRI PORPHYRIOS

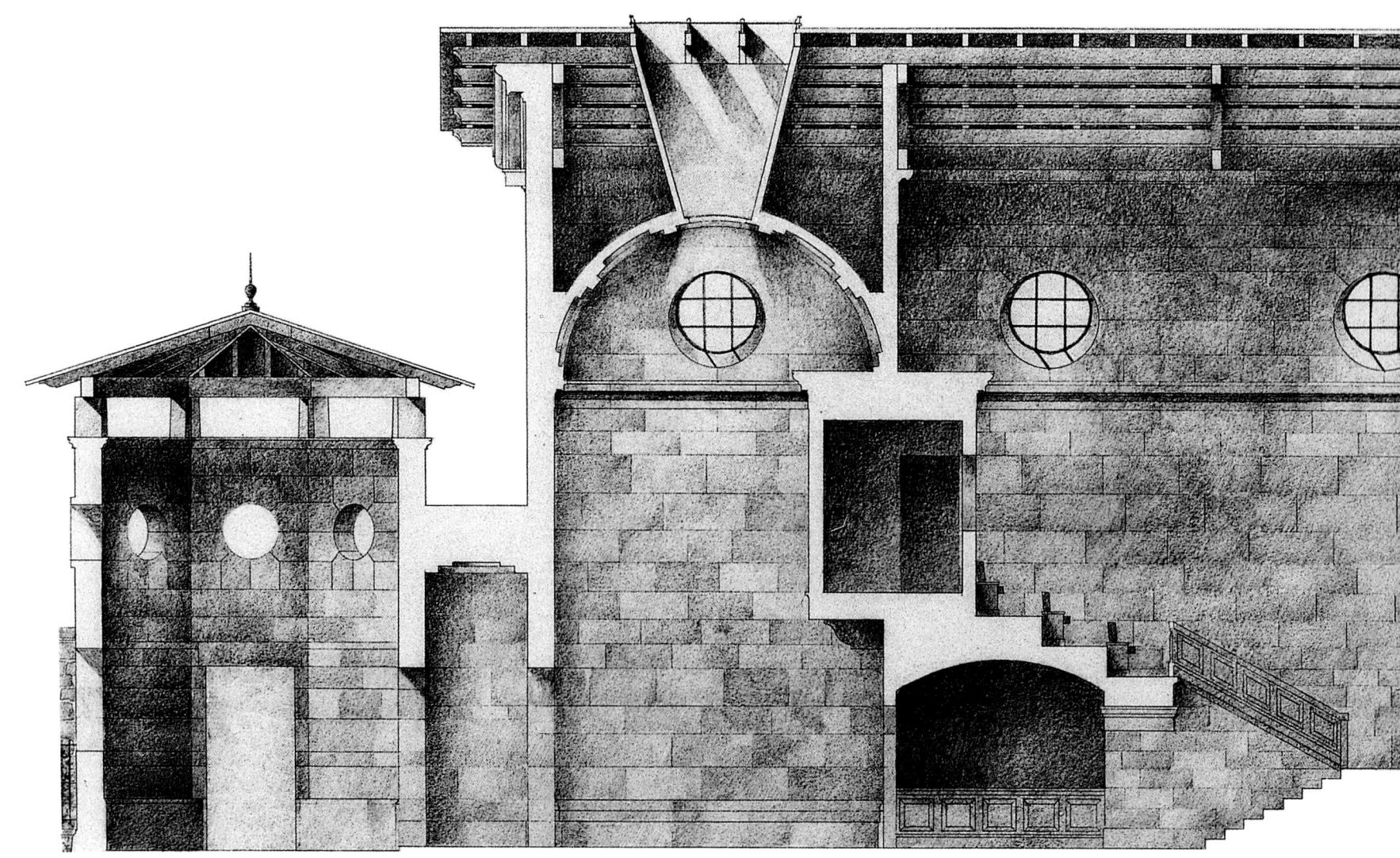

SECTION THROUGH ENTRANCE PAVILION, FOYER AND AUDITORIUM; *OVERLEAF*: SOUTH ELEVATION

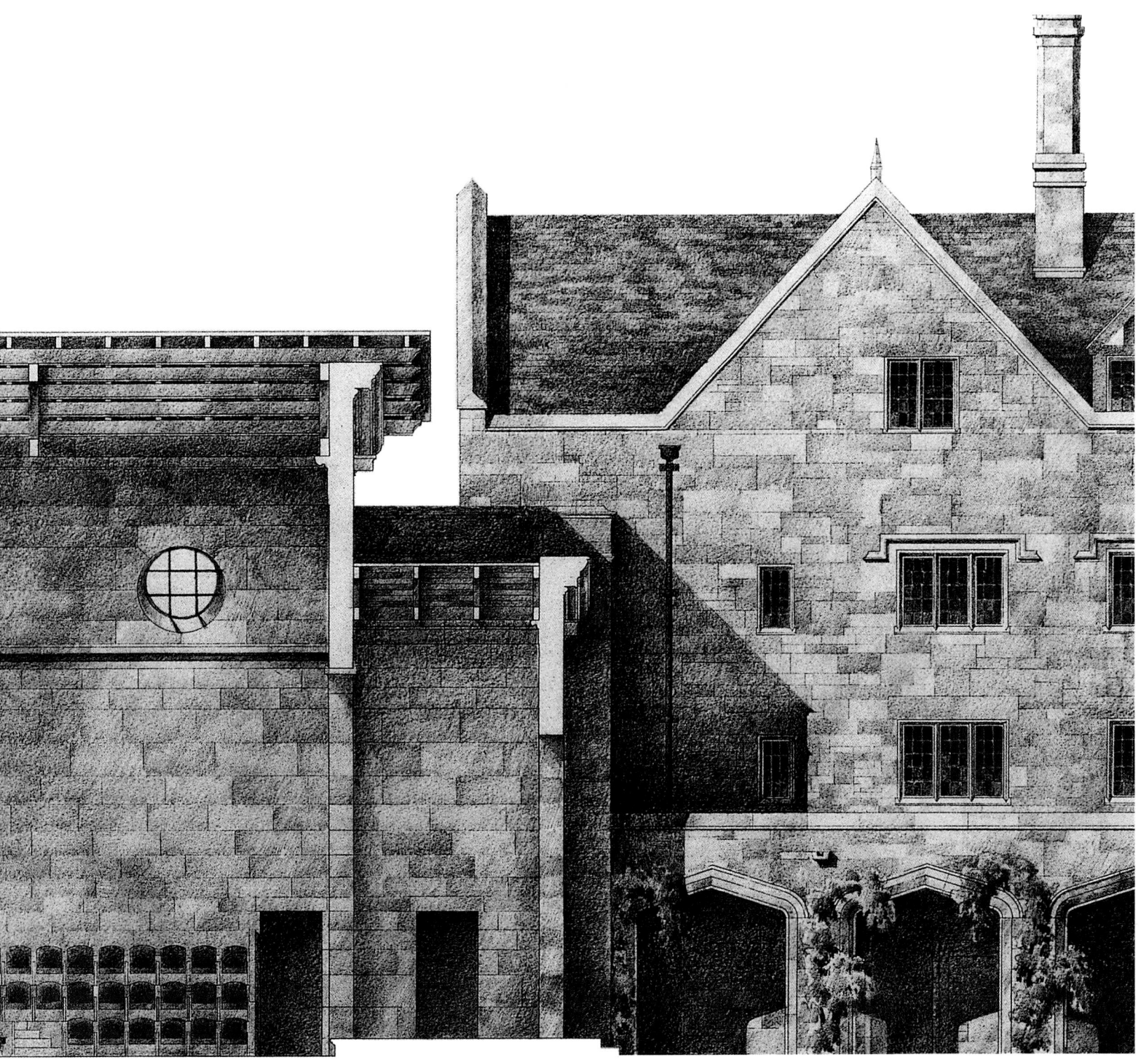

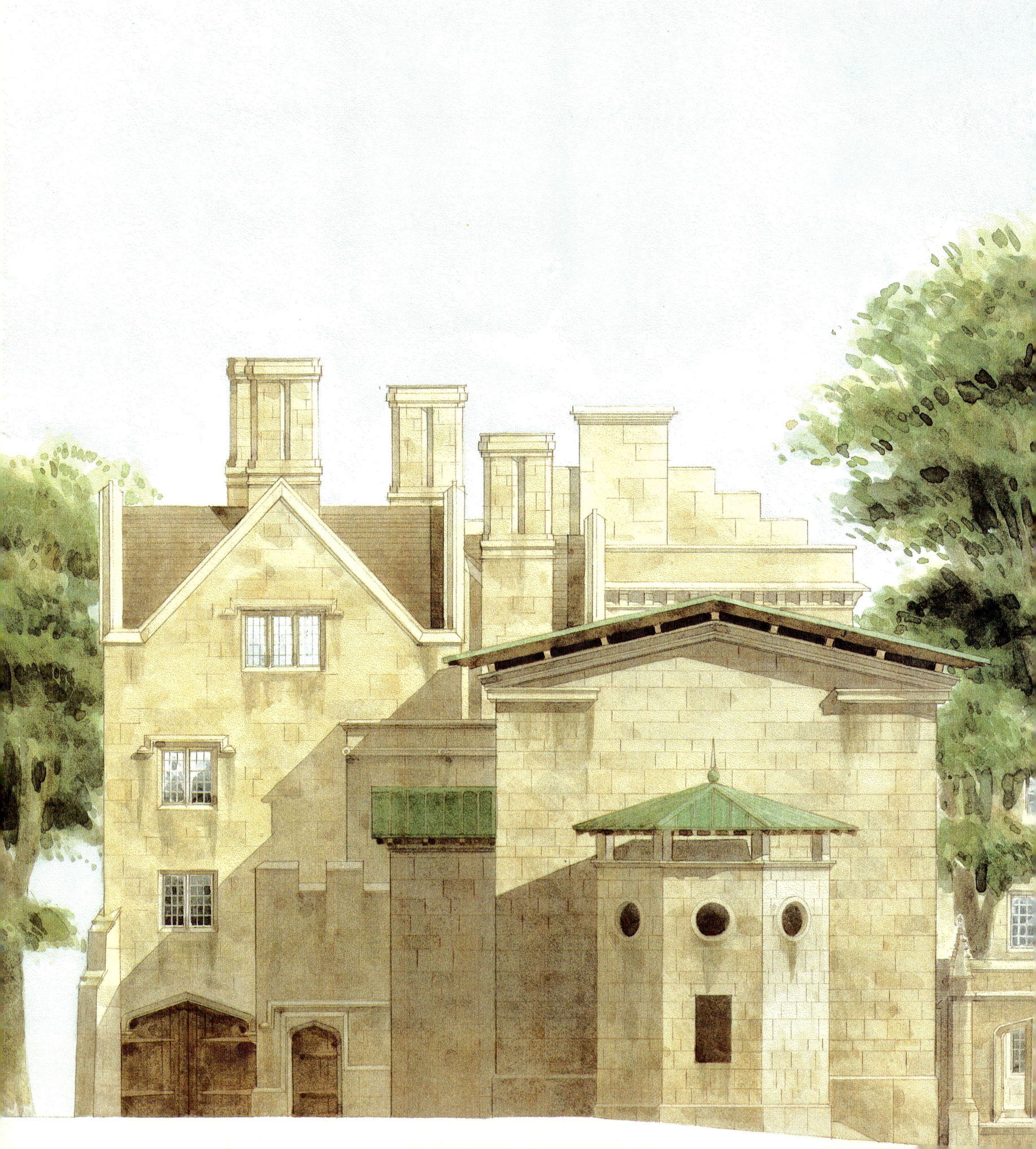

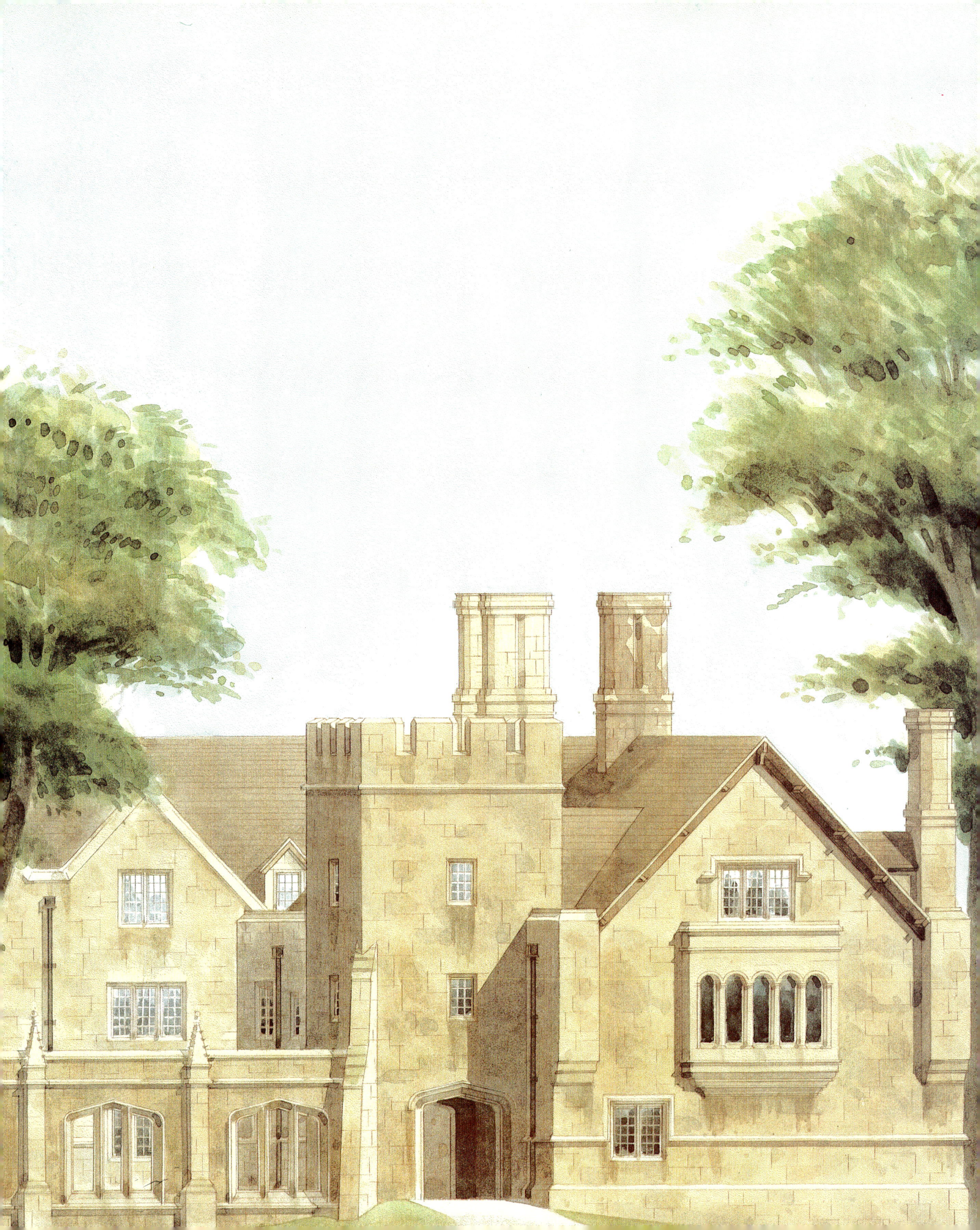

DEMETRI PORPHYRIOS

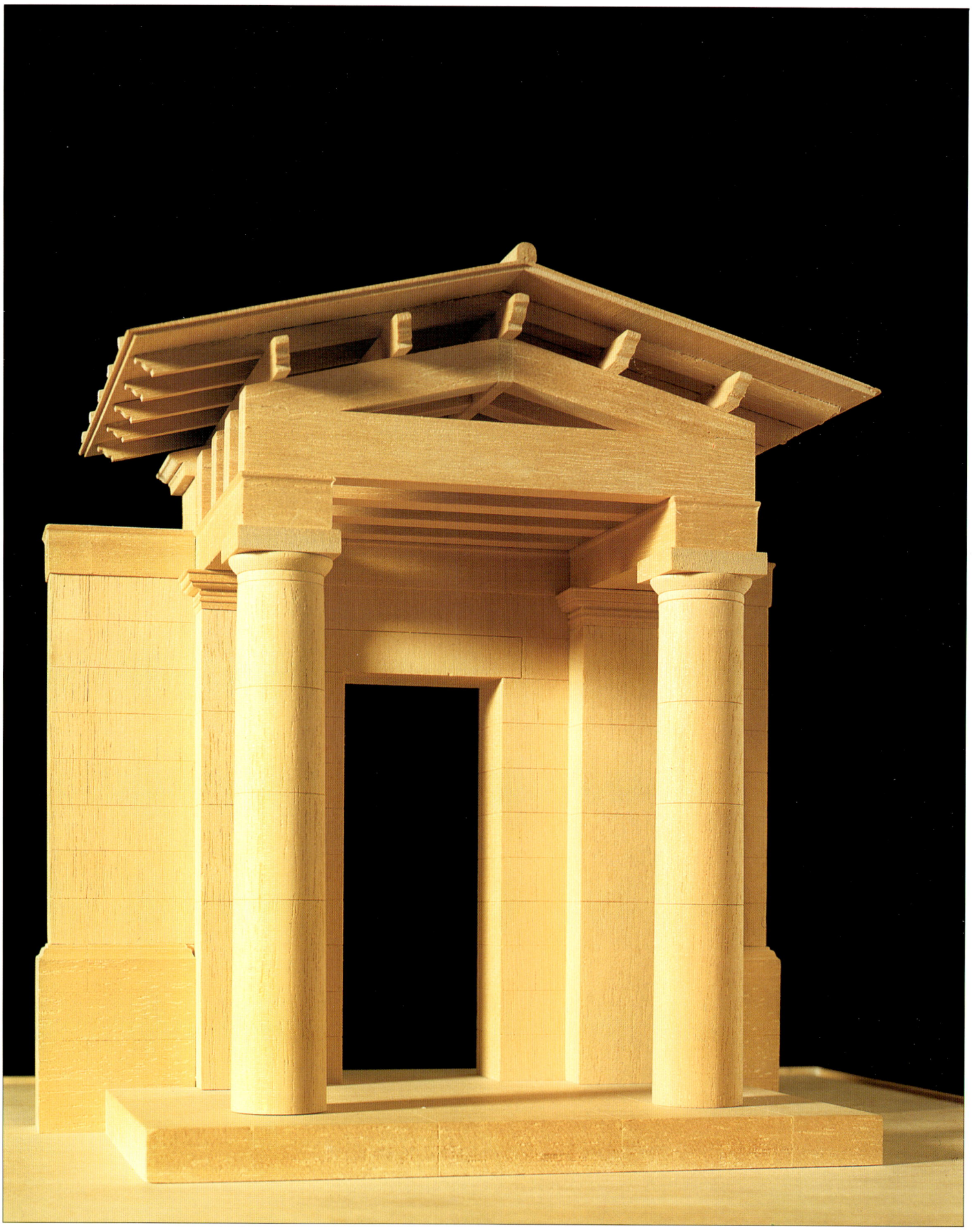

PROPYLON IN SURREY
1984

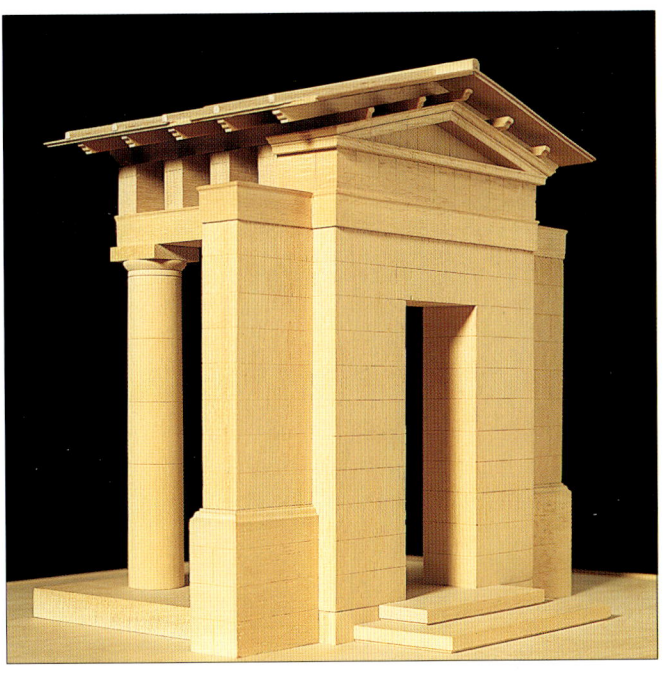

This is a votive gate for a country estate in Surrey. It is situated at the edge between the formal grounds of the estate and its forested land beyond.

The elevation facing the house has a pedimented front surmounted by a timber roof. The treatment here is highly refined with all profiles carefully proportioned and executed with precision in Portland stone. The side facing the forested land has a rather vernacular character. The pediment has given way to a series of oak trusses resting on oak architraves that are held by brick columns and engaged pilasters. The end faces of the trusses with the void metopes inbetween and the timber architrave below are juxtaposed to the refined language of the stone entablature pointing out the constructional origins of classical architecture.

The transition from the 'forest' to the 'city' is represented here as a dialogue between vernacular and the classical.

This is a trilithic construction with the didactic aim of describing the origins of the classical in the tectonics of the post-and-lintel. A tectonic experience is the sine qua non of architecture. It conveys a sense of the necessary because construction is determined by the form-giving capacity of the materials used.

At the same time a tectonic experience conveys a sense of freedom. Much like play, it sets its own rules as an image of real construction and shelter. In this sense tectonic order is an artistic fiction removed from the contingencies of the building trade, yet invested with the experience of stability, unity and balance which the craft of building describes in the first place.

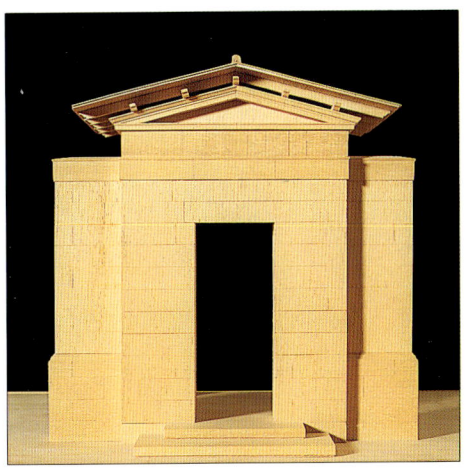

DEMETRI PORPHYRIOS

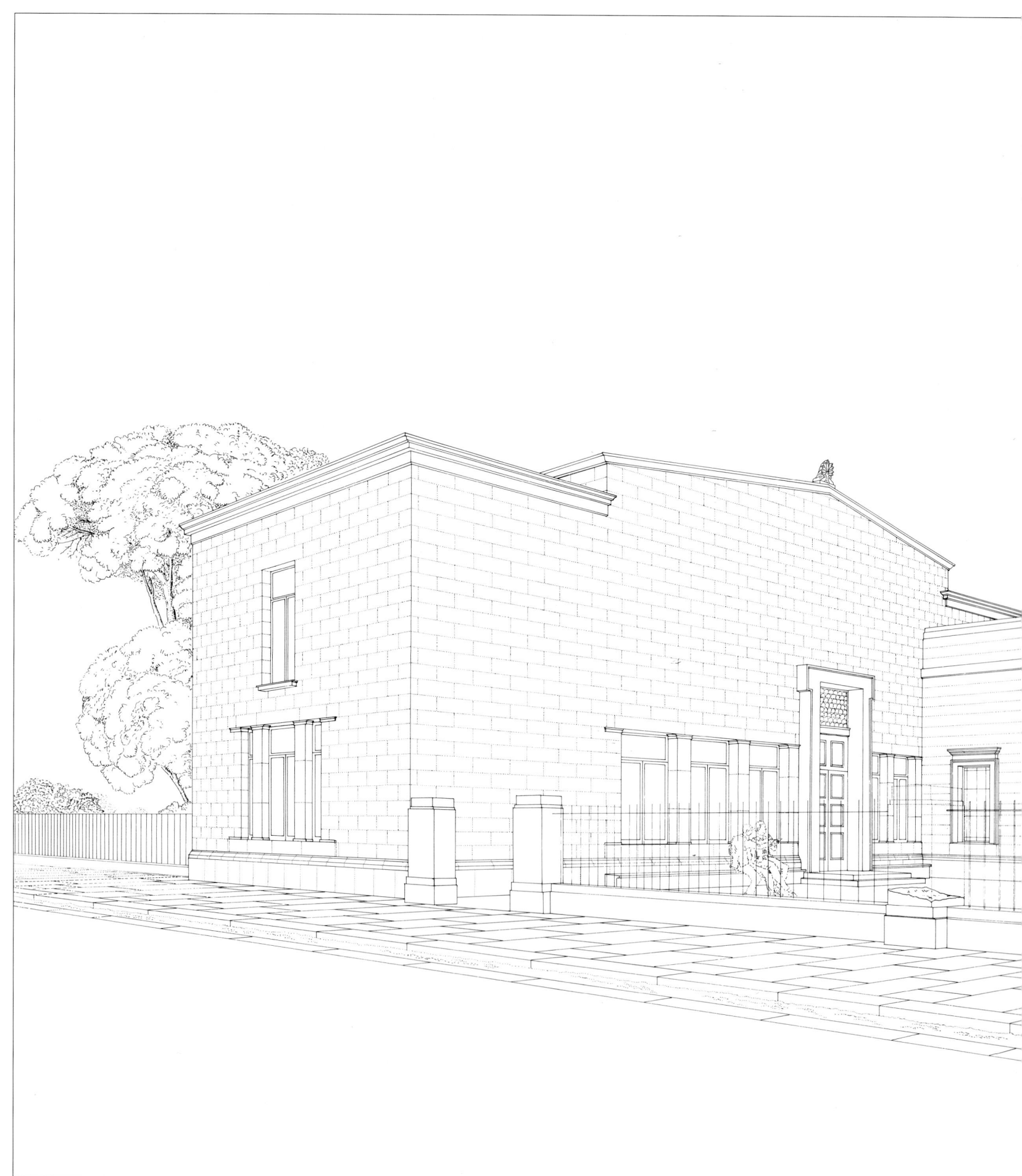

PERSPECTIVE VIEW FROM TRUMPINGTON STREET

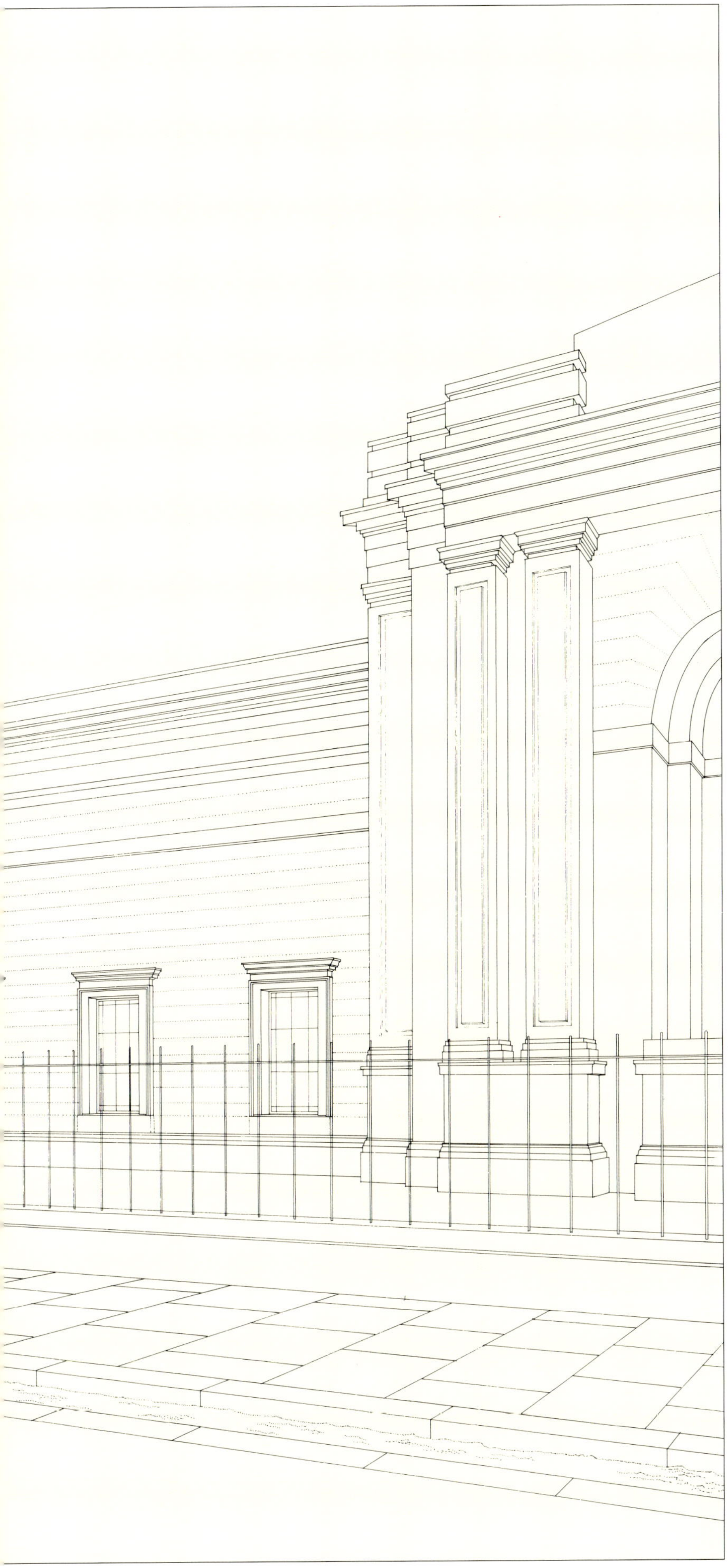

THE FITZWILLIAM MUSEUM EXTENSION
CAMBRIDGE, 1986

Our entry for the Fitzwilliam Museum competition in Cambridge was one of the final three schemes selected. The project addresses urban and architectural issues related to extending a national monument in the historic centre of Cambridge.

The new building completes the 'unfinished' side of the Fitzwilliam court and establishes a counterpoint to the views from Trumpington Street. The new extension is given the character of a free-standing building while, for programmatic reasons, it remains physically attached to the Museum.

Internally our proposed extension is organised along two routes. The primary route aligns with the axis of Basevi's lion pavilions. This is the route that visitors to the new sculpture galleries would take. The other route connects the coffee bar with the museum shop and eventually links up with the existing ground floor galleries. The lecture hall is located in the basement beneath the octagonal sculpture gallery.

The building has high quality internal finishes while the exterior walls are in flush jointed Portland stone similar to that used throughout the Museum. The massing is characterised by simplicity and decorative elements have been used sparingly. The richly sculptural pediment of the Founder's Building is echoed in the gabled front of our proposed extension. Yet the character of the proposed extension derives not so much from sculptural richness or elocution of ornament as from the contrast between areas of sculptural intensity and expanses of unadorned surface.

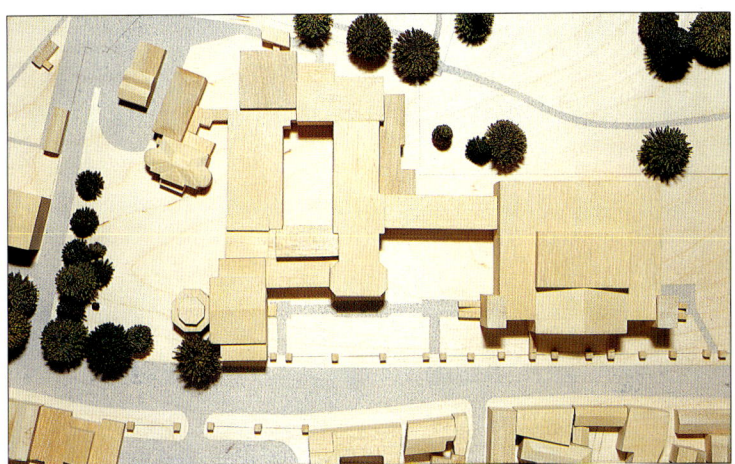

MODEL SHOWING THE EXTENSION IN CONTEXT

DEMETRI PORPHYRIOS

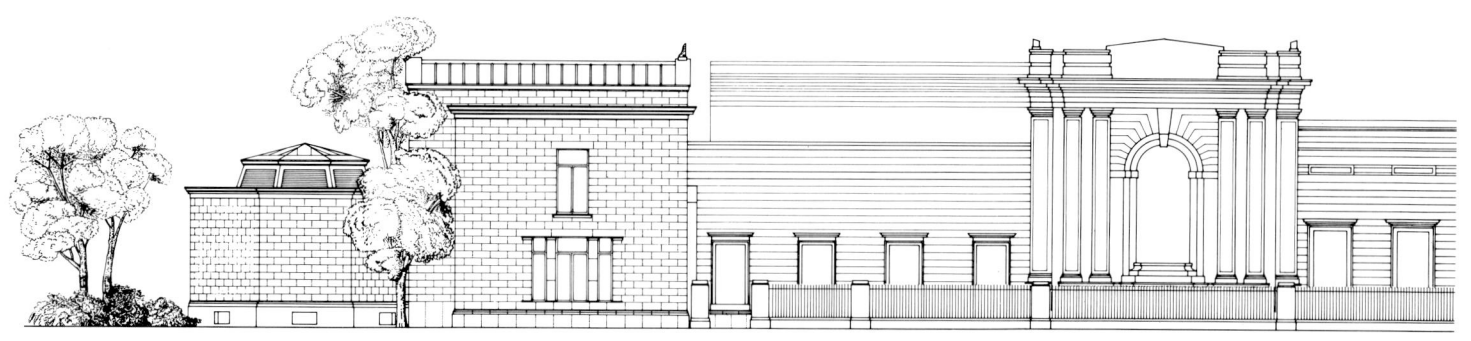

PROPOSED EXTENSION   EXISTING GALLERIES

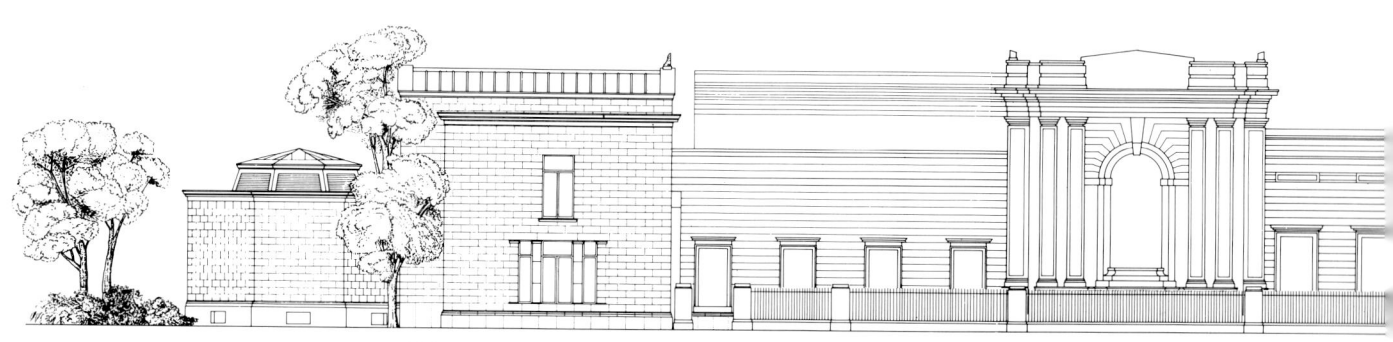

PROPOSED EXTENSION

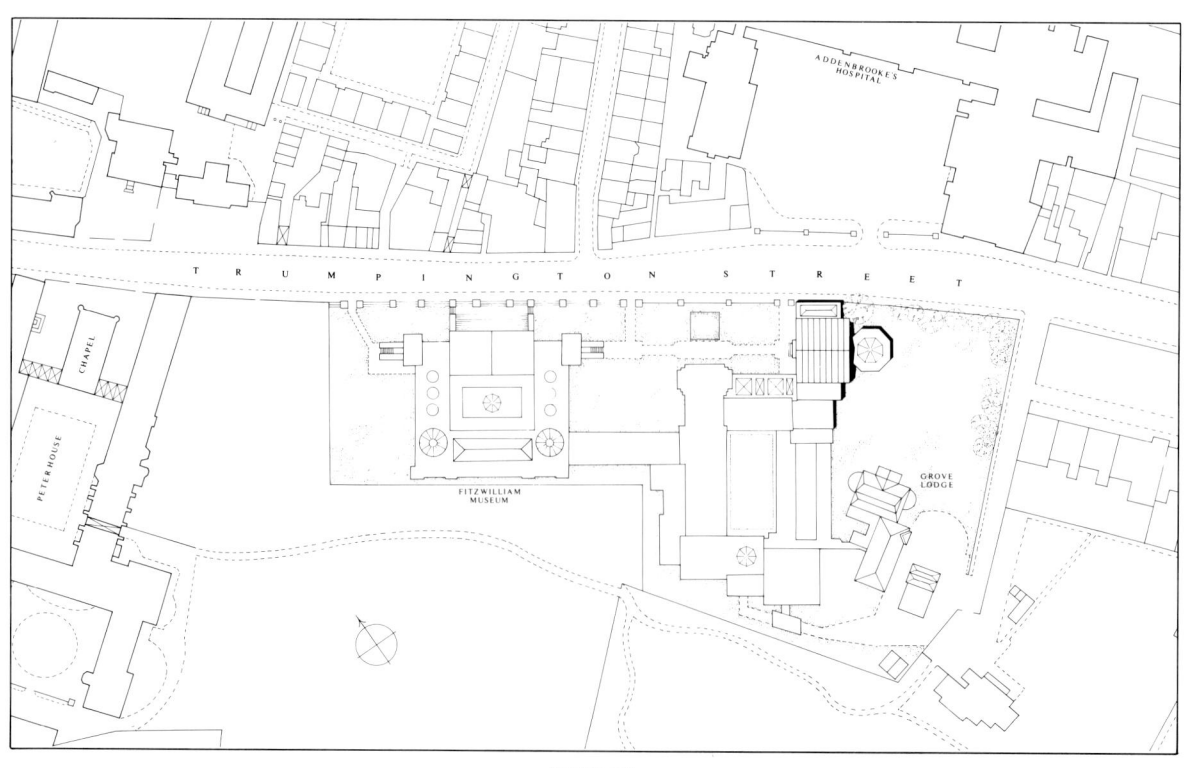

SITE PLAN

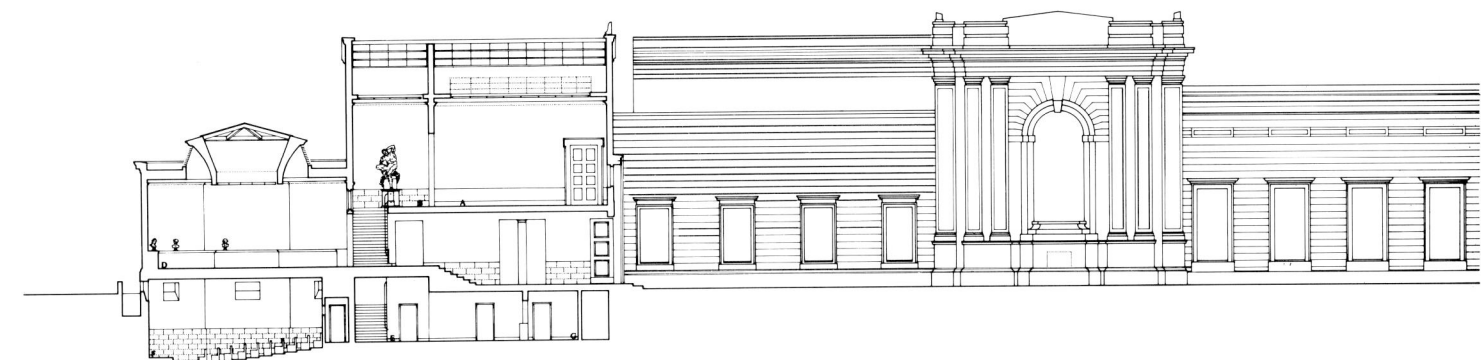

A LARGE SCULPTURE B STAIRCASE HALL C RECEPTION & CONTROL LOBBY D SMALL SCULPTURE E LOBBY F LECTURE THEATRE G CLOAKS

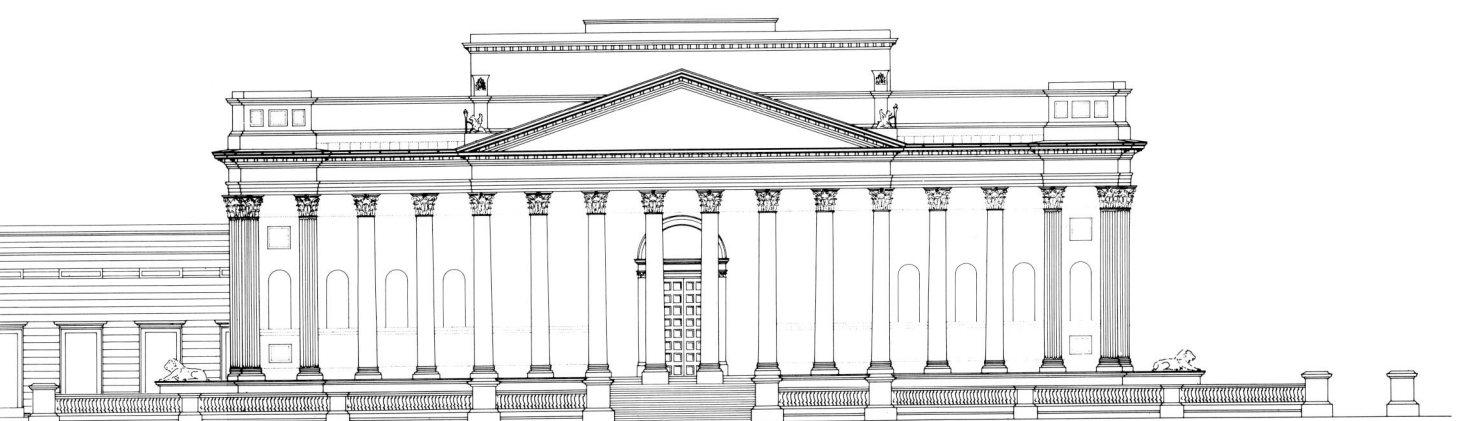

THE FOUNDER'S GALLERY BY G BASEVI

A RECEPTION LOBBY
B MUSEUM SHOP
C COFFEE SHOP
D STAIRCASE GALLERY
E SCULPTURE GALLERY
F EXISTING STAIRCASE
K EXISTING ARMOUR GALLERY

GROUND-FLOOR PLAN

VILLA IN ATHENS
1987

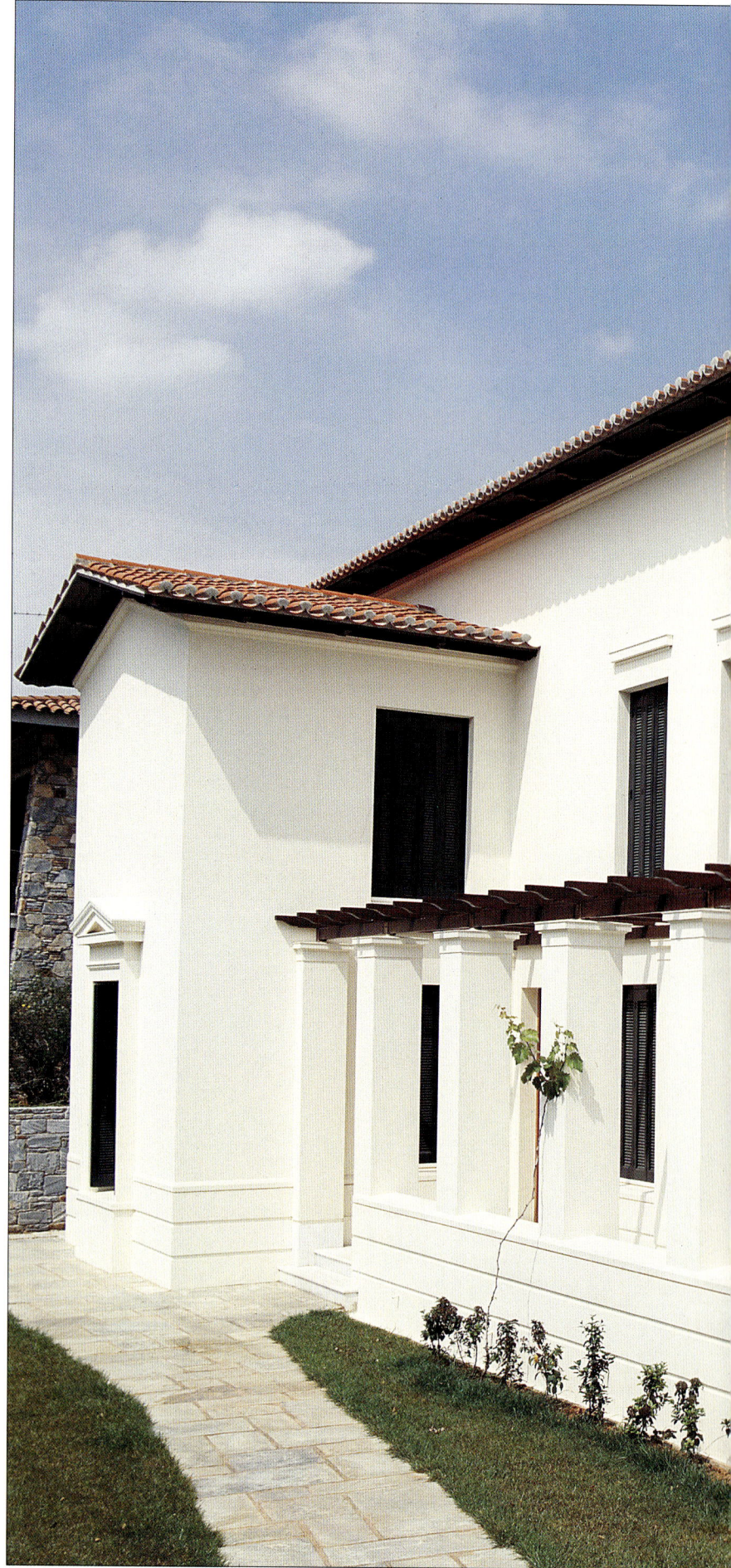

The villa is situated on a hill in a northern residential district of Athens. It is sited at the north-western corner of the site close to the street and at the highest point of the land so as to leave room for the garden and in order to gain views towards Athens and the mountain of Penteli beyond.

One approaches the villa diagonally from the street. Along the front there is a pergola which extends almost the full frontage of the site. This pergola becomes a visual boundary between the public and private realms of the site.

Upon entry one arrives at a central atrium seven metres high which marks the heart of the house. The various rooms required by the brief are all organised in an additive manner around this atrium. The austere walls of the atrium terminate in a series of finger-like piers which support the ceiling and its central skylight. This skylight is echoed on the floor marquetry much like the ancient compluvium/impluvium. The atrium has a high marble skirting which returns on itself thus emphasising its sculptural quality. A few steps lead down to the drawing room with its great fireplace. This central axis of progression between entrance door, atrium and drawing room (tablinium) is interrupted by a single doric column in marble. Here, at the centre of the house, the tectonics of post-and-lintel are celebrated.

The dining room and kitchen face the garden pool, whereas the library faces the street and it is marked externally by a pedimented window. On the first floor the bedrooms are organised around an ambulatory that surrounds the central atrium. Light filters into this ambulatory through the intercolumniations of the piers that crown the walls of the atrium.

The villa has an antiseismic concrete structure and solid brick walls finished externally in stucco. Internally, walls are plastered, floors are finished in parquet and the joinery work is in painted timber. This is essentially a simple building with extensive unadorned surfaces where sculptural profiles are used sparingly only at crucial junctions or in order to highlight the composition. Local constructional techniques and the commodious disposition of the brief have shown us the way to typical solutions which acquire their own distinct formal characteristics. This way architecture is neither an arbitrary adornment of building nor the inevitable causal outcome of building technique.

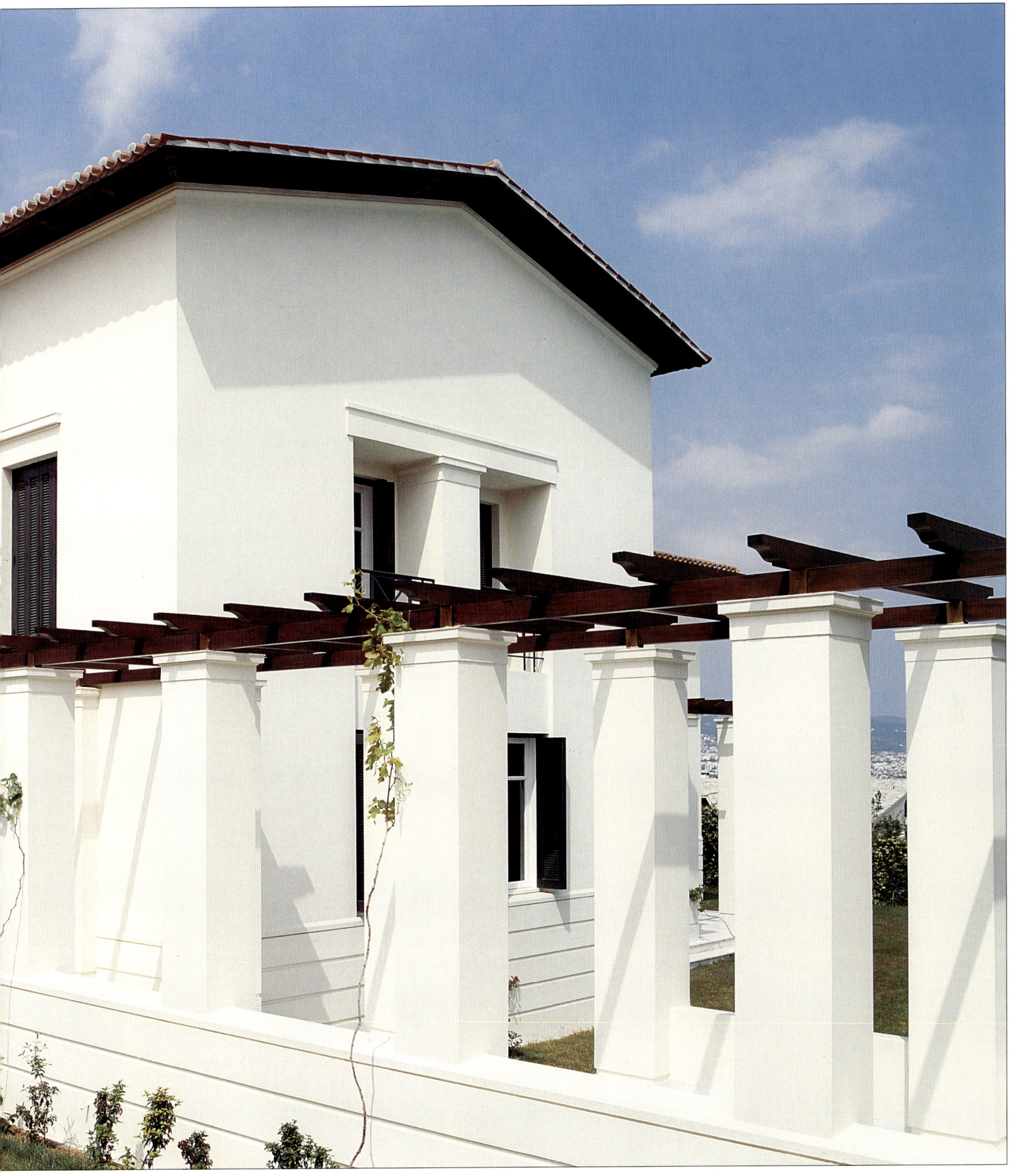

VIEW FROM THE STREET

DEMETRI PORPHYRIOS

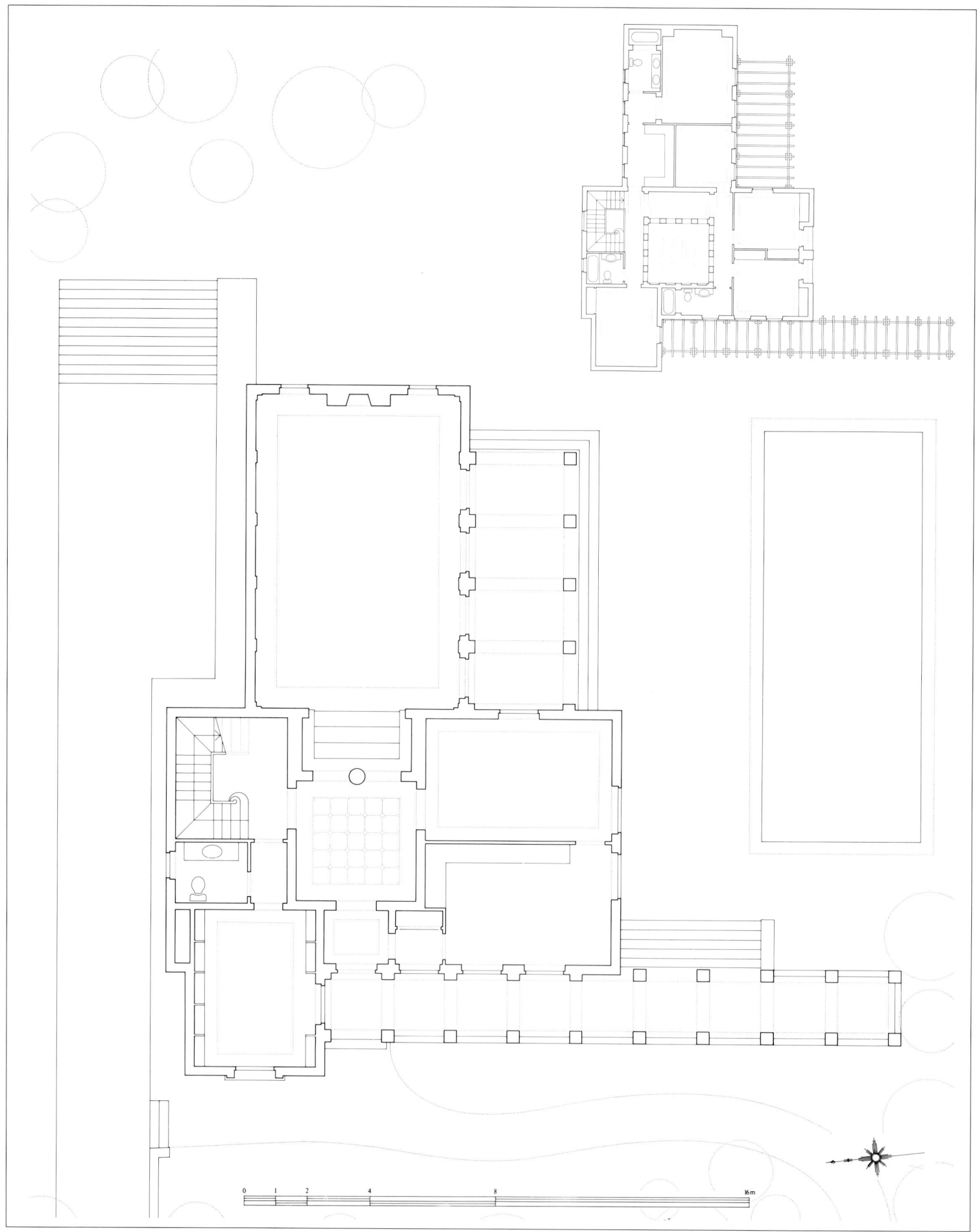

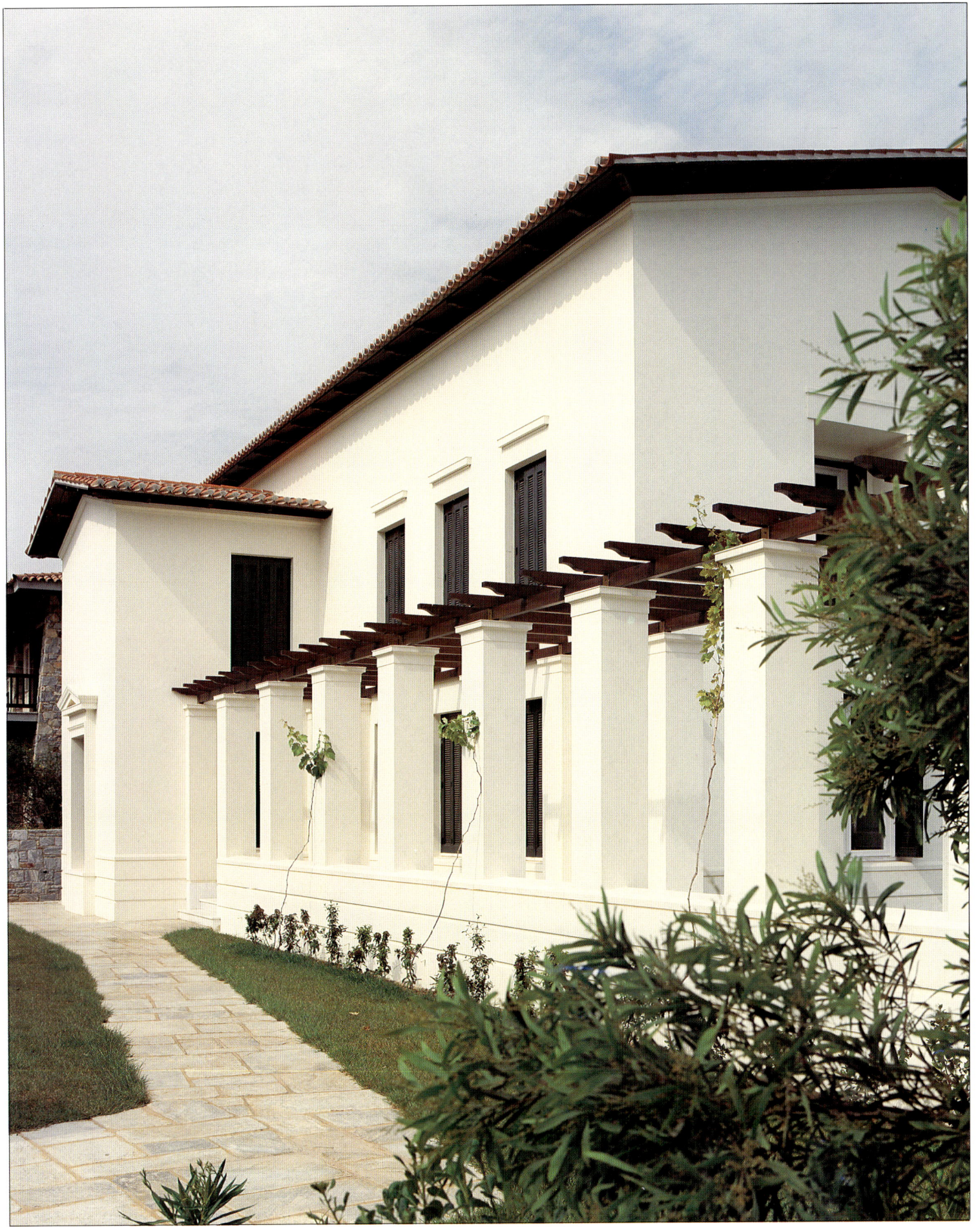

VIEW FROM THE FRONT COURT

DEMETRI PORPHYRIOS

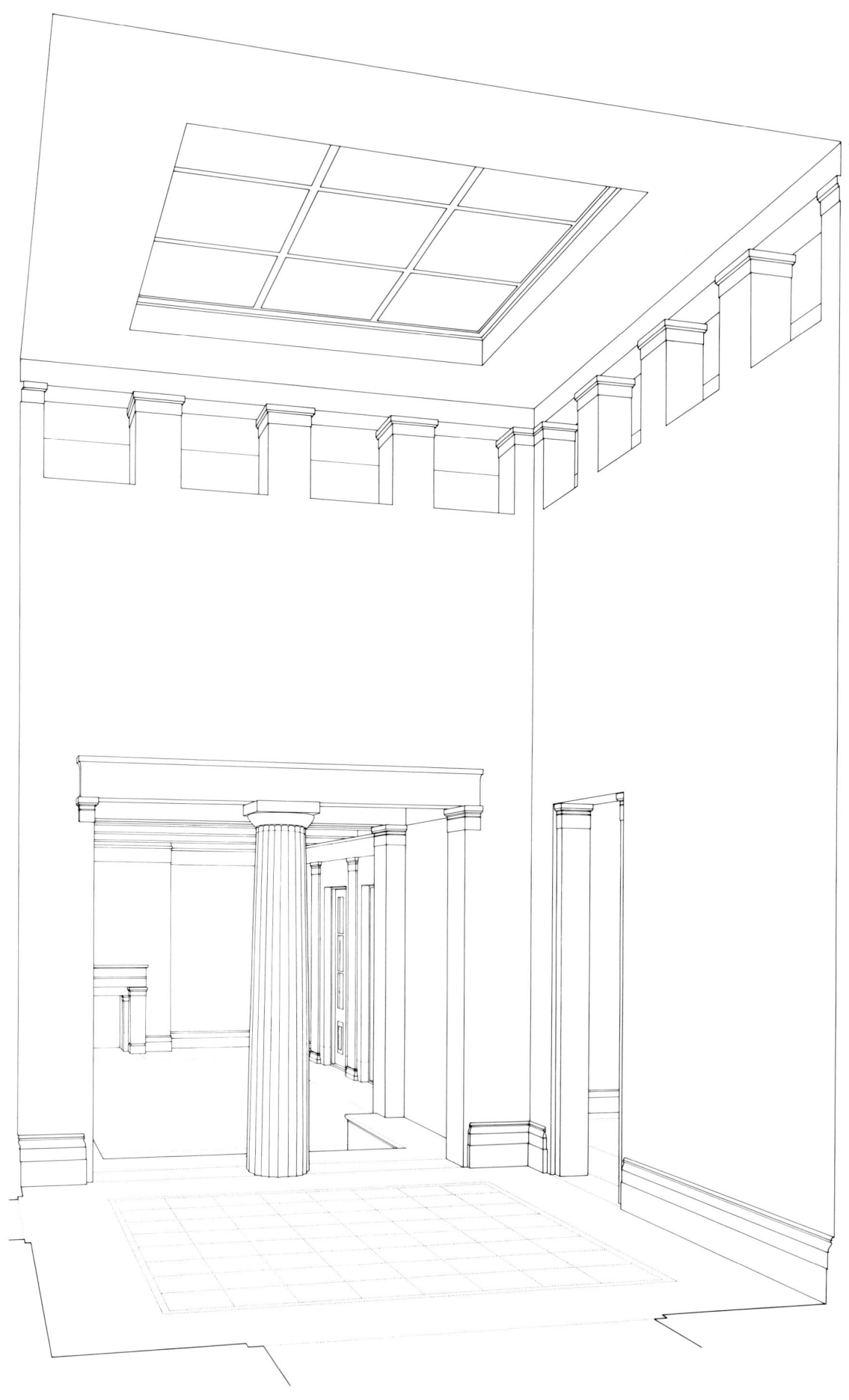

PERSPECTIVE VIEW OF THE ENTRANCE HALL

VILLA IN ATHENS

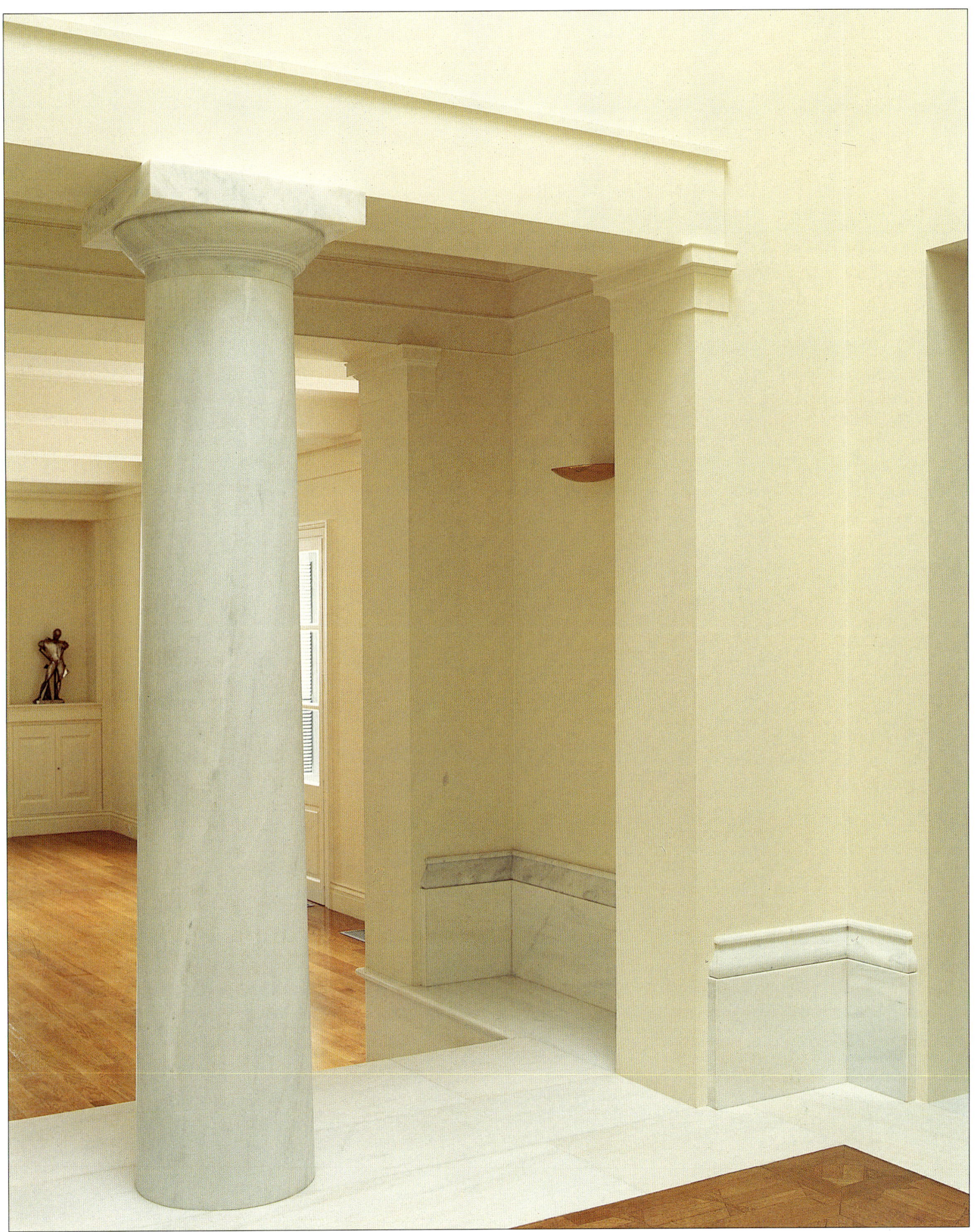

DETAIL OF DORIC COLUMN IN ATRIUM

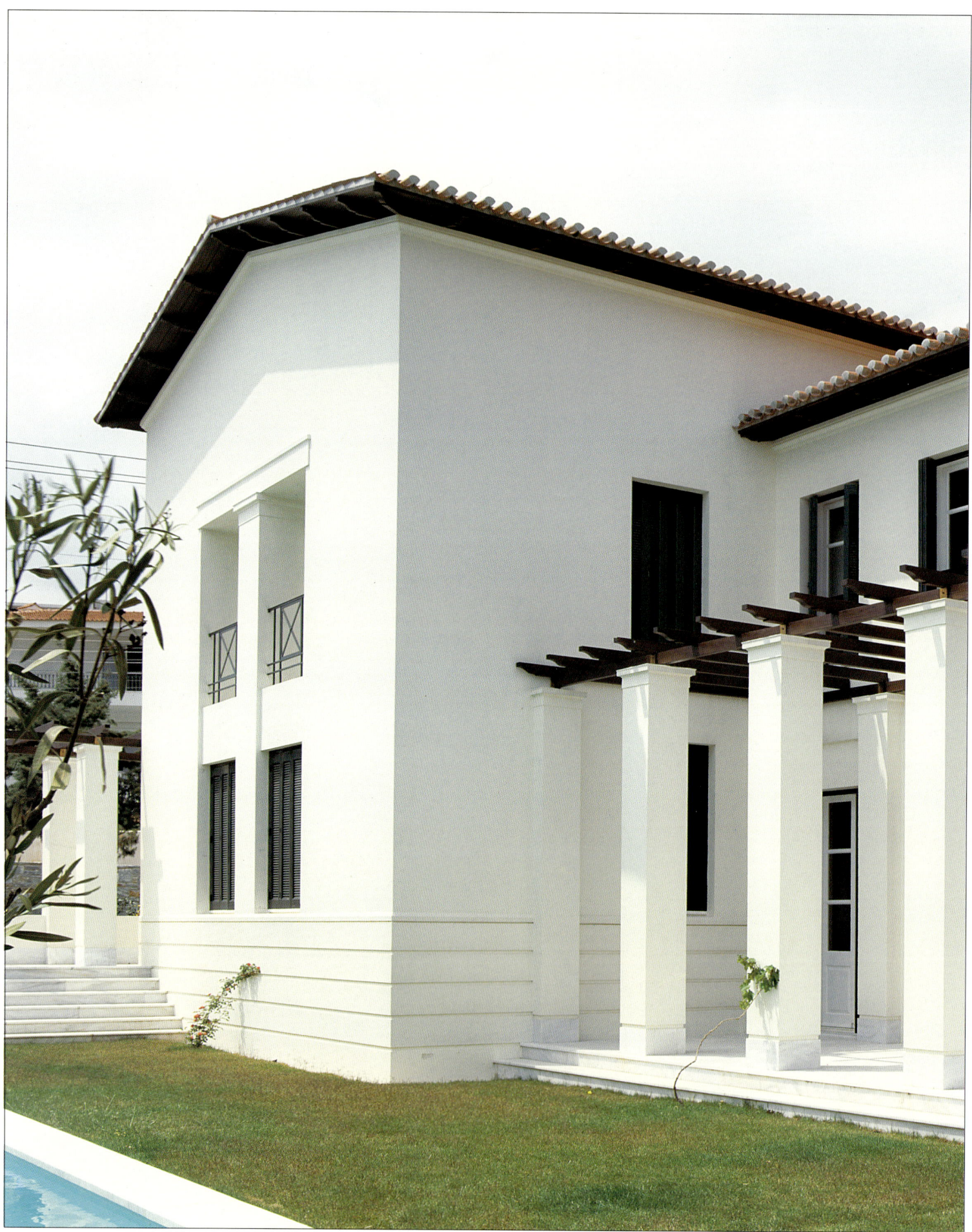

VIEW FROM THE GARDEN

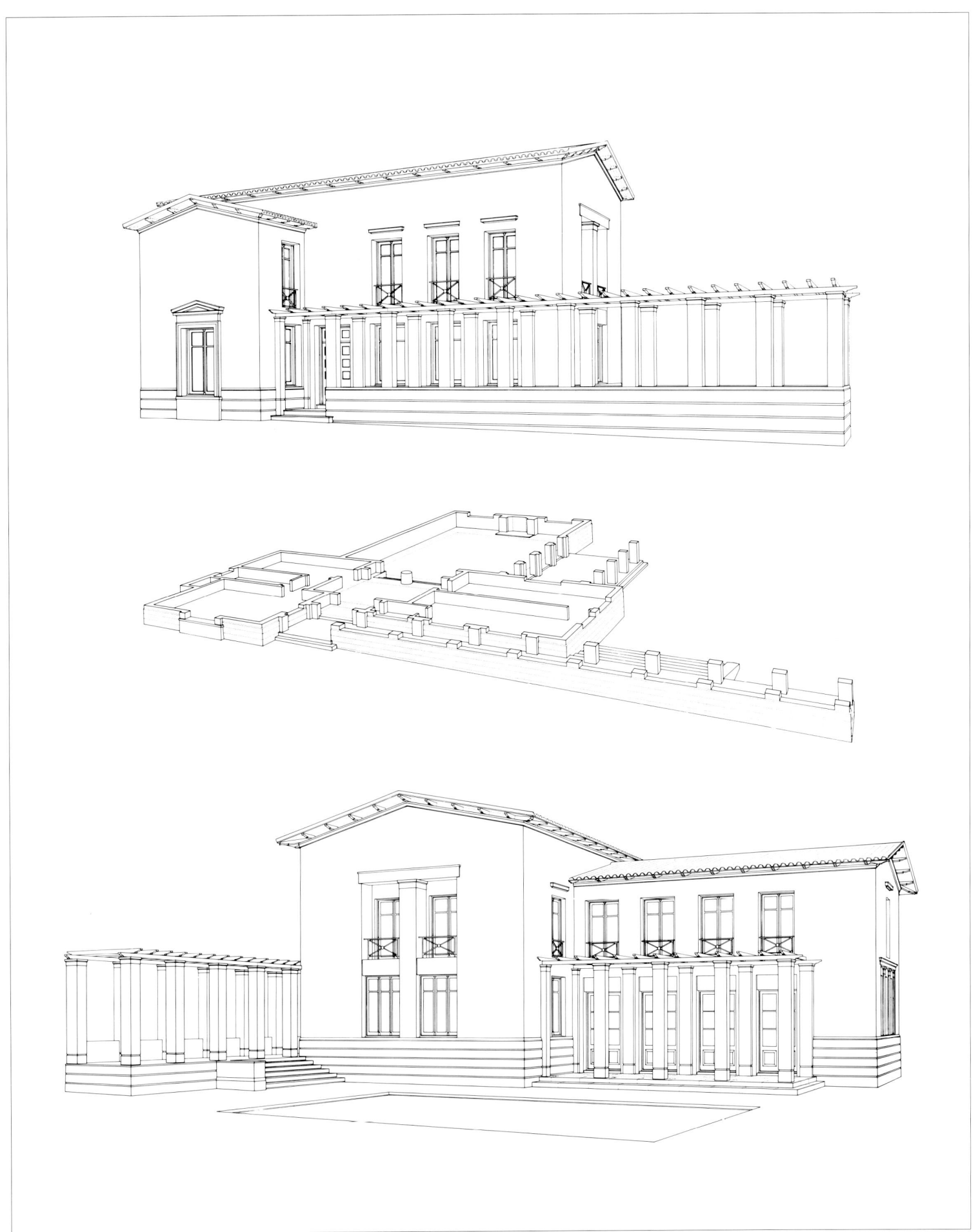

ABOVE: PERSPECTIVE VIEW FROM THE STREET; *CENTRE*: GROUND FLOOR; *BELOW*: PERSPECTIVE VIEW FROM THE GARDEN

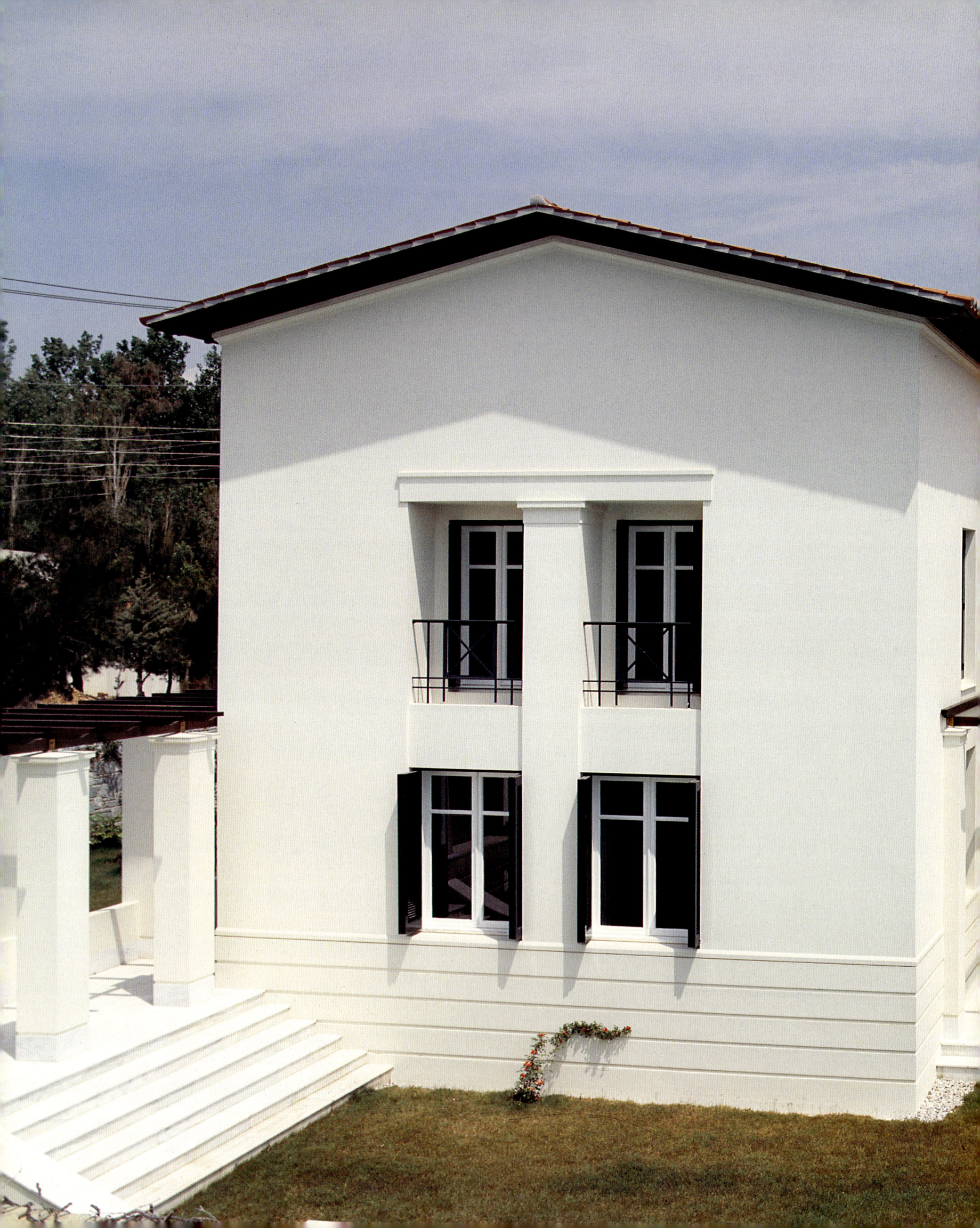

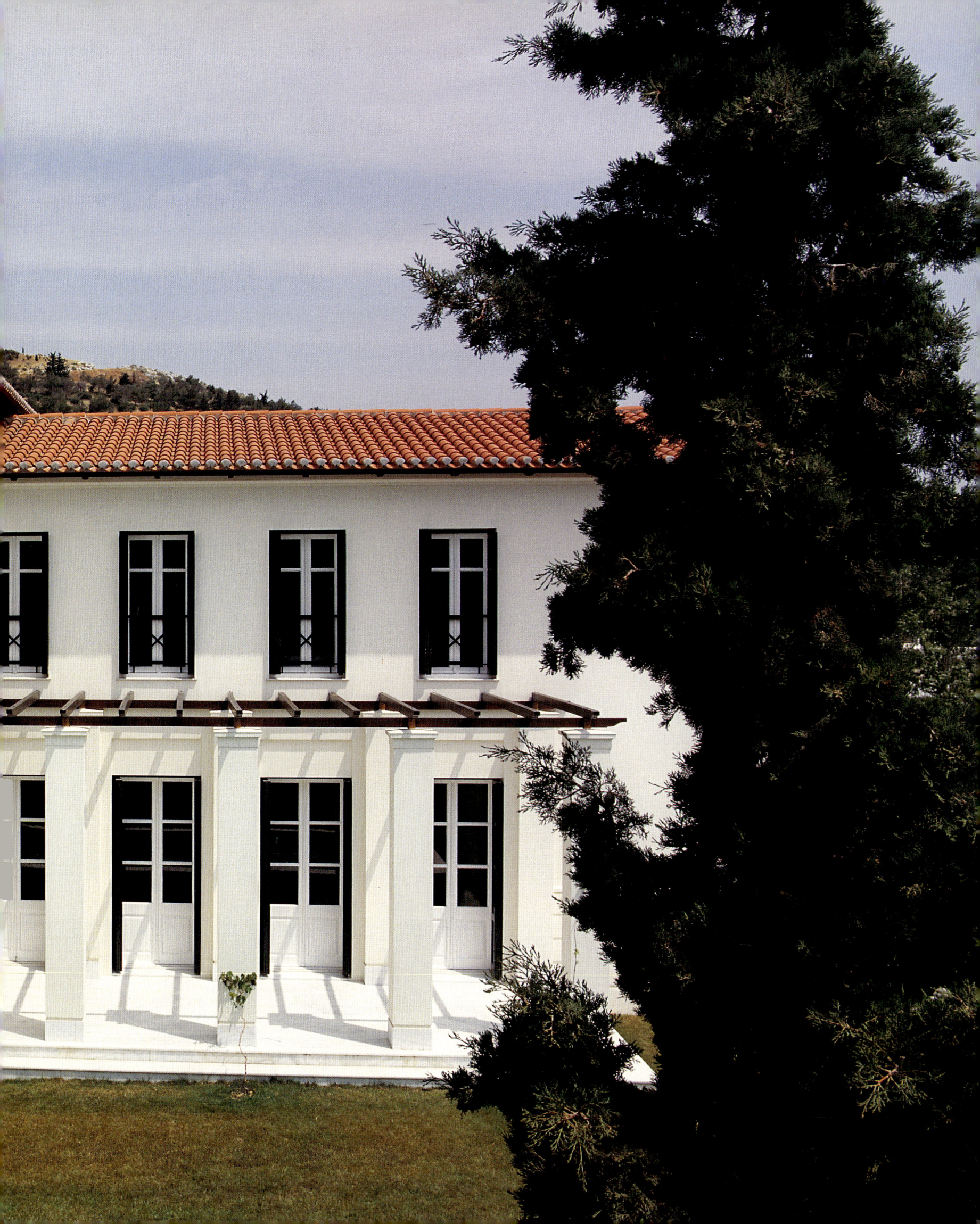

DEMETRI PORPHYRIOS

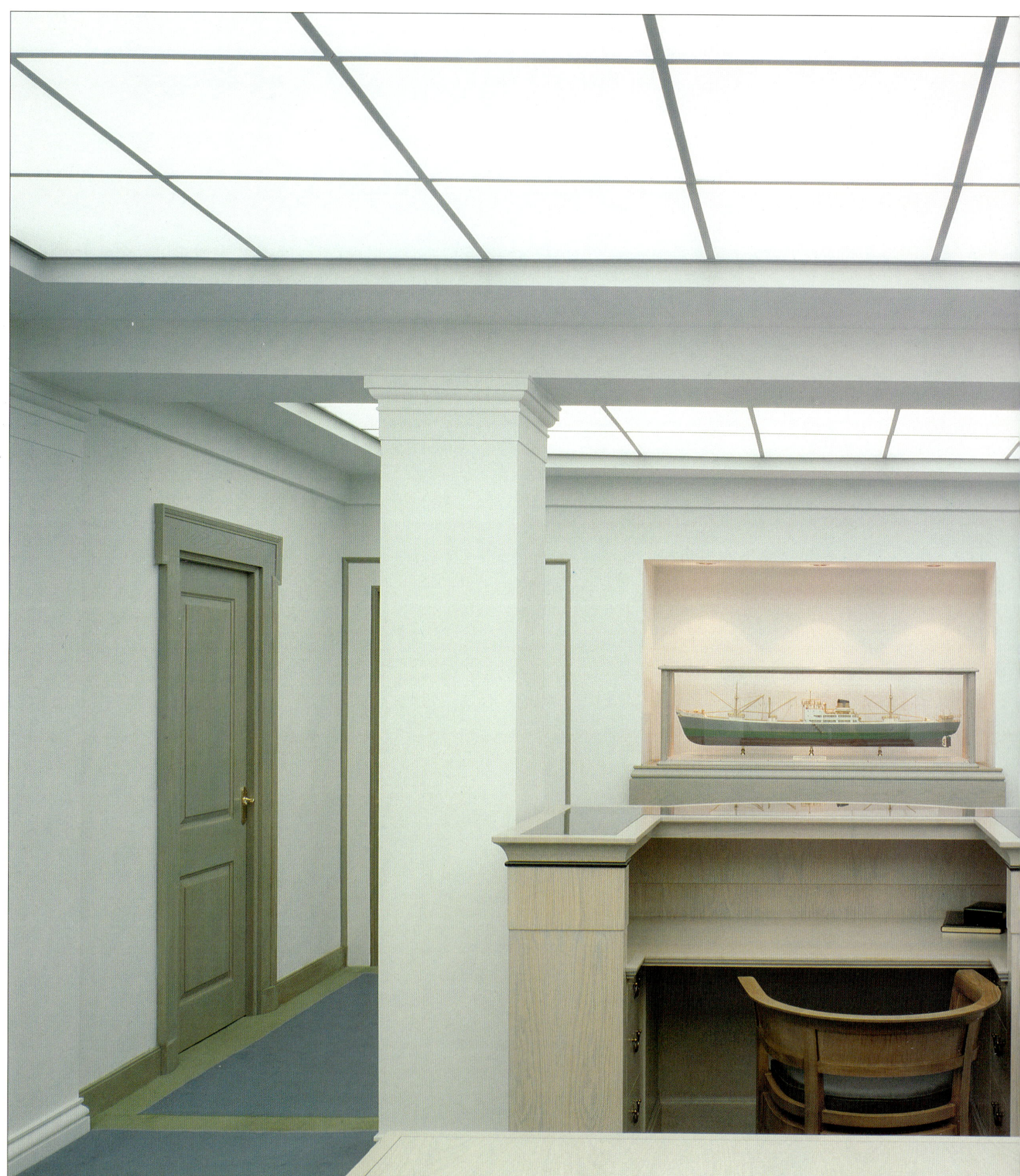

VIEW OF RECEPTION HALL

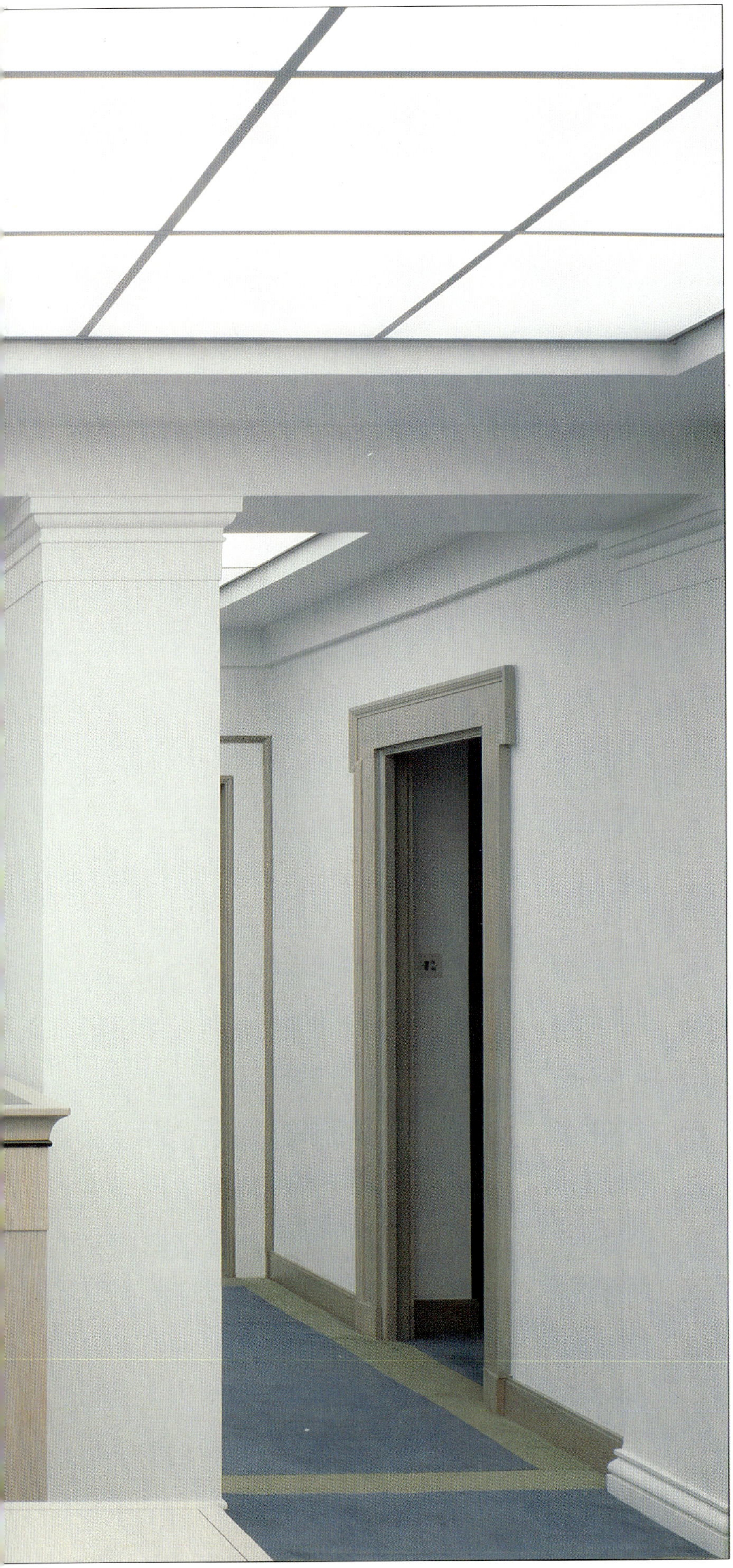

SHIPPING OFFICES
LONDON, 1987

The offices are for a firm of shipbrokers in the City of London. The client was unhappy with the open plan of the building and requested an organisation with separate rooms.

We had to work within an existing irregular envelope in which the columns of the concrete frame followed the converging long elevations of the building. Our first concern, therefore, was to devise a system of poché that would house all ancillary, storage and service requirements, and at the same time mediate between the peculiarities of the existing geometry. We thus transformed the incidental and the haphazard into a sequence of constituted rooms. The offices are organised along the two long elevations of the building and they open either onto the central reception hall or the telex and communications core. Fitted cupboards and storage spaces for every office are accommodated in the poché so that the office space is left unencumbered. The clarity of each room is emphasised by a border in the carpet and a central light grid in the ceiling. These light grids generally read as roof lights and they articulate the junction between ceiling and wall with a perimeter lintel and a ceiling border.

The perimeter of the light grids has been specially designed to house the outlets of the ventilation and air-conditioning systems. All doors, architraves, skirtings and fitted office cupboards are specially made in light-grey stained oak. We were also asked to design the furniture generally including office desks, tables, model stands, chairs and sofas, all in oak or eucalyptus.

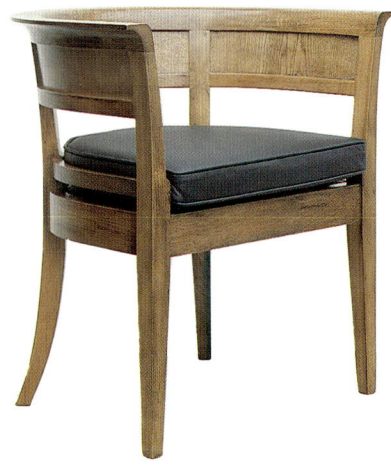

DEMETRI PORPHYRIOS

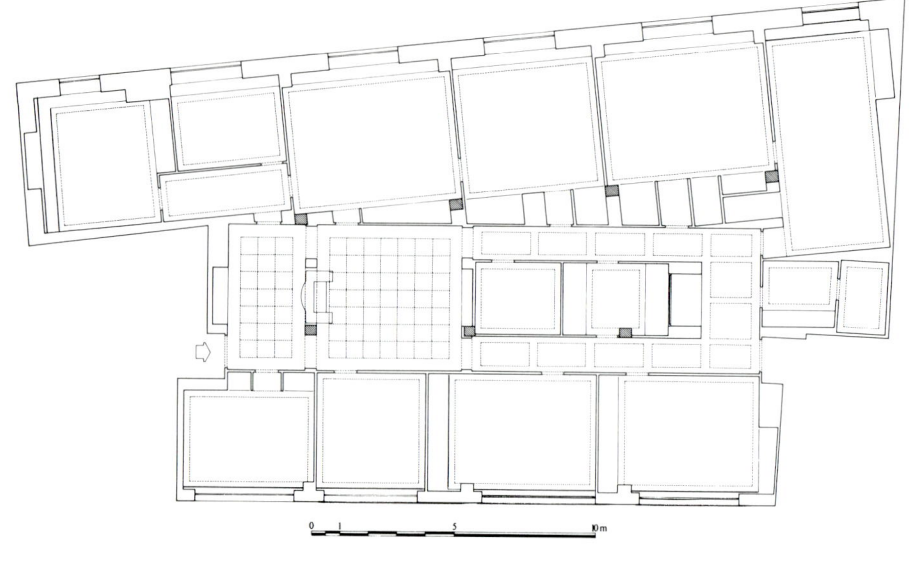

FLOOR PLAN

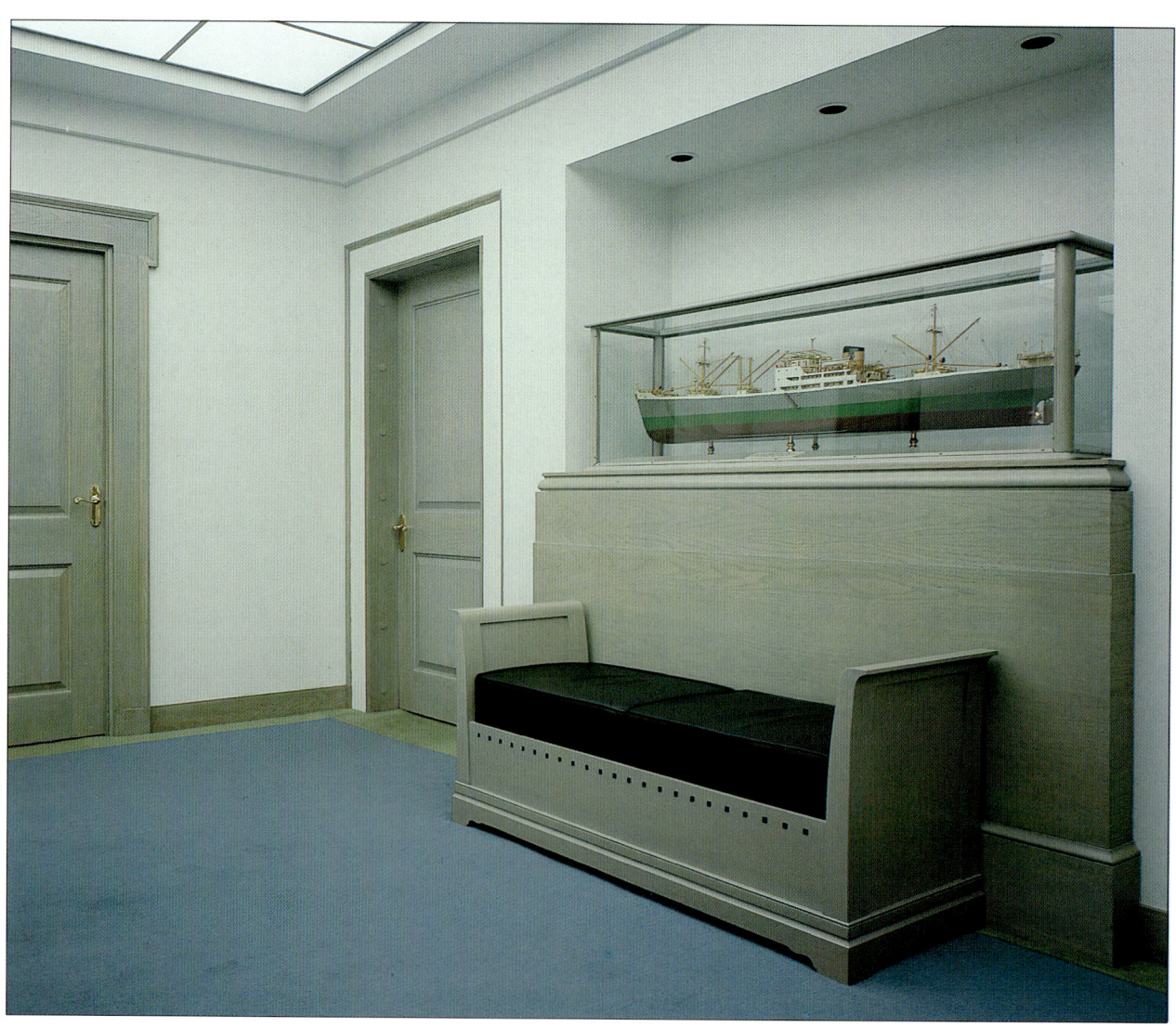

VIEW OF ENTRANCE AND RECEPTION AREA

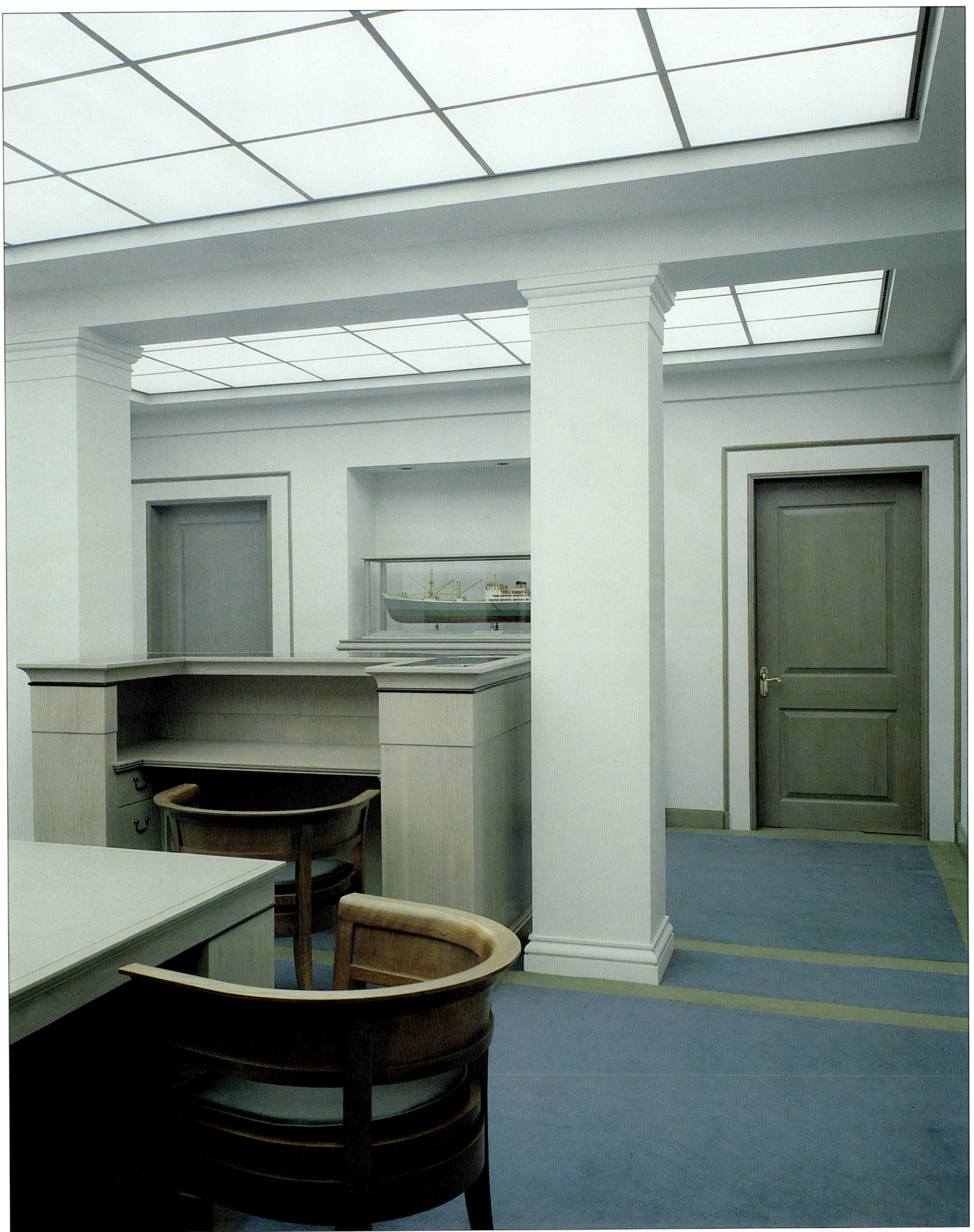

VIEW OF OFFICE POOL AND RECEPTION AREA

DEMETRI PORPHYRIOS

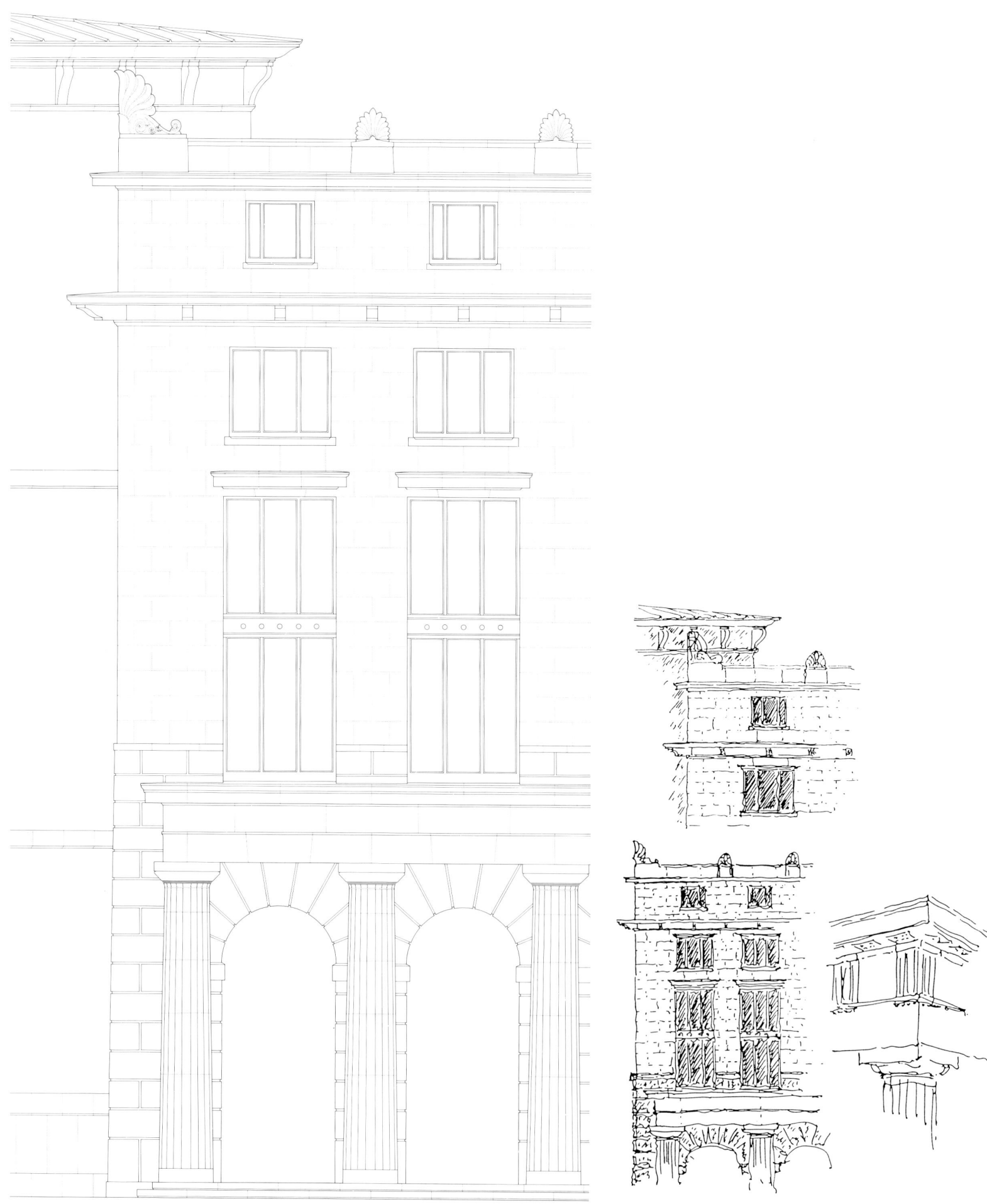

TYPICAL BAY ELEVATION AND PREPARATORY SKETCHES

OFFICE BUILDING
ATHENS, 1989

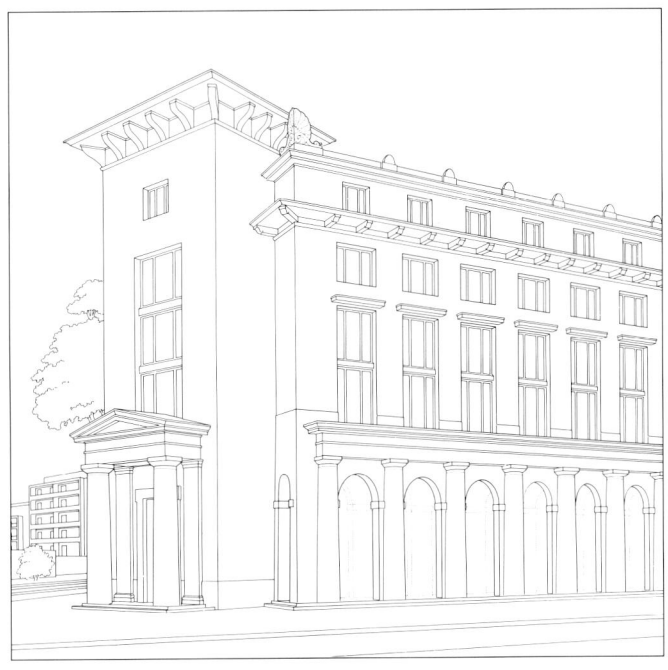

PERSPECTIVE VIEW FROM THE STREET

In the decades after the War a systematic destruction of nineteenth-century buildings defaced the city of Athens. Buildings and urban theories that are supposedly egalitarian and progressive but which, in fact, have been proven opportunistic, facile and empty have been sold to the public as the essence of modern culture. And yet the few neoclassical buildings that still remain today serve both as a means of continuity and as points of orientation in an otherwise bland cityscape.

The site we were given is a rather prominent and visible one along a vista that terminates at the Temple of Zeus and at the intersection of two major routes, one leading to Piraeus and the other to the airport. We took the view, therefore, that the buildings which marked old nineteenth-century Athens could be rebuilt. Each of these 'reconstructions' may preserve not only the essential subject of the lost city but also its basic compositional structure, which has acquired its own urban significance.

At ground and mezzanine levels the building houses a major retail unit. The upper floors provide office accommodation while parking is placed underground. Given the nature of the triangular site, the honorific entrance is at the corner marked by a tower. Vertical circulation is at the tower as well as at the rear of the building adjacent to the side entrances.

Along the street fronts the building is bounded by two-storey colonnades which shelter the ground floor and its commercial activity. The building has an antiseismic concrete structure and solid brick walls in rusticated or incised stucco. The doric columns and entablature of the colonnades as well as cornices, brackets, sills, anthemia or diestones are all in pentelicon marble.

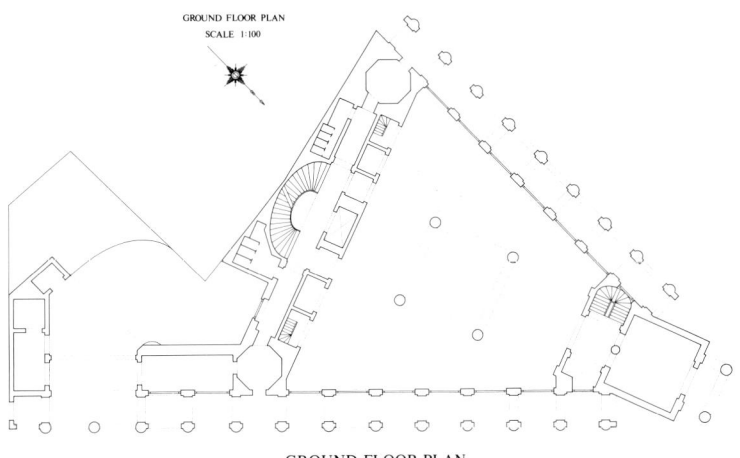

GROUND-FLOOR PLAN

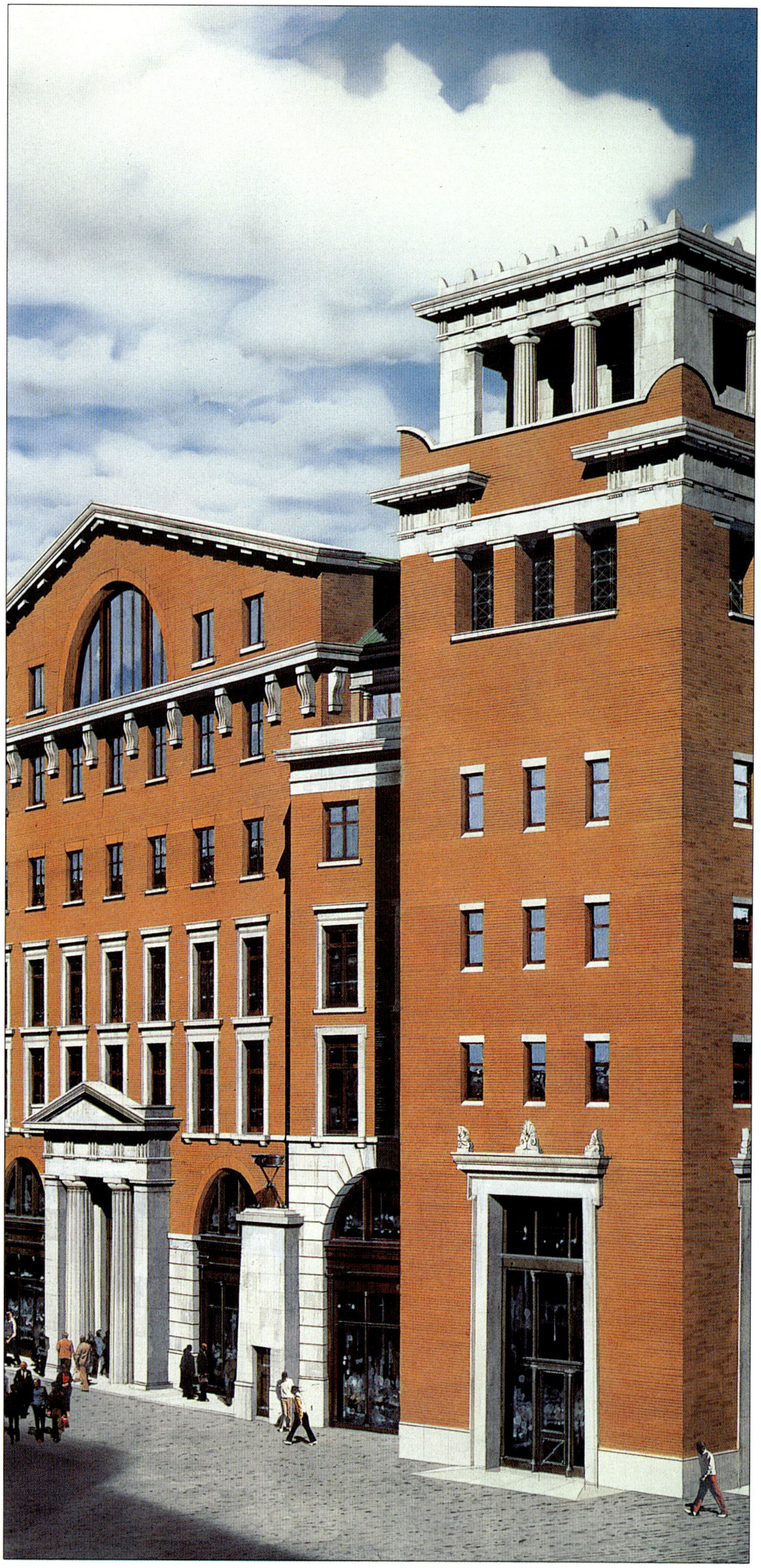

DEMETRI PORPHYRIOS

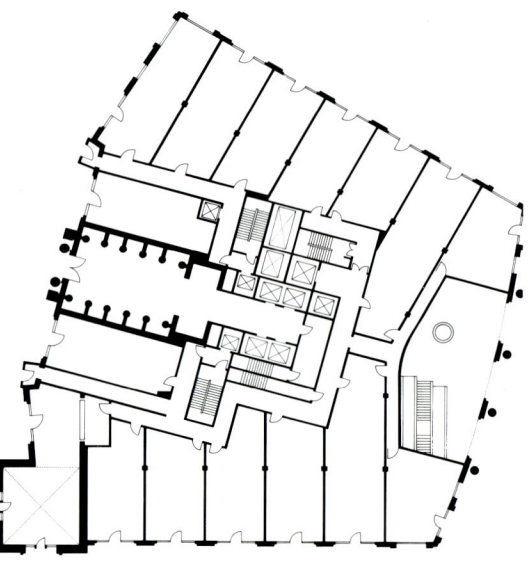

PERSPECTIVE VIEW FROM PATERNOSTER SQUARE AND GROUND-FLOOR PLAN

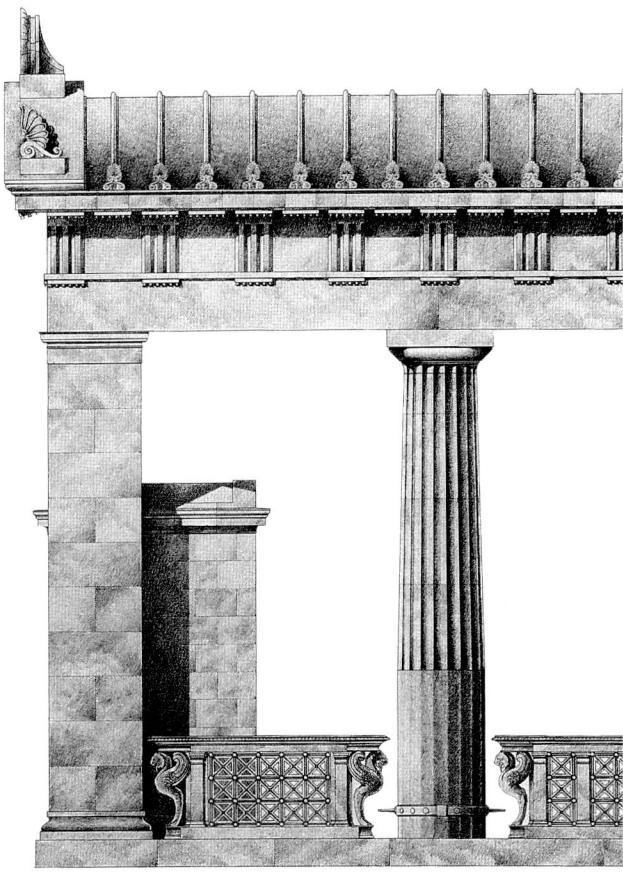
LOGGIA DETAIL

PATERNOSTER SQUARE OFFICE BUILDING
LONDON, 1991

This office building is part of a group of classical buildings which together form the proposal for the Paternoster Square development next to St Paul's Cathedral. The emphasis in our design has been on the dialogue between architecture and the urban context. The geometry of the site suggested a building with many faces that is seen in fragments and never as a whole. Its massing, therefore, is designed to unfold as the observer moves through the square and the surrounding streets.

There are two main entrances. One off Paternoster Square leading to the offices and the other giving access to St Paul's Underground Station with its link to the lower level shopping. The double height lobbies to the offices and the underground station are specially designed. At ground floor the building houses retail units and the base of the tower is given to a double height tourist information centre for the city. All typical office floors have their cores and services in the centre while the windows are coordinated with the structural and lighting grids to allow for both open-plan office organisation and perimeter cellular offices.

Along the Paternoster Square elevation the building is composed of multiple advancing and receding volumes which are ultimately centralised by the doric portico and the crowning gable above. The tower marks the whole urban ensemble of Paternoster Square. It springs from the ground in a simple and unaffected manner and its unadorned surfaces contrast with the sculptural detailing of the crowning pavilion.

Vertically the building is organised into three sections: a rusticated base, a middle and an attic floor. The ground and first floors are rusticated as are the corner pavilions. The terminating cornice lends the building a gravity and sculptural character while the gradual increase in the plasticity of the building from top to base emphasises the accumulation of weight towards the ground. Ornamental profiles underline the constructional reading of the building and motifs like anthemia, reeds, rondels and acroteria are used as punctuation devices or to soften the skyline.

The building has a concrete frame with the external walls in self-supporting brick and ashlar construction. All architectural projections and rusticated surfaces are in Portland stone, all joinery work for windows and doors is in stained hardwood while roofs are in lead sheeting.

Novel materials have been avoided for they have proven utterly unreliable in performance and have also resisted domestication. It is instructive that although twentieth-century applied science and technology have made unprecedented strides, few of these have been of any real consequence to architecture. It is as if technology has distanced itself from architecture, perhaps in order to tell her that she has long ago reached maturity and perfection.

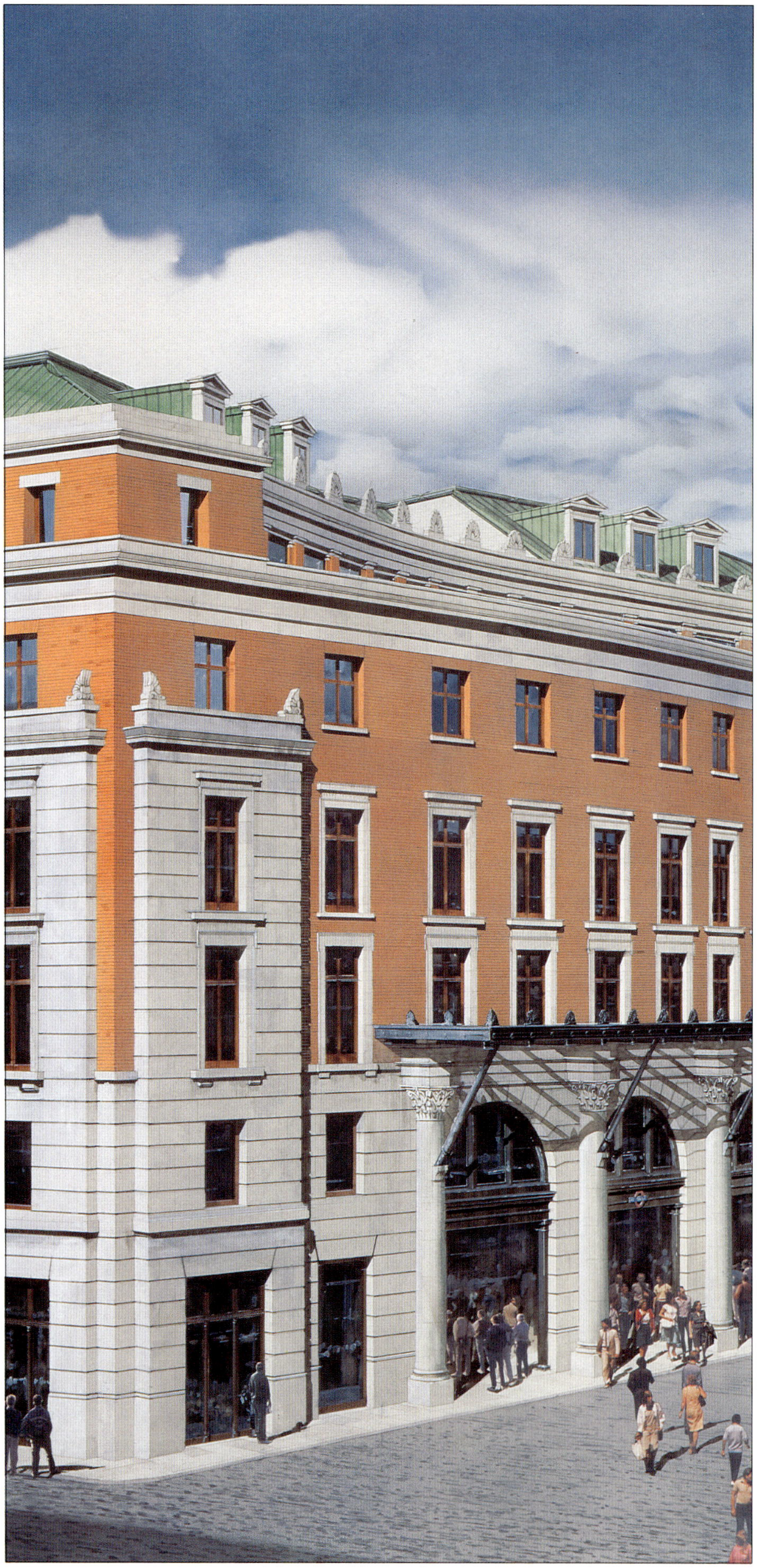

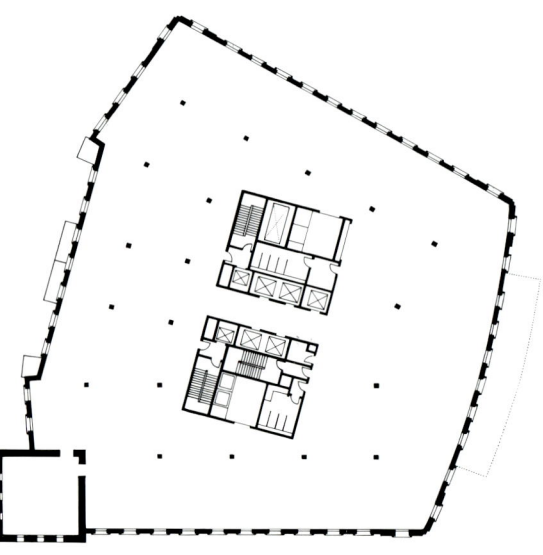

PERSPECTIVE VIEW OF LONDON UNDERGROUND ENTRANCE AND TYPICAL FLOOR PLAN

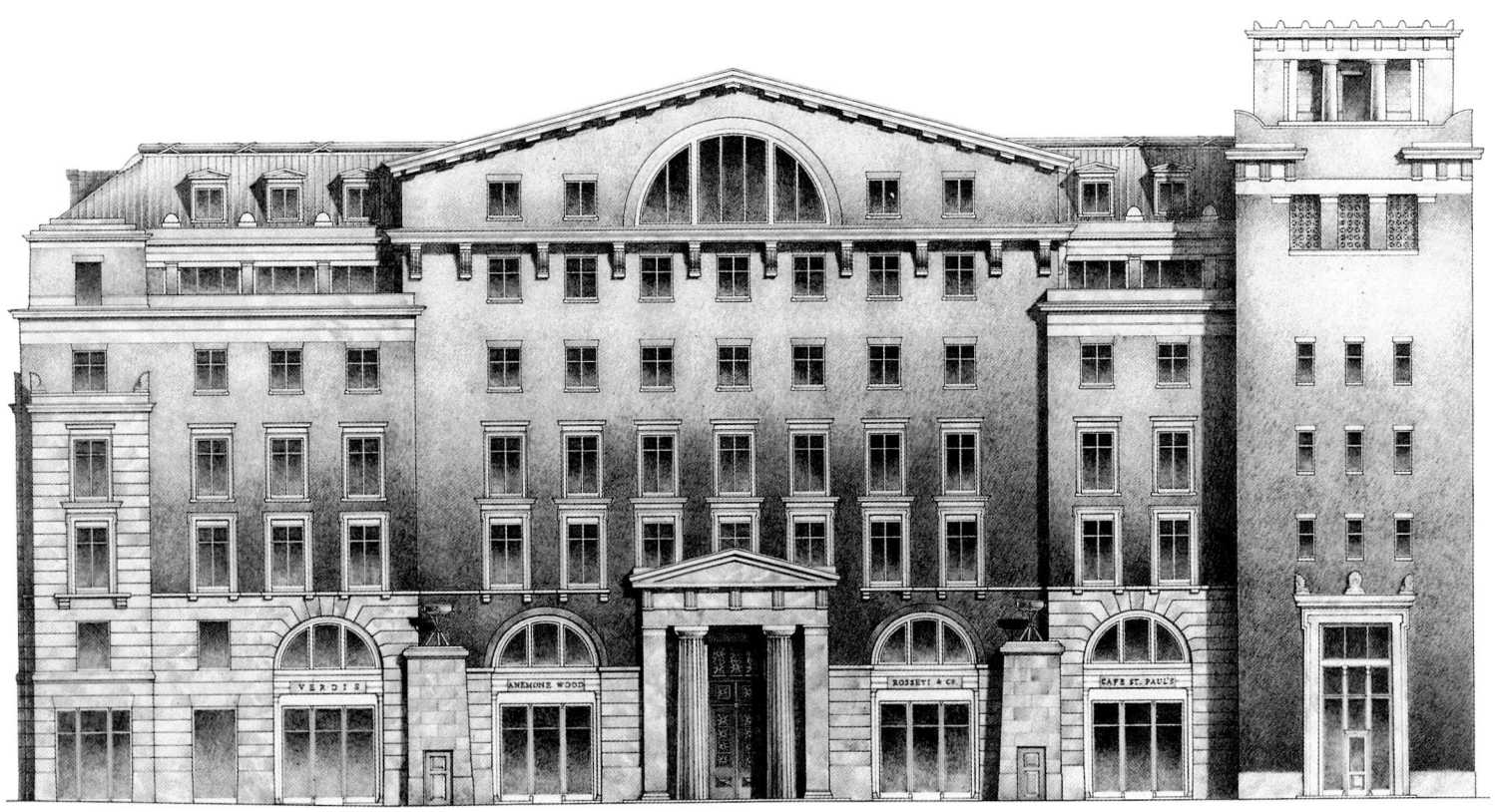

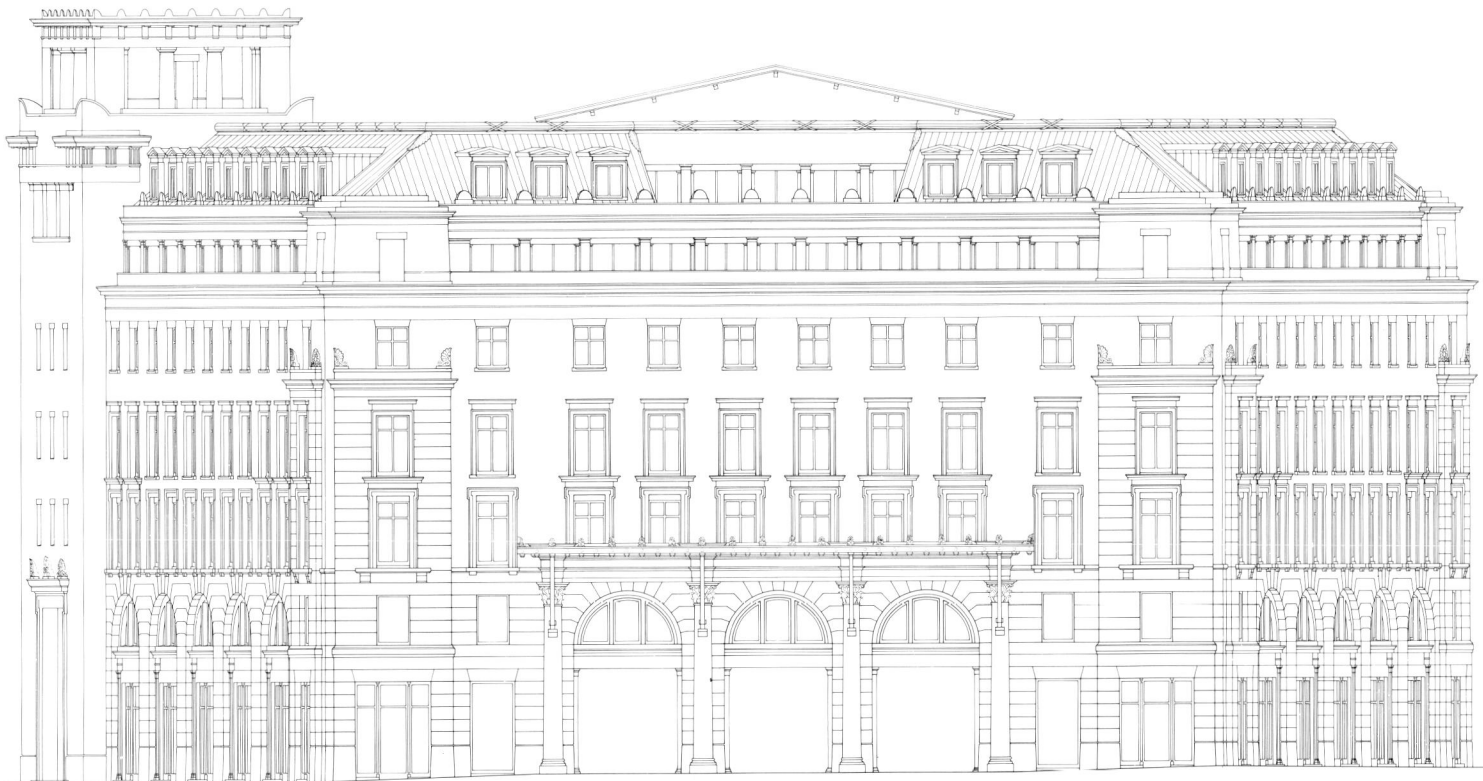

ABOVE: OFFICE ENTRANCE ELEVATION; *BELOW*: LONDON UNDERGROUND ENTRANCE ELEVATION

DEMETRI PORPHYRIOS

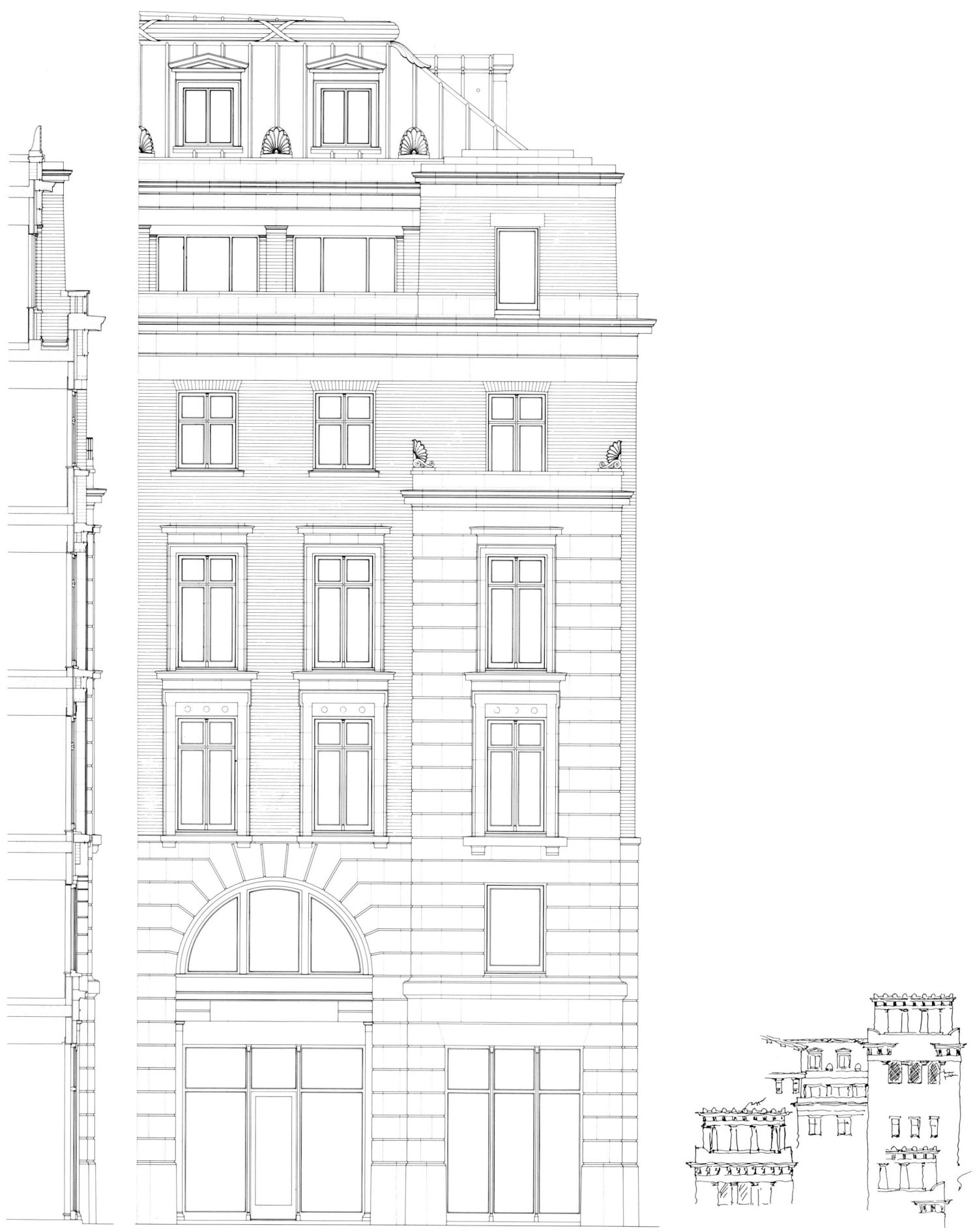

TYPICAL SECTION WITH BAY ELEVATION AND PREPARATORY SKETCHES

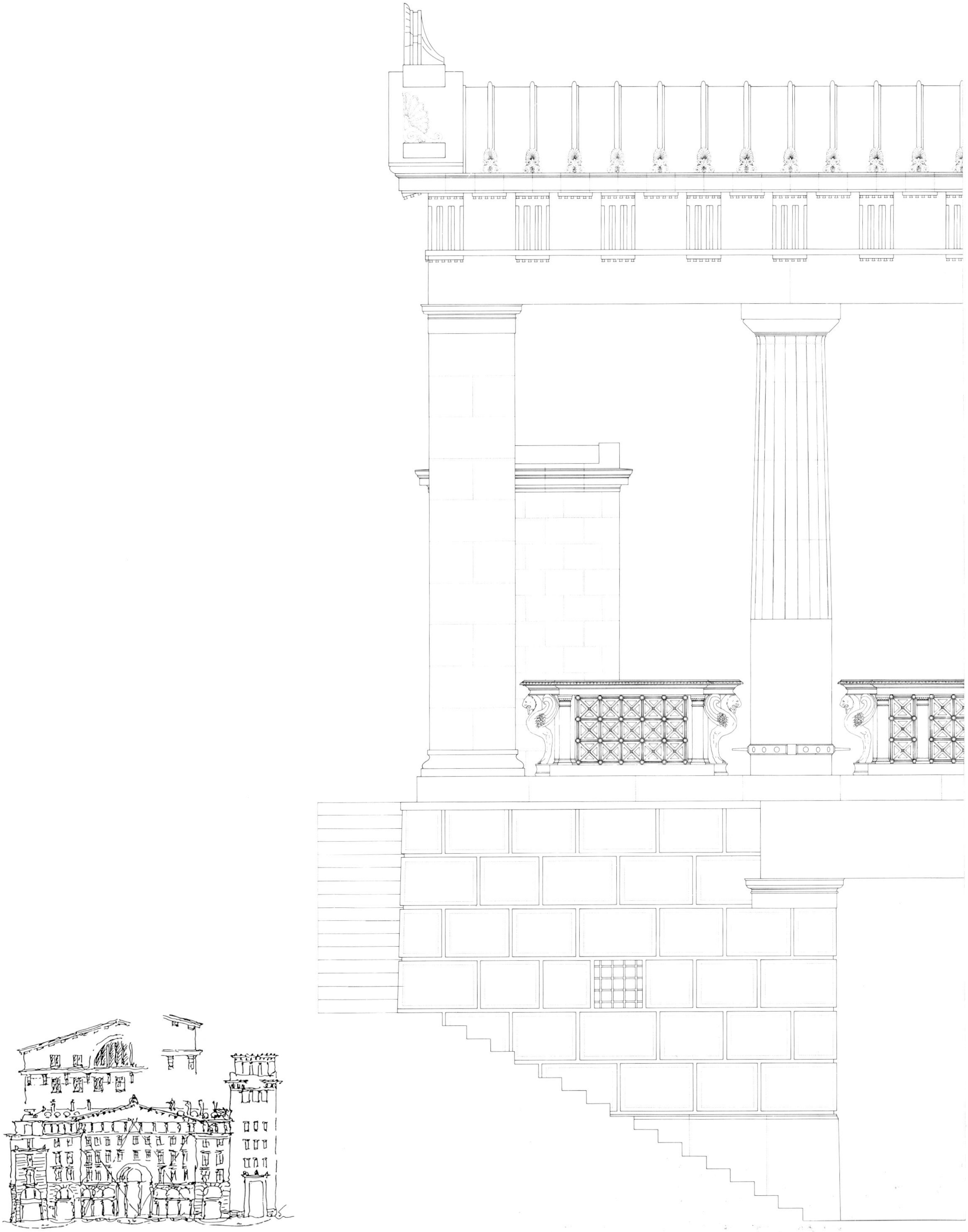

PATERNOSTER SQUARE OFFICE BUILDING

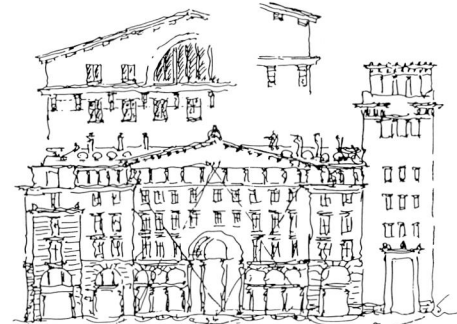

PREPARATORY SKETCHES AND TYPICAL BAY OF LOGGIA

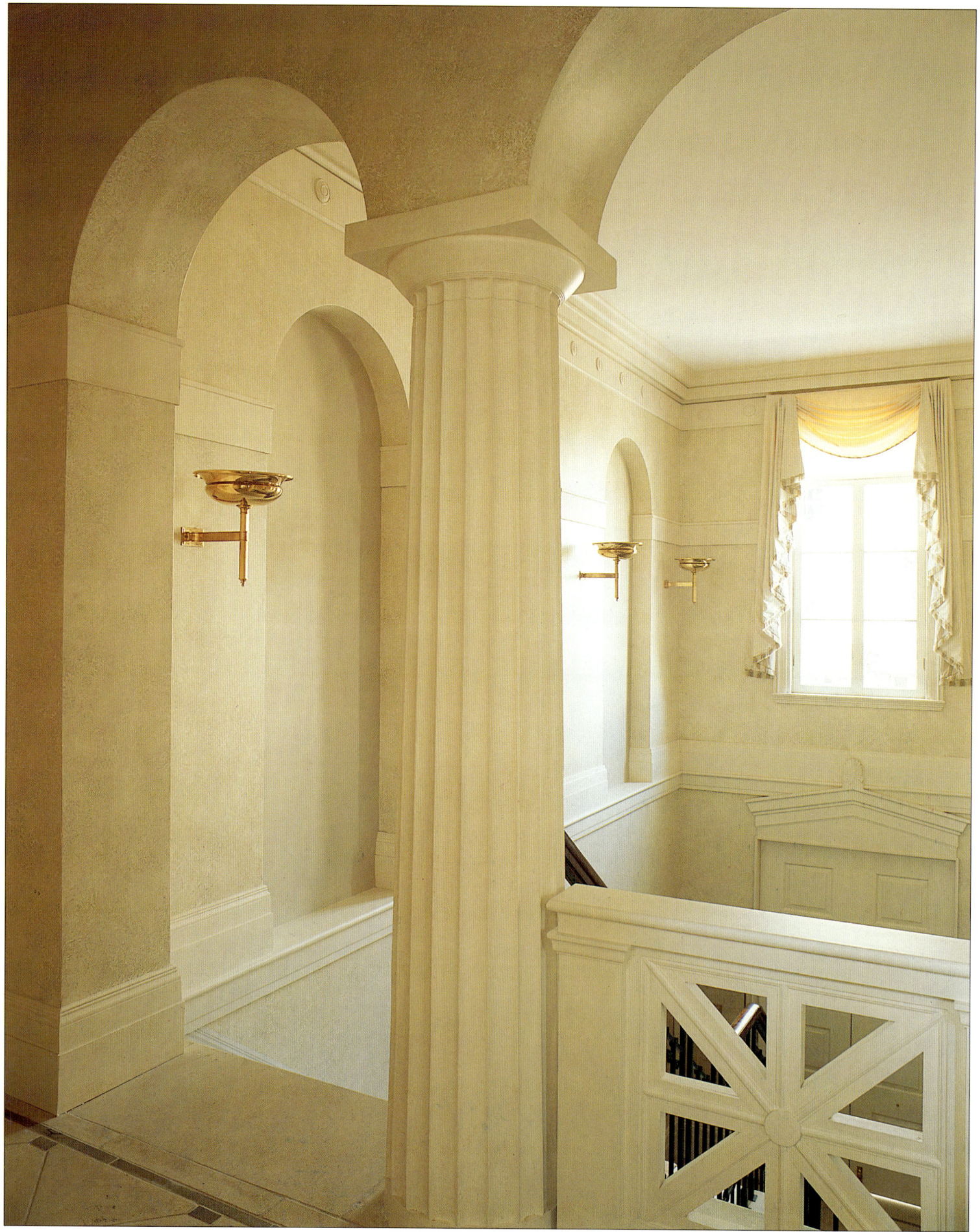

VIEW OF HALL FROM LANDING

HOUSE IN KENSINGTON
LONDON, 1987

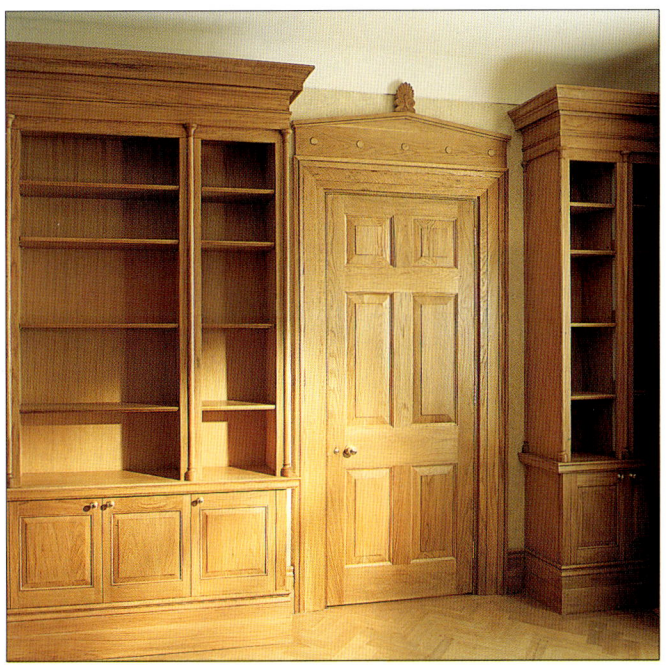

VIEW OF THE LIBRARY

This new five-storey family house in the residential area of Kensington replaces an existing dilapidated building. It is in a well maintained terrace that dates from the late eighteenth century. The overall character of the street is Neo-Classical.

The site is rather restricted by a frontage of only nine metres. We decided to follow the plan organisation typical of such houses. Laterally, the building is organised in two unequal bays; a sensible and time-honoured solution that groups circulation and ancillary spaces along the narrow bay thus freeing the rest of the frontage for reception rooms.

Traditionally, the staircase connects all floors without distinguishing between public reception areas and private bedrooms. Here, however, due to the size of the house, we felt such a distinction was necessary. The entrance hall is seven metres high and connects the library and dining-room with the first floor reception rooms. At ground floor the library connects with the dining-room which opens onto a terrace overlooking the garden. At garden level are the family room, kitchen and all ancillary and service spaces. The master bedroom suite occupies most of the first floor with bedroom, dressing room and bathroom organised in an enfilade fashion that reveals the full depth of the house.

The street elevation is rendered and painted off-white, while the rear elevation is faced in brick. Walls are plastered internally and painted or finished in stretched fabric. All internal cornices, coffers, anthemia and pediments have profiles in fibrous plaster. The doric columns are in plaster of Paris. All joinery is custom made in hardwood for painting. The panelling and bookcases for the library are in English oak, stained and polished. We also designed the light fittings for the entrance hall and all metalwork for railings internally and externally.

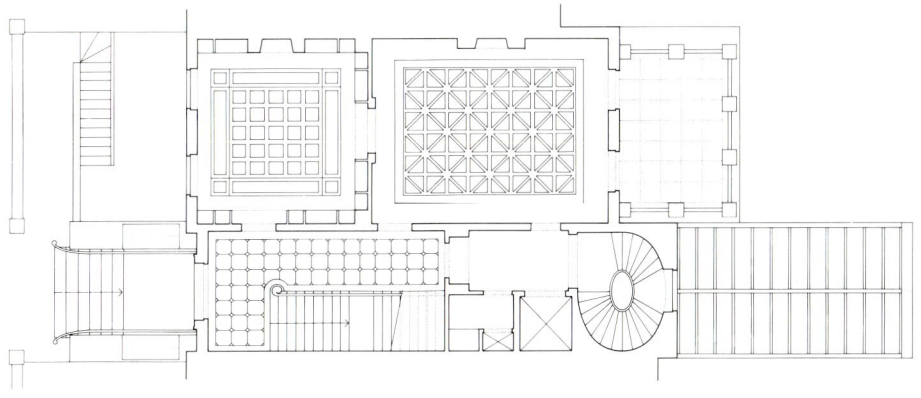

GROUND-FLOOR PLAN

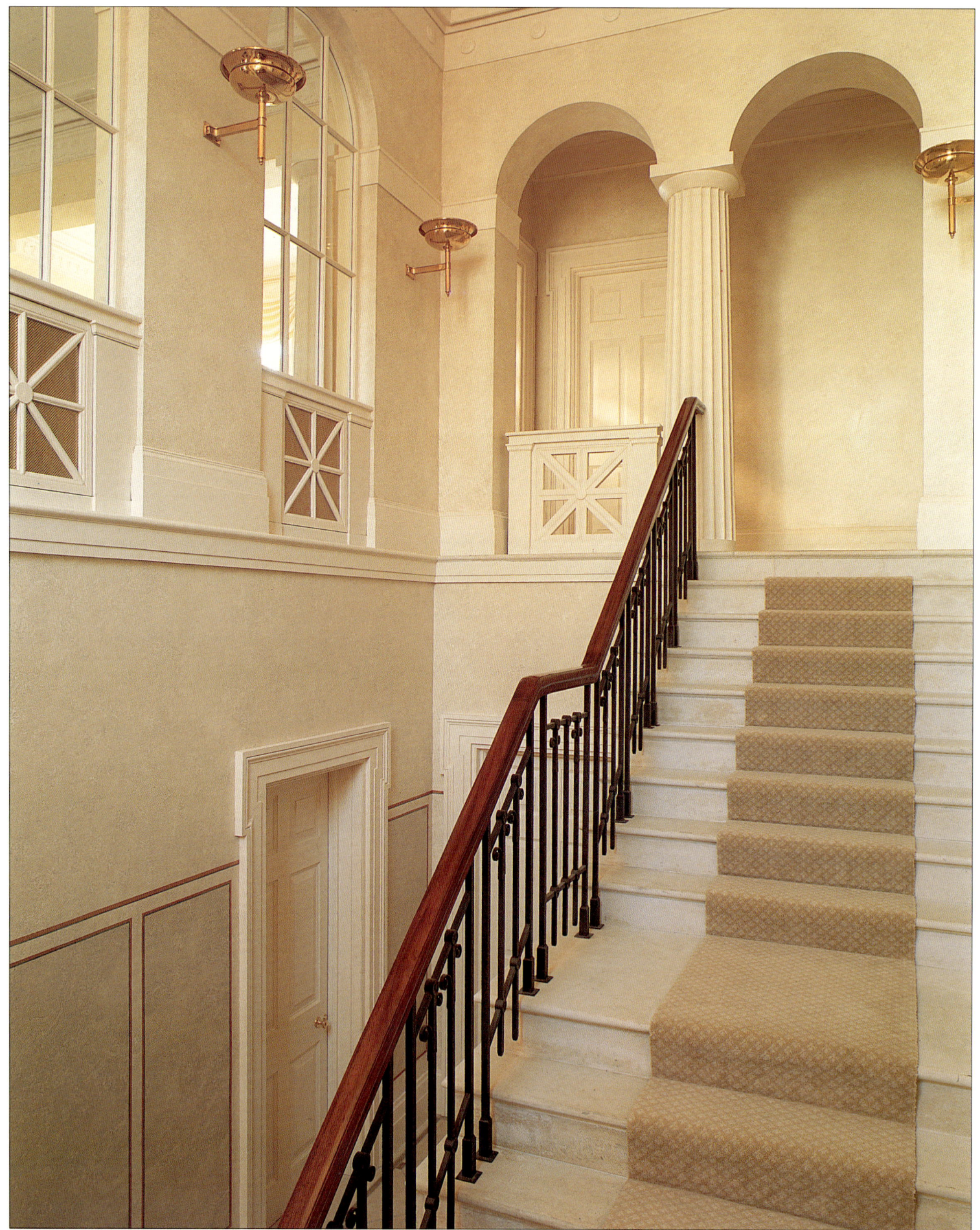

VIEW OF ENTRANCE HALL

HOUSE IN KENSINGTON

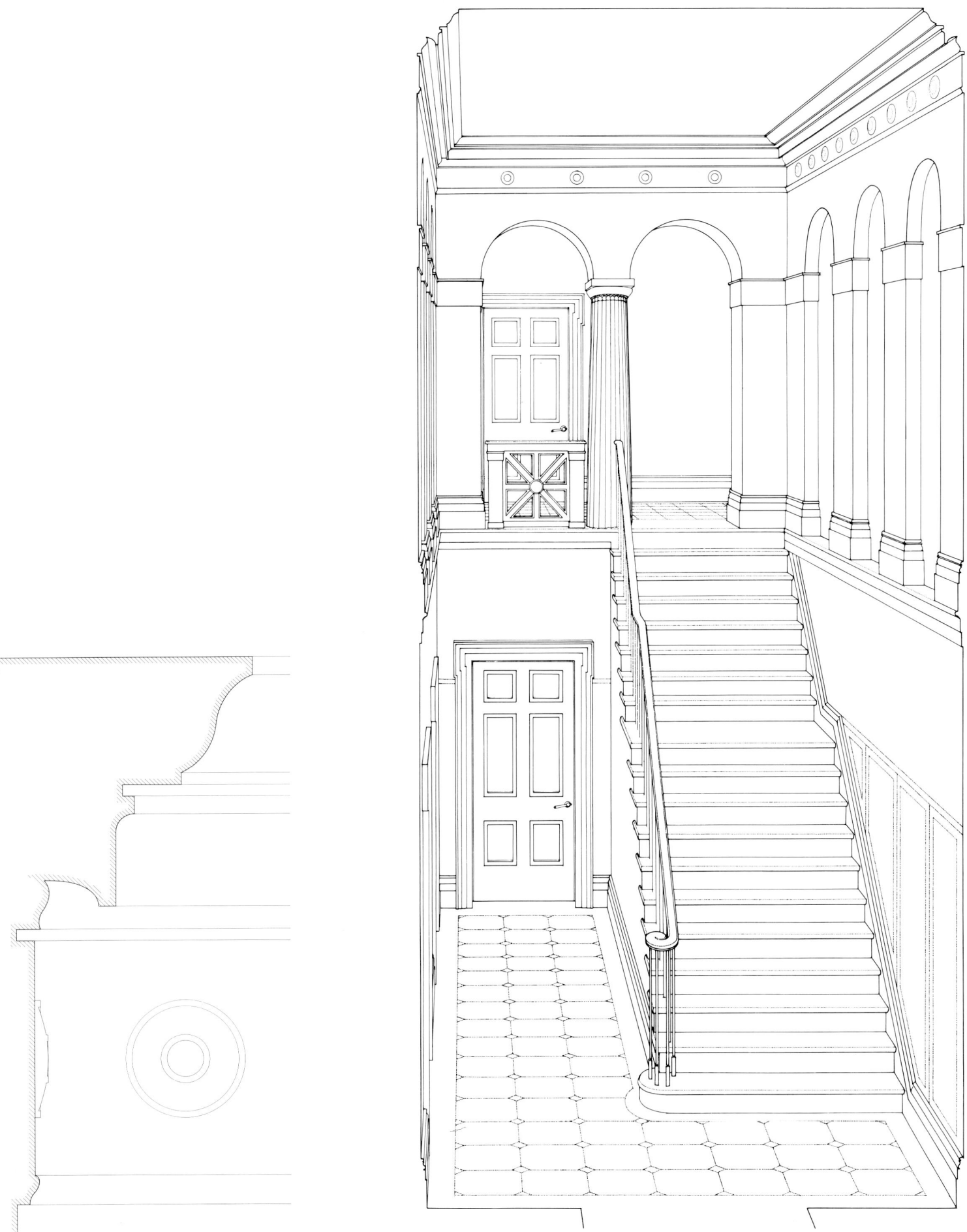

PERSPECTIVE VIEW OF ENTRANCE HALL AND CORNICE DETAIL

DEMETRI PORPHYRIOS

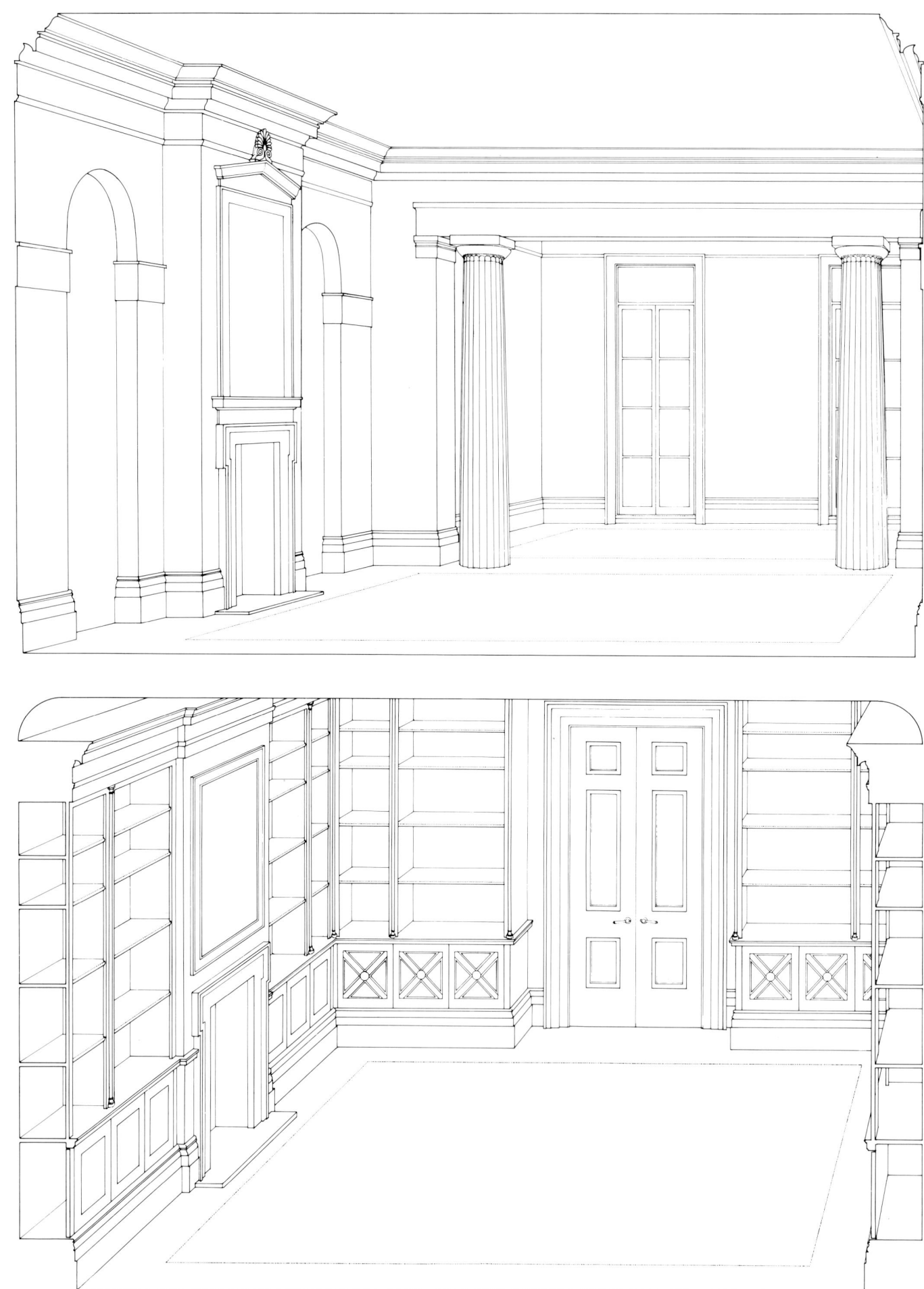

PERSPECTIVE VIEWS OF DRAWING ROOM AND LIBRARY

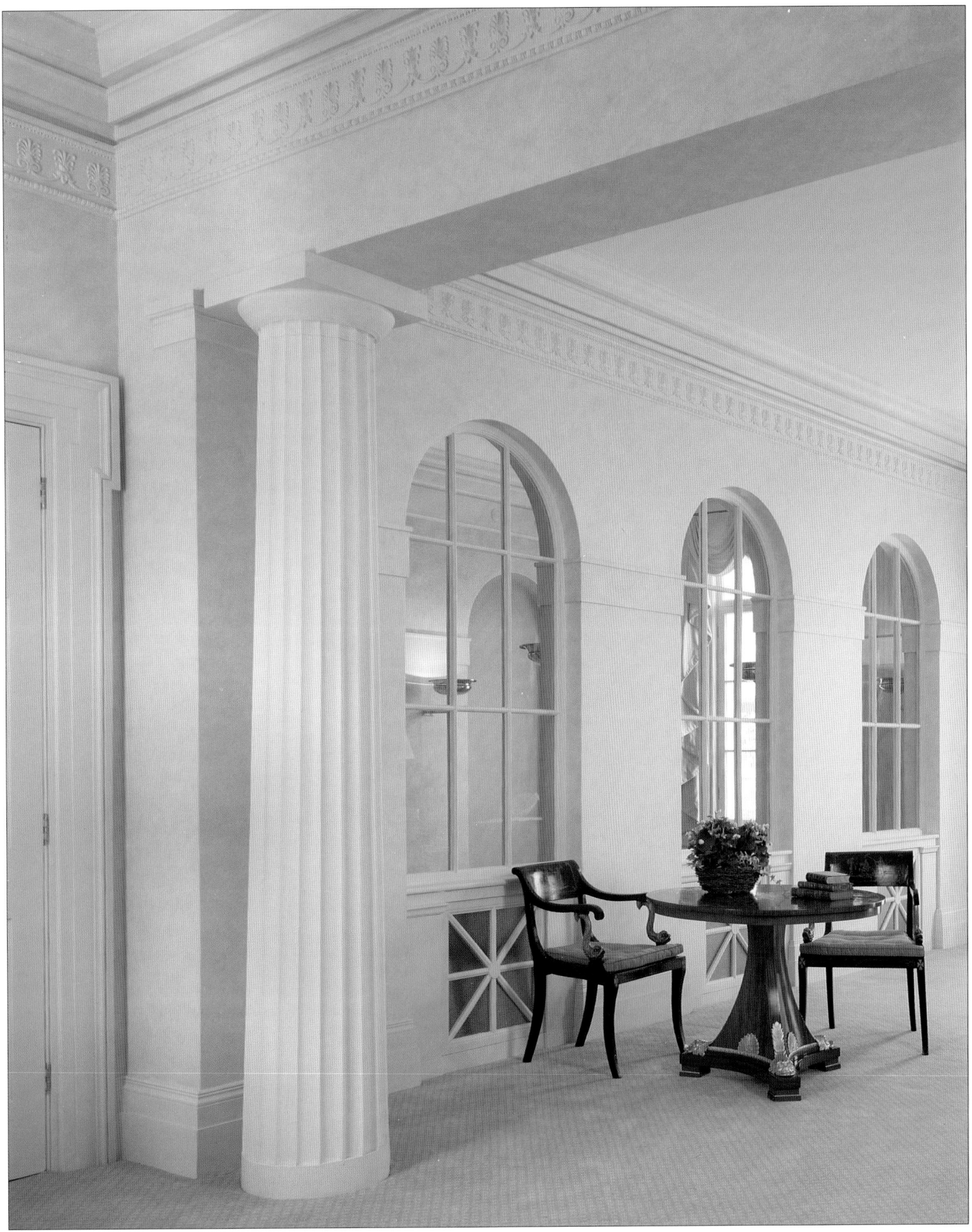

VIEW OF DRAWING ROOM

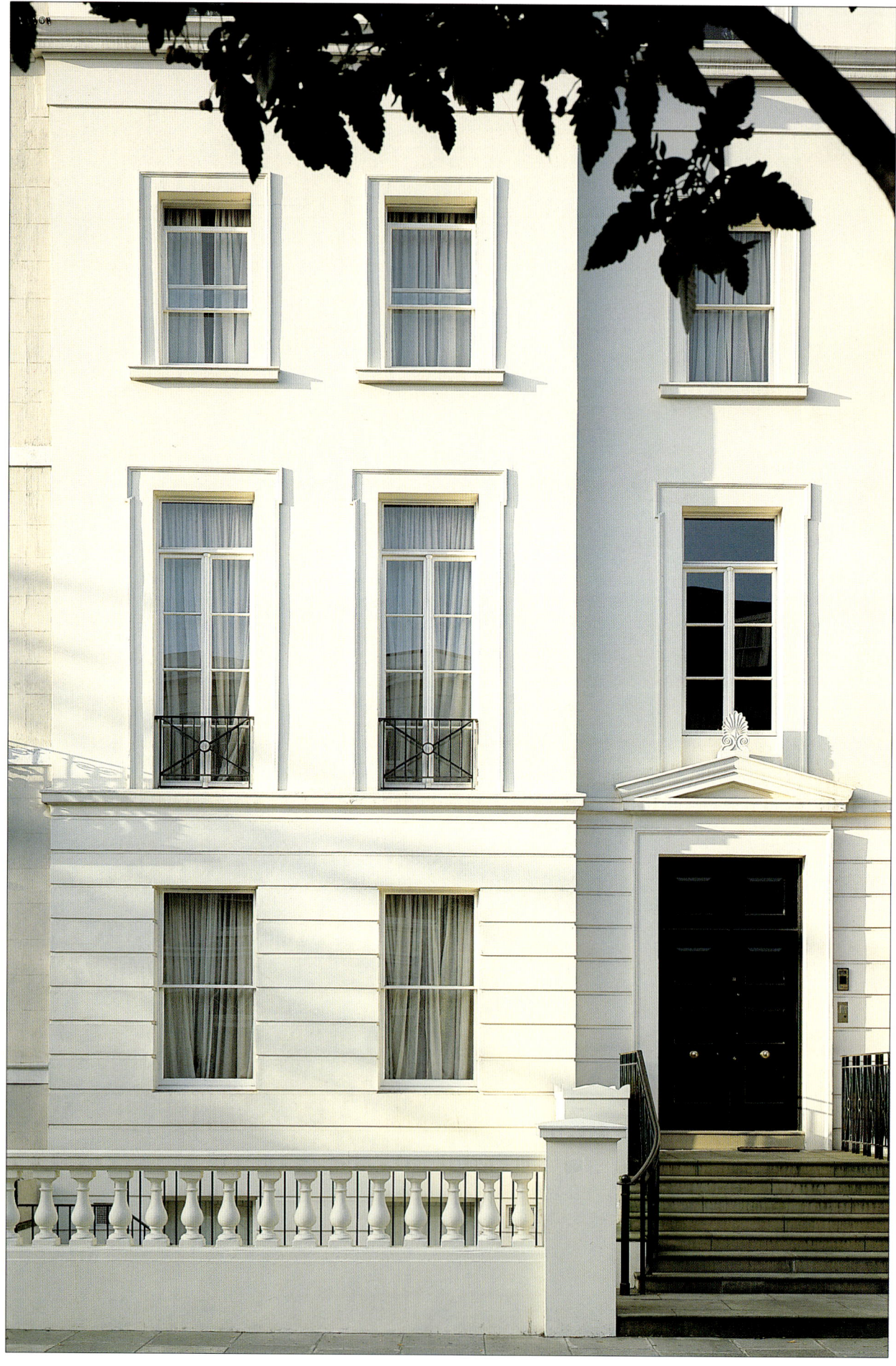

VIEW FROM THE STREET

HOUSE IN KENSINGTON

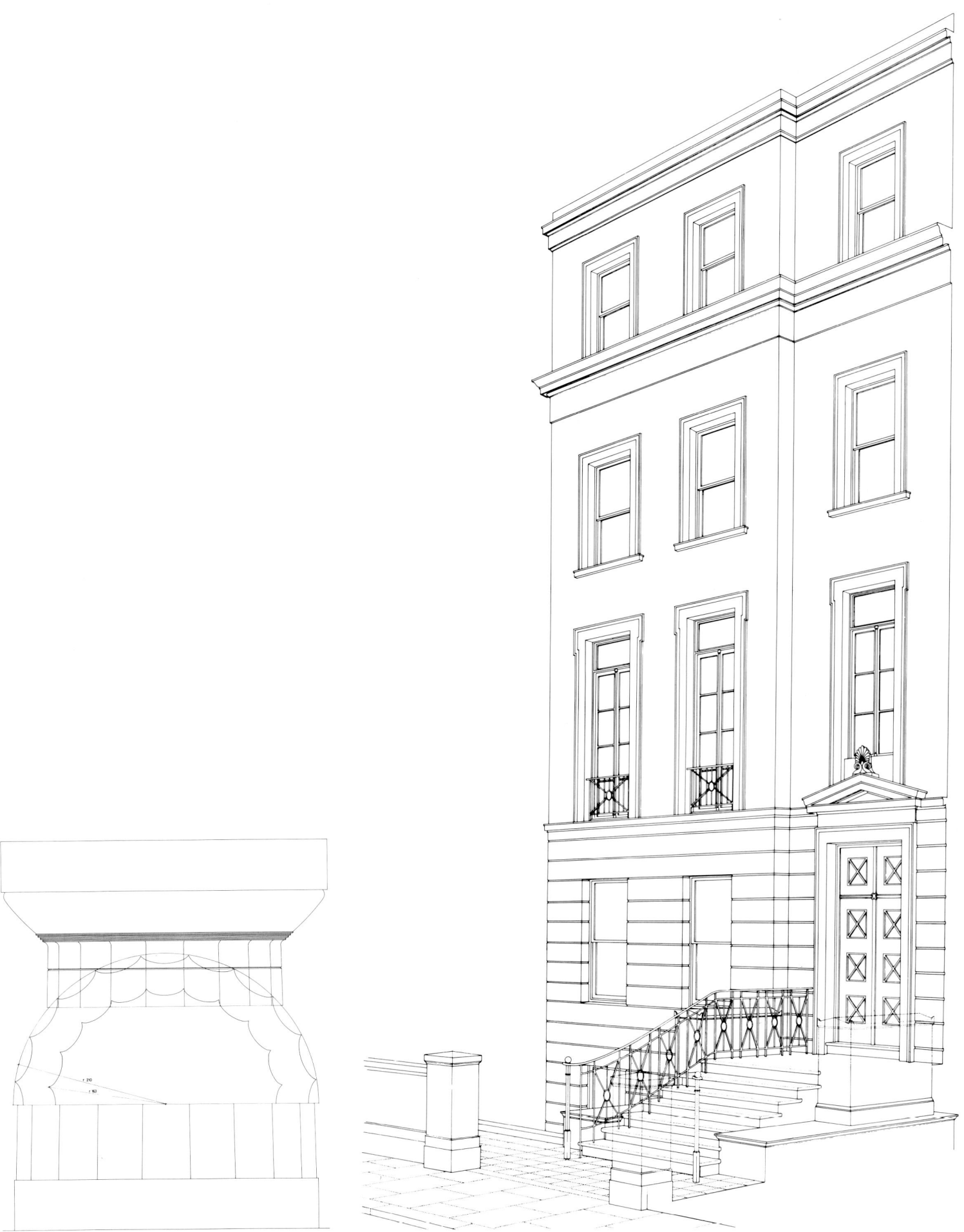

PERSPECTIVE VIEW FROM THE STREET AND DETAIL OF DORIC COLUMN

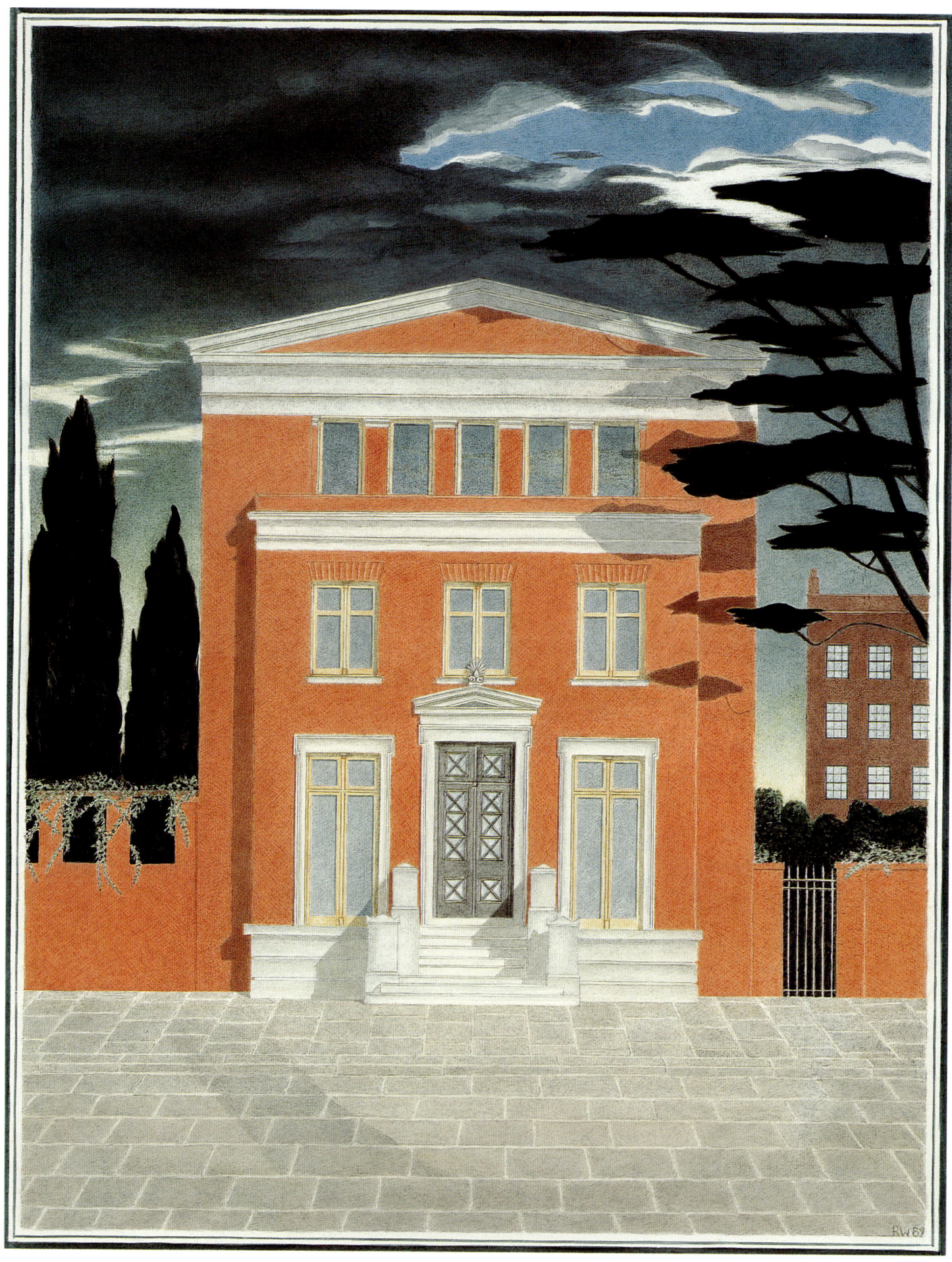

VIEW FROM THE STREET (PAINTING BY RITA WOLFF)

HOUSE IN CHELSEA
LONDON, 1989

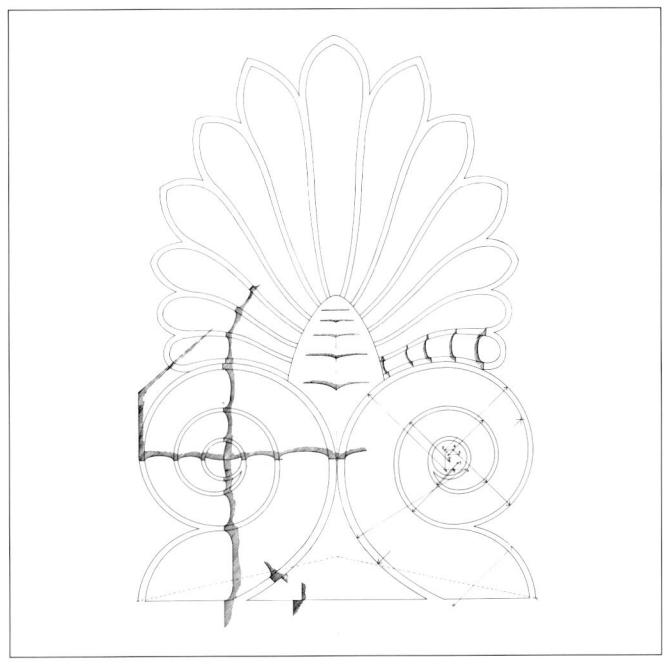

DETAIL OF ANTHEMION

This house is located in the residential area of Chelsea and it is adjacent to a number of free-standing and semi-detached eighteenth- and nineteenth-century urban villas. The buildings are generally close to each other and as such they are essentially frontalised with contingent side elevations and a simple vernacular treatment on the side of their gardens.

The house is organised in a compact pedimented volume that makes maximum use of the permitted development. Along the street a lower projecting volume helps scale down the building and allowed us to proportion the various parts. The walls generally are in brick. Facing the street, architectural elements like pediments, cornices, entablatures, rustication, diestones and window surrounds are all in Portland stone and highly refined.

By contrast the garden elevation is in red brick with a simple gable and a timber awning that shelters the drawing room balcony. Two flights of stairs flank the projecting conservatory and lead to the patio and the garden beyond.

At ground floor the house is organised around a central foyer with the library and dining room facing the street and the drawing room looking over the garden. The staircase to the bedrooms winds around a podium with the top landing projecting much like a balcony. The bedroom floors are organised around a central skylit atrium with a perimeter gallery.

In the trilogy of the houses at Kensington, Chelsea, and Chepstow Villas we have worked with the same classical elements and within the confines of domestic London typologies. Tradition is always the framework within which one works. Yet the boundaries of the classical are always permeable and endlessly renegotiated. The classical does not speak of a single canon. It is rather a field of interplay between commodity, firmness and delight.

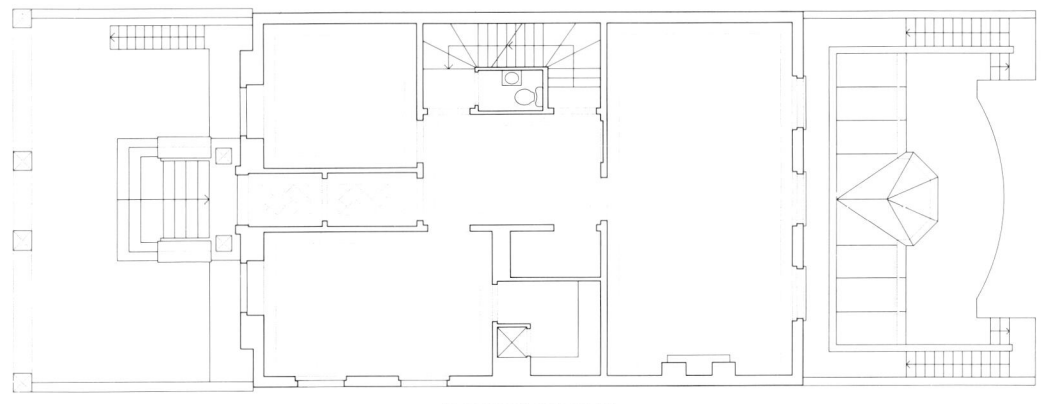

GROUND-FLOOR PLAN

DEMETRI PORPHYRIOS

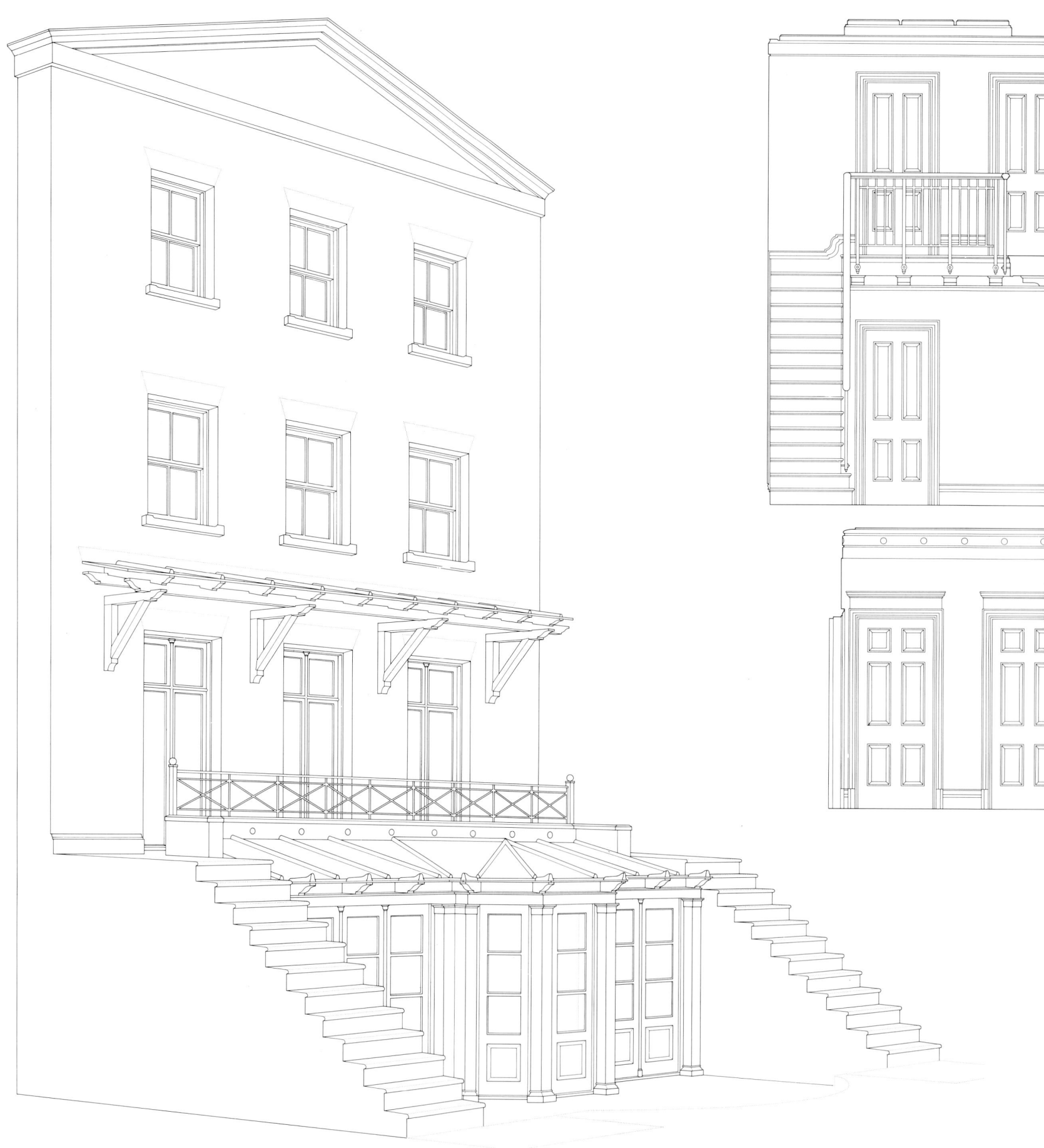

PERSPECTIVE VIEW FROM THE GARDEN; SECTION THROUGH ENTRANCE HALL AND ATRIUM ABOVE

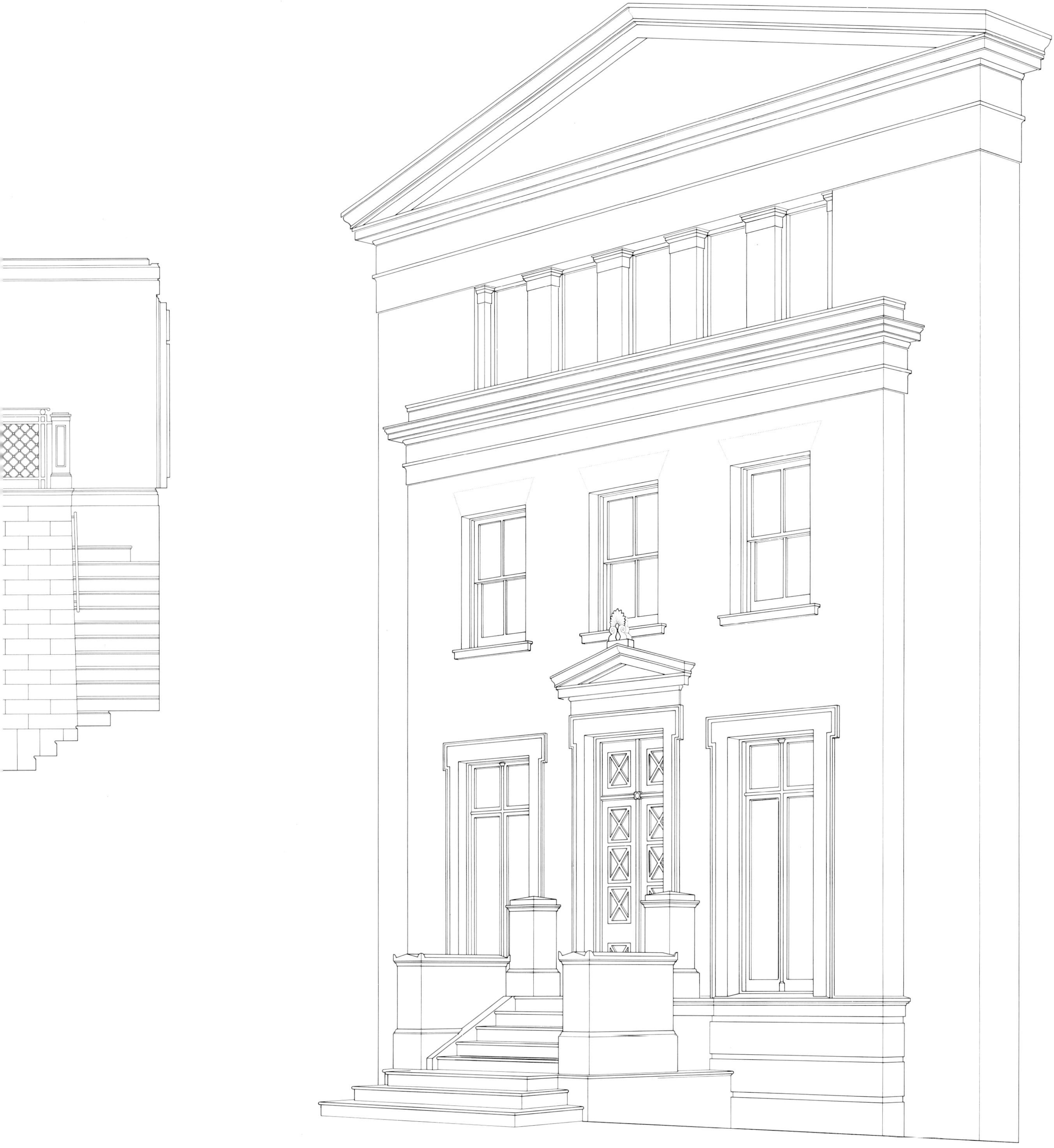

HOUSE IN CHELSEA

PERSPECTIVE VIEW FROM THE STREET

CHEPSTOW VILLAS
LONDON, 1988

This is a new building in the residential area of Holland Park. A fifties structure had replaced the nineteenth-century urban villa destroyed in the War. This modernist building was a rather unfortunate intrusion into the undisturbed urban fabric of the street and we took the view that it should be demolished.

Early in the design we decided to maintain the existing urban and iconographic rules of the street. But whereas originally these were single family houses, our brief asked for maisonettes and apartments of different size. We had to devise a scheme, therefore, that respected the urban hierarchies of the street while providing accommodation of a repetitive nature.

Along the street elevation the centre bay is a soaring void that becomes a portico roofed by the broken pediment. By contrast, the garden elevation is a simple wall pierced by windows. It is here that the repetitive nature of the brief is revealed. A separate skylit volume houses the conservatories of the two maisonettes. The projecting timber eaves and perimeter trusses give the conservatory an appropriate rustic quality without compromising its reading as a 'machine in the garden' that derives from its scale and tectonic rationality.

The plan is organised front to back and around a central lift and service staircase. This is a masonry wall building on a raft foundation with concrete floors. Externally the whole is rendered and all profiles are formed on site. The entrance lobby has a marble floor, incised and rusticated walls and a coffered barrel-vaulted ceiling. All internal cornices, coffers and anthemia have specially made profiles in fibrous plaster.

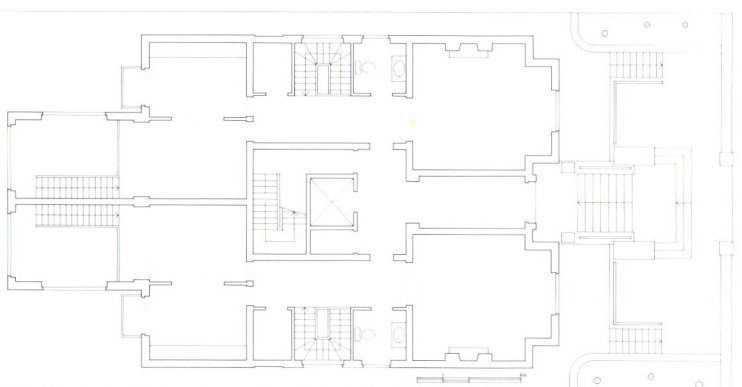

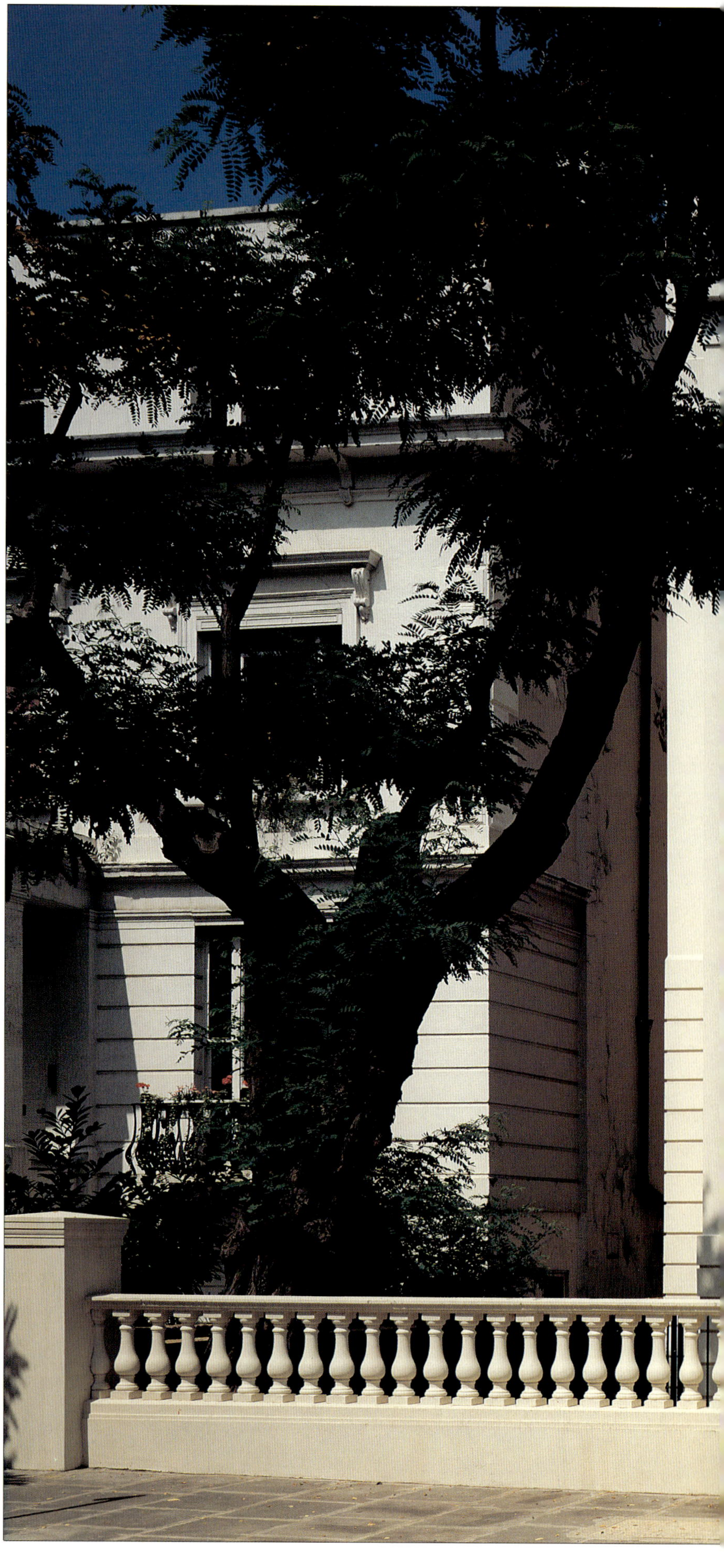

GROUND-FLOOR PLAN AND VIEW FROM THE STREET

112

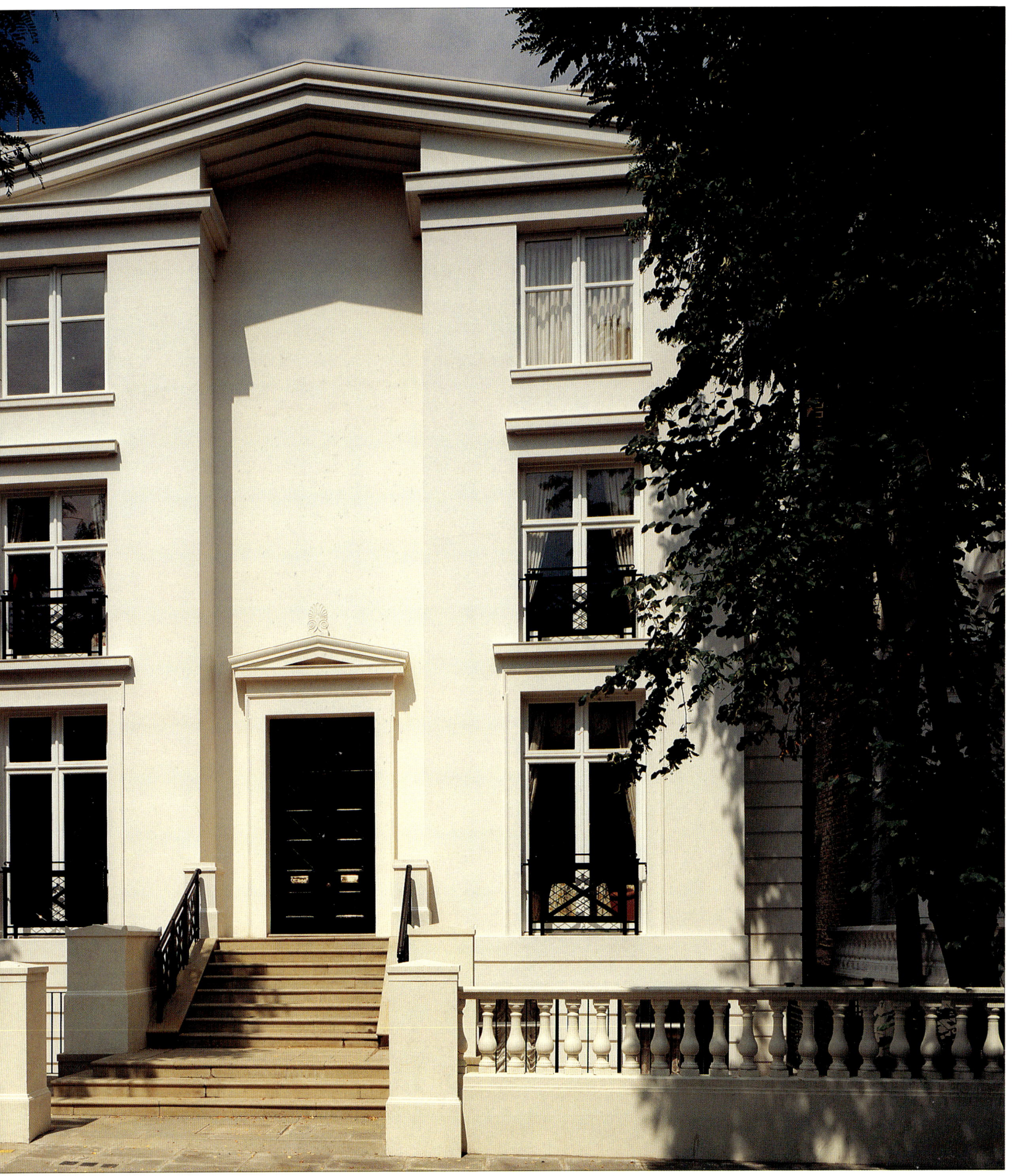

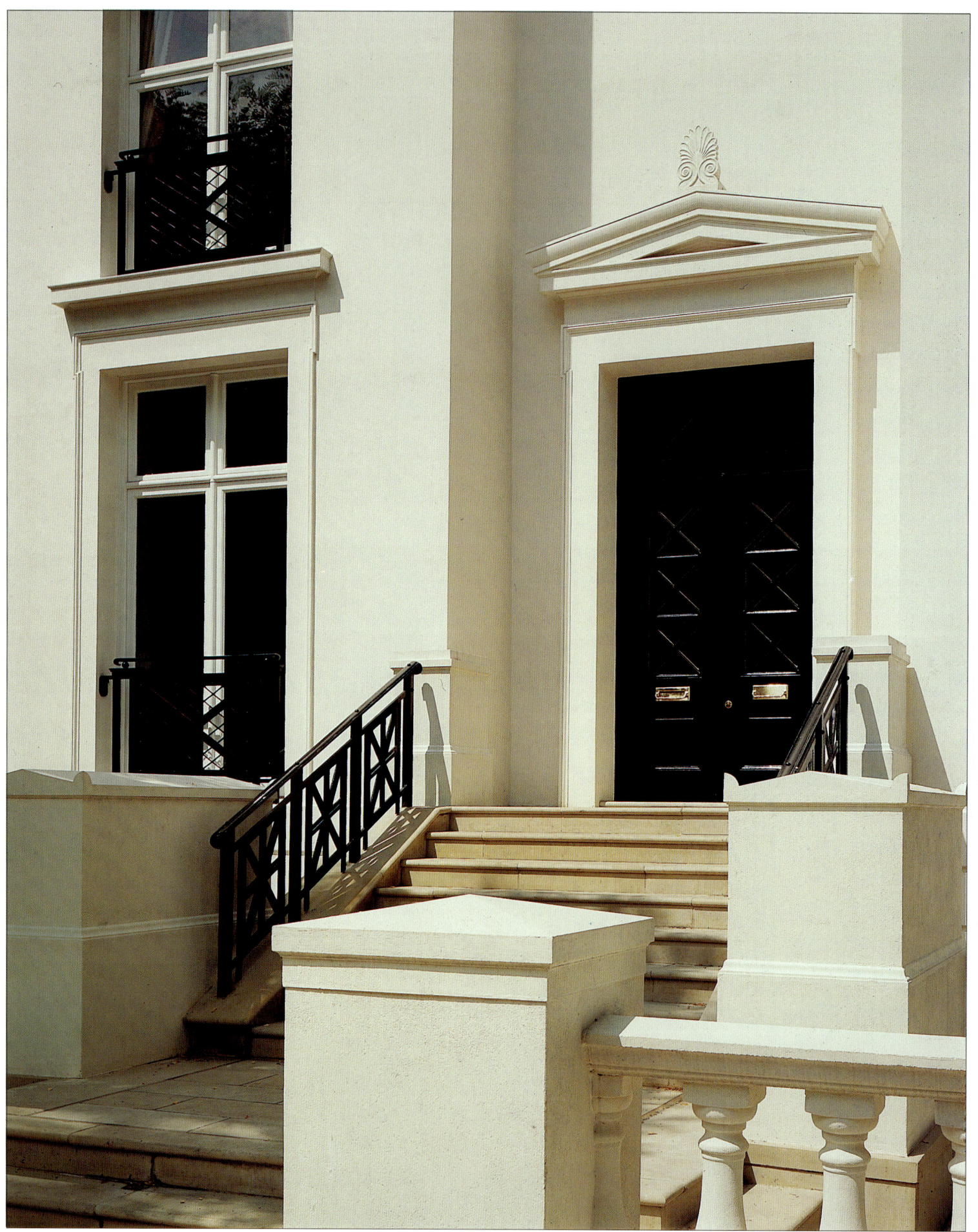

VIEW OF FRONT ENTRANCE

CHEPSTOW VILLAS

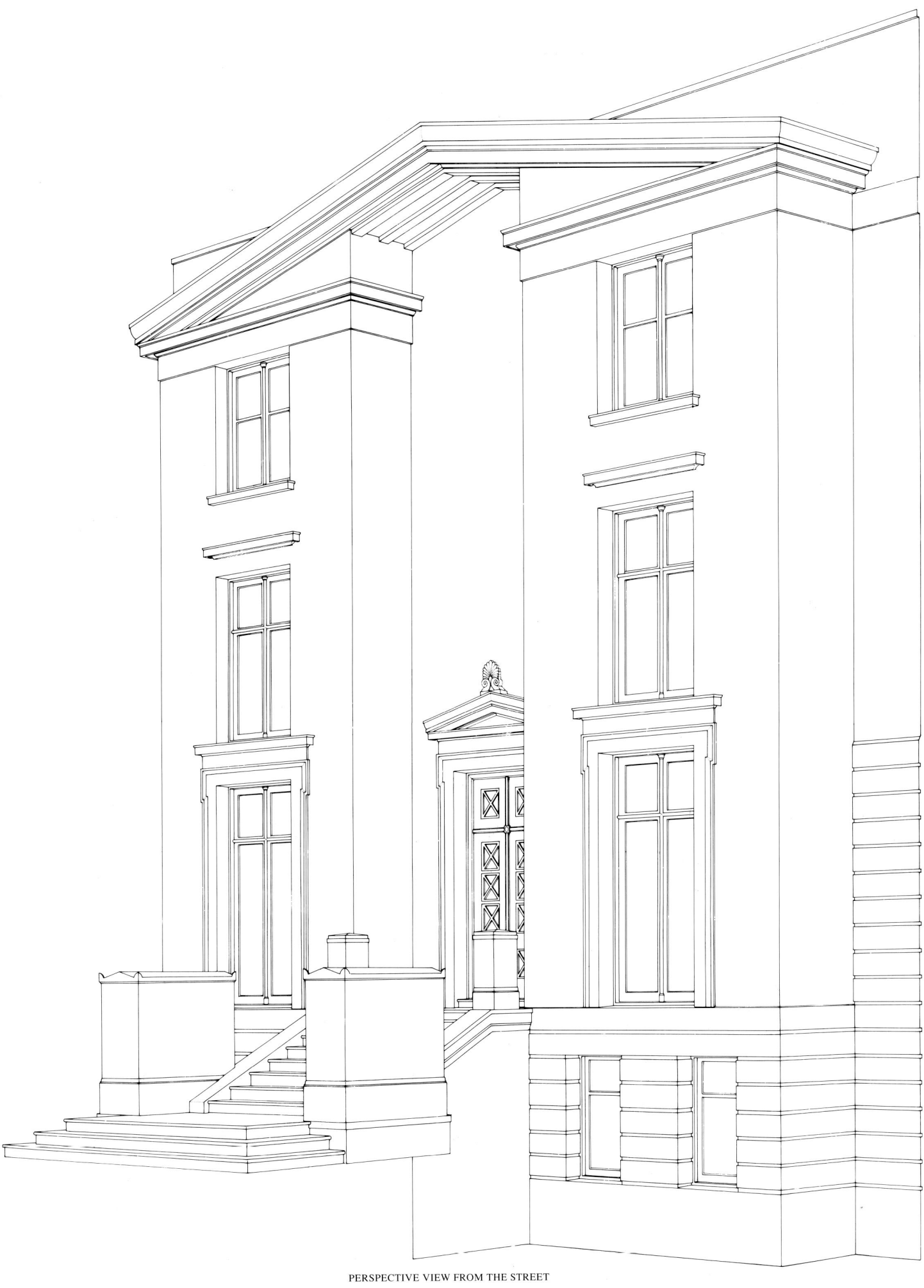

PERSPECTIVE VIEW FROM THE STREET

DEMETRI PORPHYRIOS

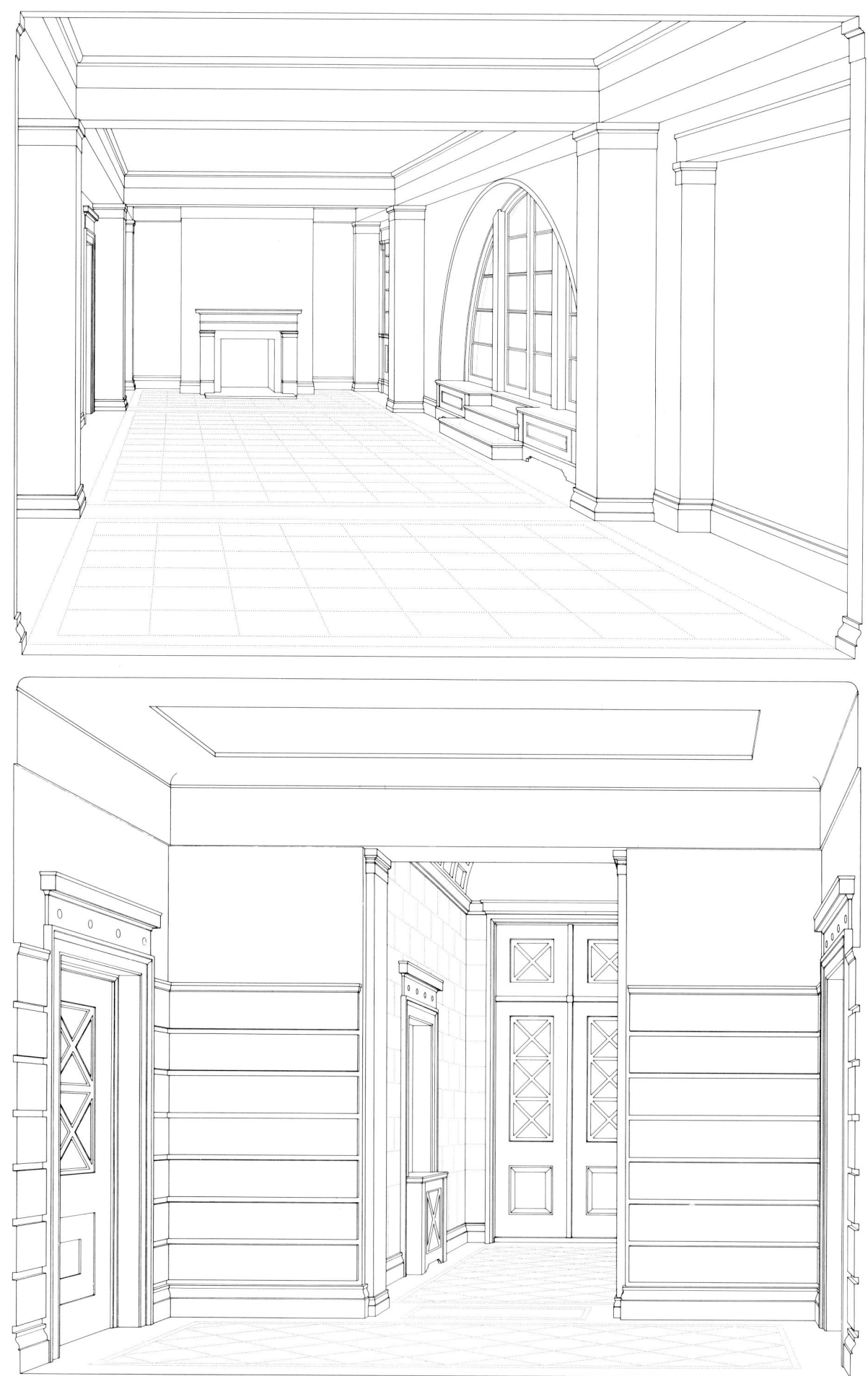

ABOVE: PERSPECTIVE VIEW OF PENTHOUSE DRAWING ROOM; *BELOW*: PERSPECTIVE VIEW OF ENTRANCE HALL

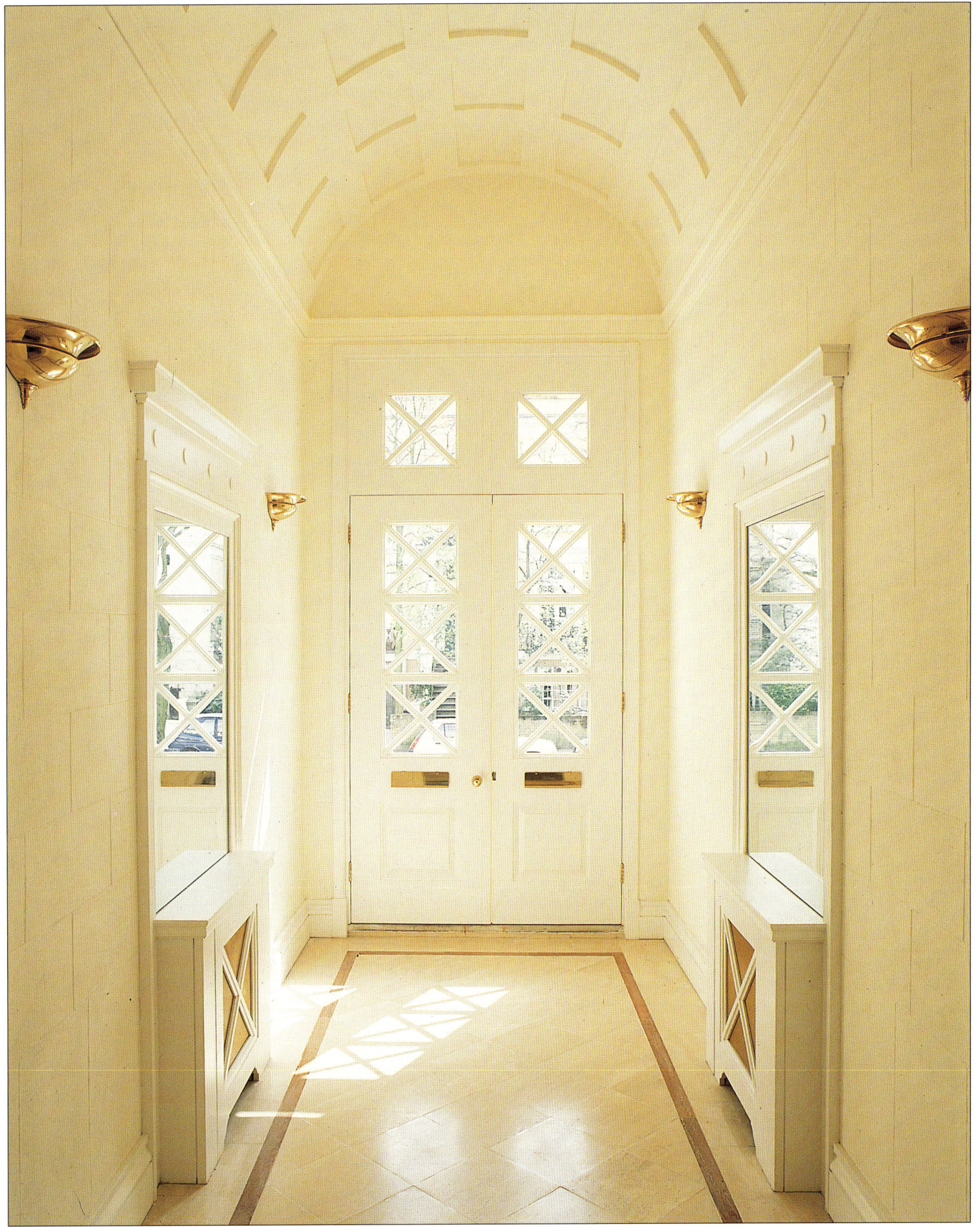

VIEW OF ENTRANCE HALL

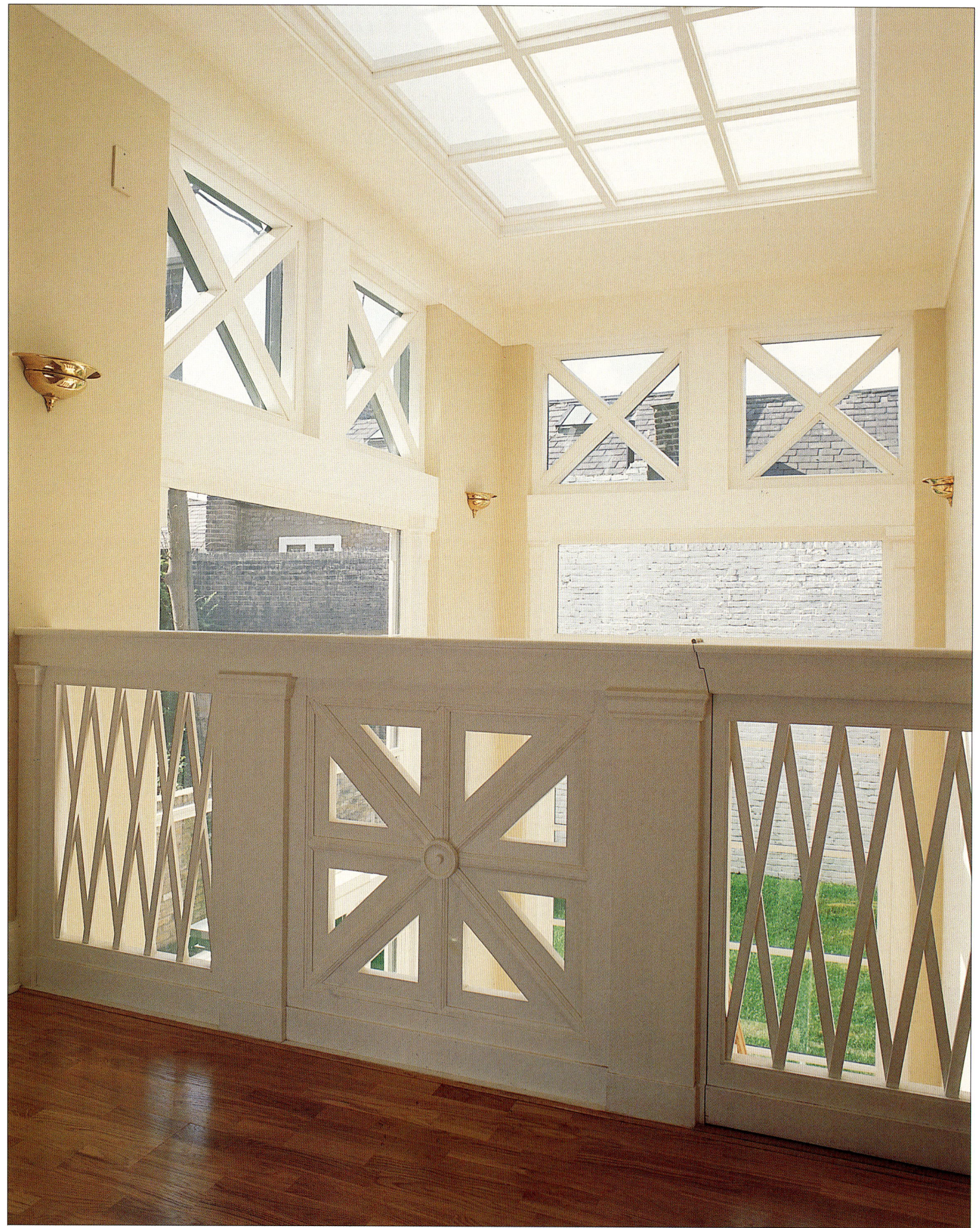

INTERIOR VIEW OF THE CONSERVATORY

CHEPSTOW VILLAS

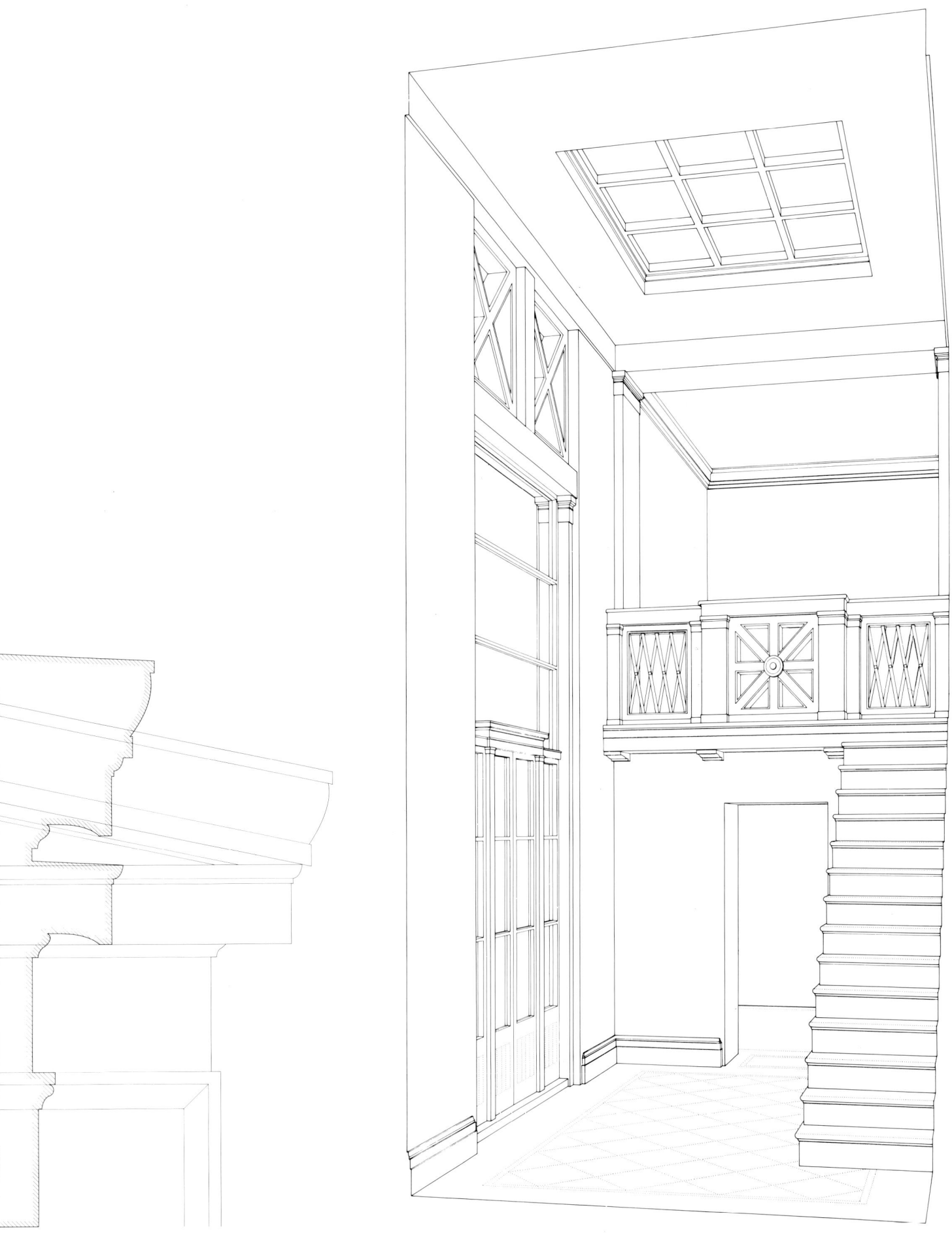

PERSPECTIVE INTERIOR VIEW OF THE CONSERVATORY AND DETAIL OF ENTRANCE PORTICO PROFILES

DEMETRI PORPHYRIOS

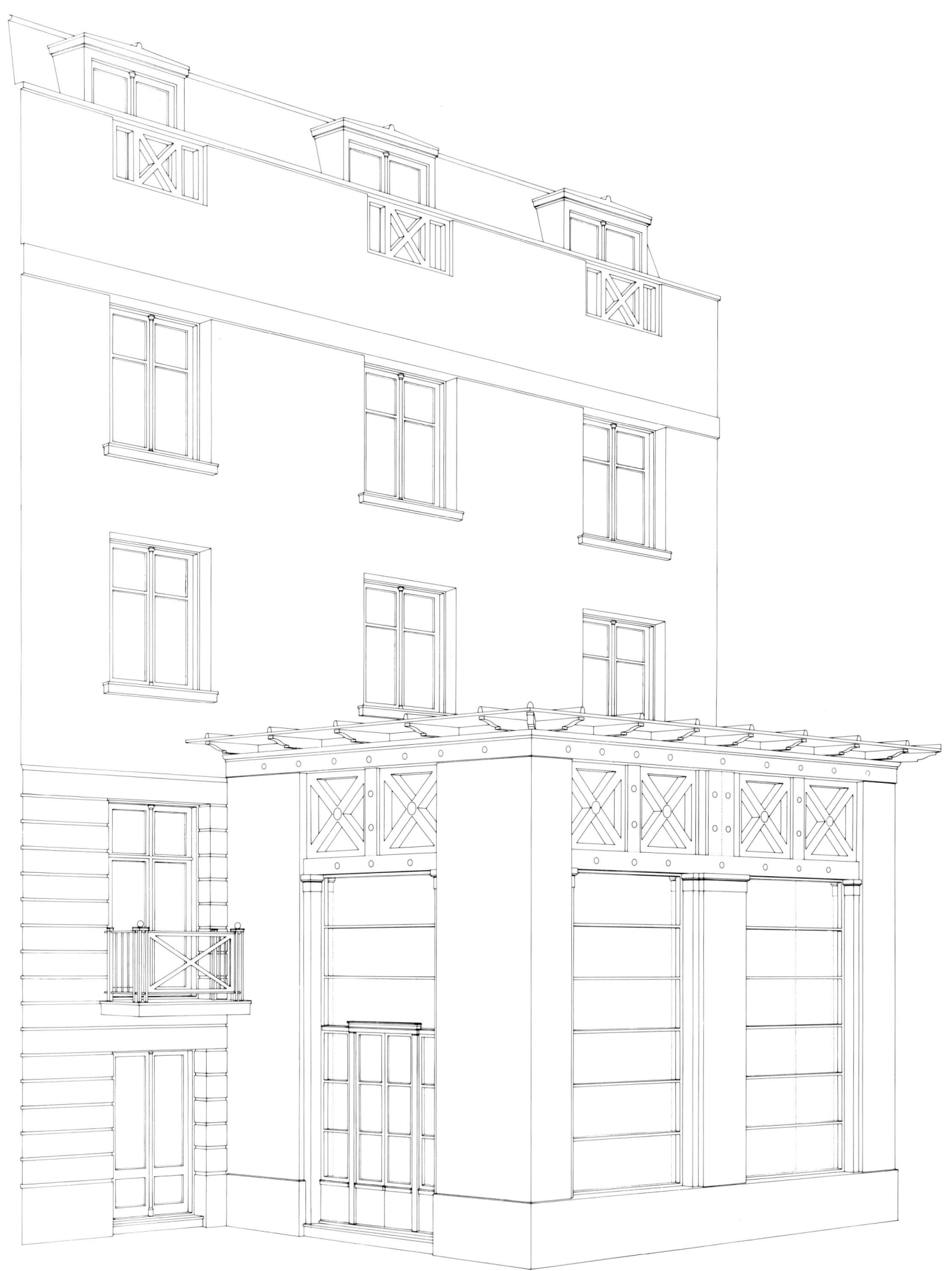

PERSPECTIVE VIEW FROM THE GARDEN

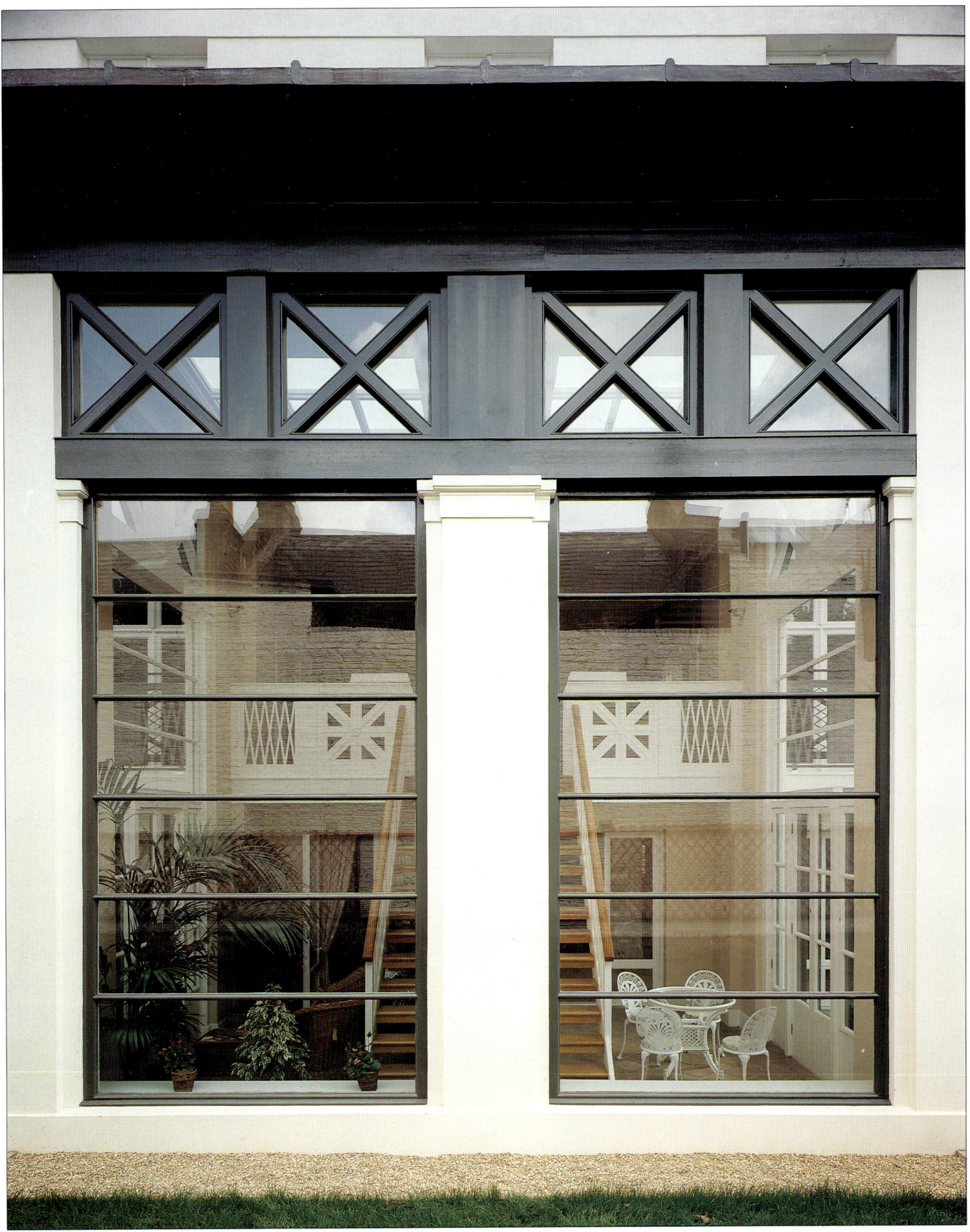

DETAIL VIEW OF THE CONSERVATORY

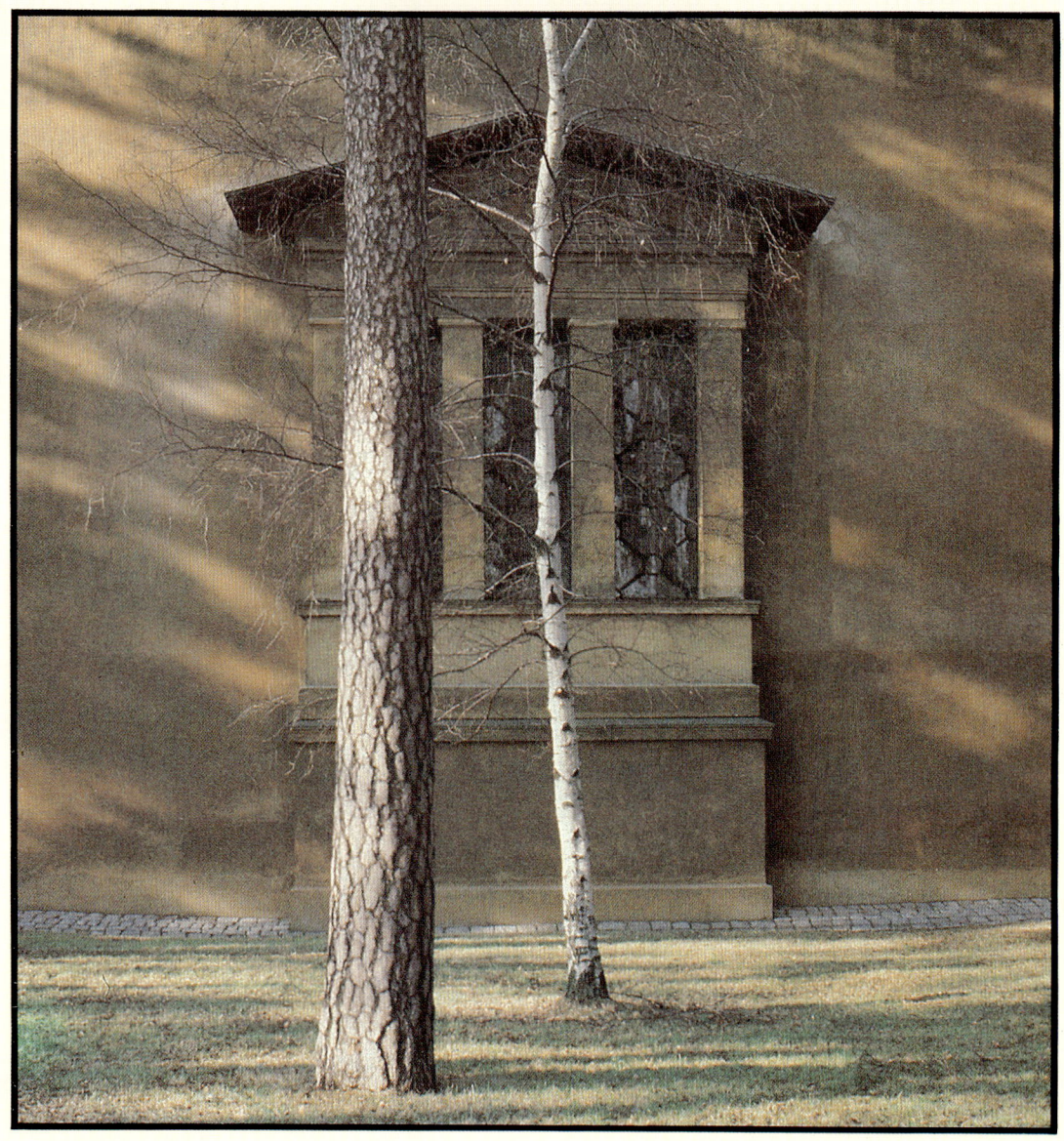

CLASSICISM
IS NOT A STYLE

Guest-Edited by Demetri Porphyrios

CLASSICISM IS NOT A STYLE

In the twenties Modernism concerned itself not simply with a wholesale revision of architectural values, but more significantly with the transvaluation of petty-bourgeois values. The conventions of conduct which once bore radiant witness to the fact that civilised men spoke the same language and could communicate with urban ease, now threatened to become a universal *paradisus artificialis*.

By the late forties, the socialist dreams of the intelligentsia of Modernism were realised – ironically enough – by the democratic capitalist state, retaining from the spirit of *Sachlichkeit* only a certain scientism of vision and a distinct documentary quality. The myth of Modernism, namely that industrial emancipation would lead to social egalitarianism, was given a specific content: democracy was to be understood as synonymous with unsolicited distribution of industrial goods. Yet the distribution of goods and freedom of choice that industrial capital had promised aimed not so much at making public life more democratic as at the creation of vast markets of consumption. By the late sixties, following the contradictory experiences of Welfare State housing programmes and the make-believe high-tech culture of Metabolism, it became clear that the global project of democratisation hailed in the twenties had suddenly shrunk to a calculated strategy of creating 'circuses of bread and spectacle'.

This socio-economic trend was parodied in the conspicuous 'consumption of culture' that shaped Modern Eclecticism. From the middle sixties onwards, operating under the moralising pretext of democratic pluralism, the culture industry emerged as the dominant ideology of twentieth-century America and Europe. The second half of our century has surely proven to be the age of pluralism 'visiting the beliefs of all countries and all ages, admitting for observation everything, without fixing any part, since truth is everywhere in bits and nowhere in its entirety, in no country, no period, and no man'.[1] Once appropriated by industrial capital Modernism became an instrument for the ideological reproduction of the very priorities of industrial capital itself. The critical vision of Modernism was lost and the original utopia of social egalitarianism was turned successively into petty-bourgeois humanism in the fifties, into expendable high-tech phantasmagoria in the sixties, and into stylistic eclecticism in the seventies.

Contemporary architecture bathes in the pantheistic limbo of eclecticism. Torn between the dilemma for a frenetic search for novelty and an inherited social mission for a popular language, architecture leafs through history caricaturing remembrances. Who influenced this trend? Virtually everybody:

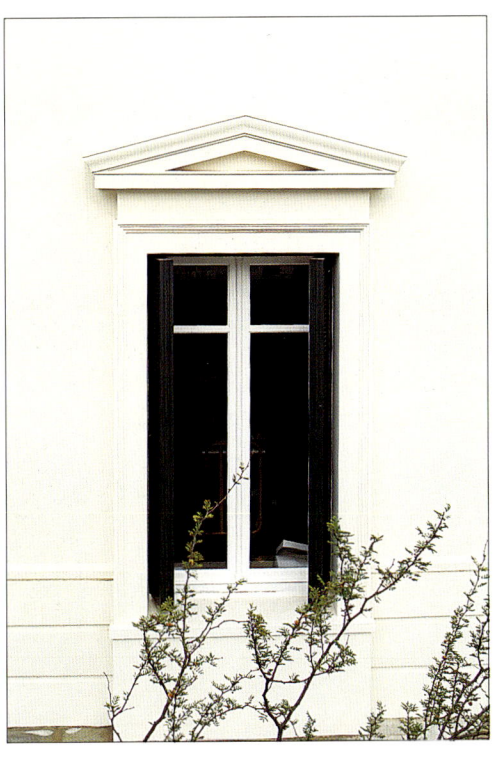

VILLA IN ATHENS, WINDOW DETAIL

the American shingle style revival, the lyrical neo-Corbusianism, neo-Constructivism, the Queen Anne revival, or the recent Hollywood 'neon'-classicism. The incomprehensibility of designed and non-designed kitsch is reified into culture by the literati of post-Modernism. Lack of common conviction and indiscriminate style-mongering are mistaken for democratic freedom and inventiveness. Collective myth is systematically fractured into countless individualistic trivia, into fastidious and uncompassionate evasions of the human situation.

The tactics of Modern Eclecticism have been clear. In an effort to recapture culture, Modern Eclecticism has plunged into history. Making use of the techniques of metaphor and quotation, Modern Eclecticism has undertaken to construct culture overnight. The 'culture' it inaugurated, however, has been a kind of shorthand whereby through abbreviation one caresses the confused multiplicity of stylistic genres, esteeming all but none in particular, creating in this way the illusion of authenticity cherished by the collector of reproductions. Modern Eclecticism started as a quest for the lost 'aura' and has grown into the exemplar of industrial kitsch.

Suffusing the entire sense of Modern Eclecticism has been the belief that industrial kitsch could be turned into an aesthetic experience that would clear the way for a healthy growth of ideals. In an effort to endow industrial kitsch with cultural value, the literati of eclecticism attempted to aestheticise reality and the process of communication.

The technique of aestheticising the real was, of course, well known to the Dadaists and Surrealists. Dada and Surrealism, however, was a fundamentally subversive movement infused with a deep moral concern to regain a lost purity. Instead, Modern Eclecticism has been an attempt to reify the strategies of an economy which, by its own nature and for its own priorities of profit, has been founded exclusively on the 'production of waste'. In that sense, Modern Eclecticism has attempted to aestheticise the real by moralising infatuation. For 'it is only infatuation . . . that does justice to what exists . . . Something that must be thought beautiful simply because it exists, is for that very reason ugly.'[2]

The second strategy, that of aestheticising the process of communication, is fundamentally linked to the experience of kitsch. For kitsch demands of its users the violent jerkiness of advertisement. We know only too well the source of violence in advertisement: its rhetorical figures of speech are used not in order to please, or to incite us to reflect and thereby gain knowledge of our situation, (as is invariably the case with art) but rather in order to abbreviate a message and send it home by tapping our image of the world. Advertisement is by nature aggressive for when it shocks or tactfully seduces us, we are left with a pervasive feeling of having been cheated; while when due to its boldness or irrelevance it fails to touch us, we are left idiotically embarrassed and trivialised.

In a manner similar to advertisment, Modern Eclecticism, by aestheticising the process of communication, links experience to mere reading or decodement. Such an architecture tolerates no aesthetic surplus that would resist consumption and thereby survive as the core of experience. Instead,

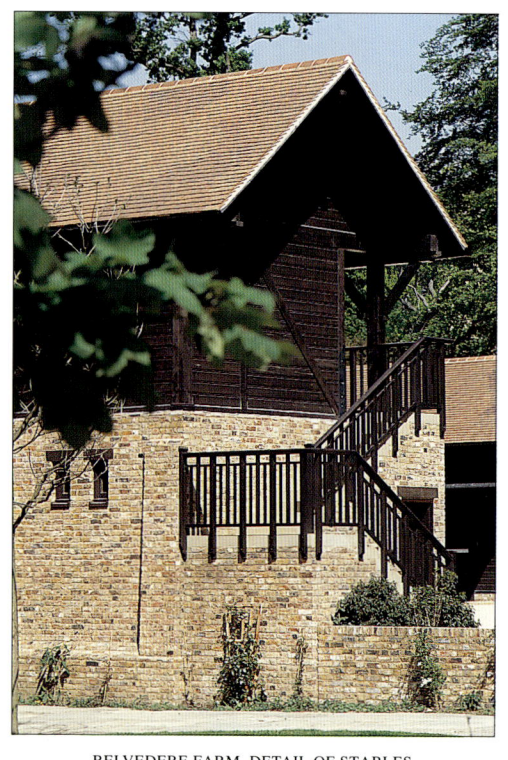

BELVEDERE FARM, DETAIL OF STABLES

figurative sensuality takes on the quality of nightmare: weightless pediments, 'neon'-classical cornices, emasculated orders, metopes enfeebled by the arrogance of architects in search of fame, engrossed voussoirs, drooping garlands, neo-constructivist pirouettes, high-tech styling, and androgynous plans, in short all sorts of upholstered coteries degenerate into a mere 'style-heap', without essential meaning other than the cult of 'irony' and the illusion of a make-believe culture. This is an architecture with no discourse; simply quotations, parentheses, brackets, and a kind of disjointed, insidious whisper that spells: advertisement.

It is exactly that quality of advertisement which accounts for Modern Eclecticism's ability to capture the illusion of culture cheaply. The word 'cheaply' should be understood here in its most literal sense. By focusing on the techniques of communication at the expense of tectonics and sound building, Modern Eclecticism side stepped the fundamental concern of architecture for reconciling construction with symbolic form.

Instead, the 'decorated shed' has functioned exactly as a strategy for discriminating between shelter and symbolism, that is between need and delight. The theory of the 'decorated shed' provided for a system of thought which would separate the budgets to be allocated to shelter and symbolism. It encouraged a figurative enrichment of modernist construction but at the same time it safeguarded against the reorganisation of the building industry that any fusion of construction with style would have necessitated. Such a reorganisation was (and still is) highly unpopular to industrial capital since it would have upset all three levels of the building industry: capital expenditure, skilled labour, and profit distribution. By means of a resourceful twist, the 'decorated shed' took the modernist precept of 'flexibility' and displaced it from the realm of spatial distribution to that of symbolic attribution. 'Pragmatics, Technics and Semantics' were to be defined by Modern Eclecticism as three independent budgets to be shifted around in a game which aimed at delectable fantasy at minimum cost.

The predicament of contemporary architecture, therefore, stems from our twofold inheritance: on one hand, the symbolically mute elements of industrial production inherited from Modernism, and on the other the expendable historicist and high-tech signs of industrial kitsch inherited from Modern Eclecticism. This raises, in my opinion, the crucial problem we face today: if there is an opposition between the economic priorities of mass industrial society and the yearning for an authentic culture that could sustain individual freedom in public life, under what qualifications is it possible to practise architecture at all? Paradoxically, the only possible critical stance for architecture today is to build an alliance between building construction and symbolic representation. To construct, that is, a tectonic discourse which, while addressing the pragmatics of shelter, could at the same time represent its own tectonics in a symbolic way.

It is from such a perspective that classicism should be re-evaluated today: not as a borrowed stylistic finery but as an ontology of building. Classicism is not a style. Its lesson lies in the way by which it raises construction and shelter to the realm of the symbol.

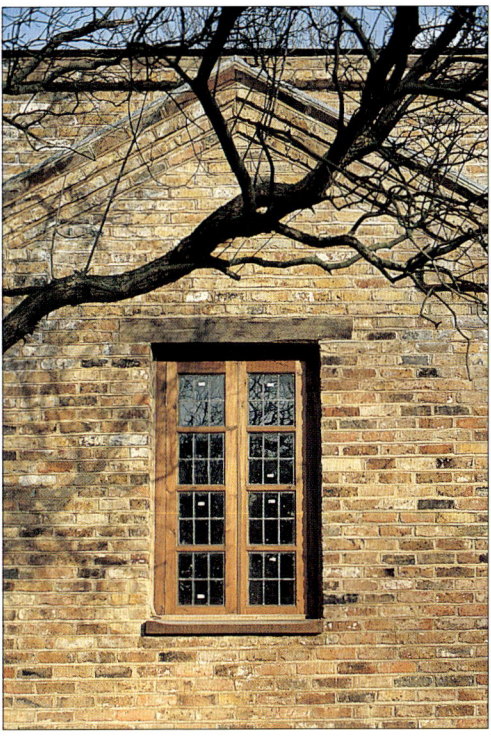

PAVILION IN HIGHGATE, DETAIL

The constructional logic of vernacular

Despite the superficial associations with rusticity that the word 'vernacular' brings to mind its essential meaning is different. The idea of vernacular has nothing to do with stylistics. It rather points to the universal ethos of constructing shelter under the conditions of scarcity of materials and operative constructional techniques.

By invoking vernacular, one does not seek the primitivism of pre-industrial cultures. The temptation to turn one's back on contemporary society in order to return to some pre-industrial order, when pursued, leaves us suspended amid the reverberations of Plato's ghost: 'what then?' Instead, the essential meaning of vernacular refers to straightforward construction, to the rudimentary building of shelter, an activity that exhibits reason, efficiency, economy, durability and pleasure. Certainly, varying materials and techniques attribute regionalist characteristics to vernacular. But beyond appearances, all vernacular is marked by a number of constructional *a prioris* which are universal and essentially phenomenological.

To begin with, building – by its very nature – involves the experiences of load-bearing and load-borne, the primary manifestations of which are the column and the lintel. Secondly, it involves the experience of horizontal and vertical enclosure, the primary manifestations of which are the roof and the wall. The floor, since it repeats the original ground, is flat for it is meant to be walked upon; whereas the roof is inclined since, in addition to its shedding off water, it marks the terminus and should appear as such. Finally, since all construction is construction by means of finite elements, the act of building involves necessarily the experience of demarcating, the primary manifestations of which are the beginning and ending.

When applied to the making of shelter, these constructional *a prioris* give rise to a set of constructional forms: as for example the gable which marks the sectional termination of the roof and thus points to the primary experience of entry; or the engaged pilaster, which manifests the confluent experiences of load-bearing and enclosure; or the window and door, which manifest the experience of suspending enclosure locally for purposes of passage; or the colonnade, which demarcates the experience of boundary; and so on.

Classicism: the symbolic elaboration of vernacular

Such constructional *a prioris* and their ensuing constructional forms can be identified – it would appear – beyond fear of interpretative dispute and could serve as the core of a common architectural knowledge.

Yet architecture cannot remain at this 'starting point'. Its vocation is to raise itself above the contingencies of building by commemorating those very contingencies from which it sprung in the first place. What distinguishes a shed from a temple is the mythopoeic power the temple possesses: it is a power that transgresses the boundaries of contingent reality and raises construction and shelter to the realm of the symbol.

This is the sense in which we can say that classicism is not a style. The classical naturalises the constructional *a prioris* of shelter by turning them

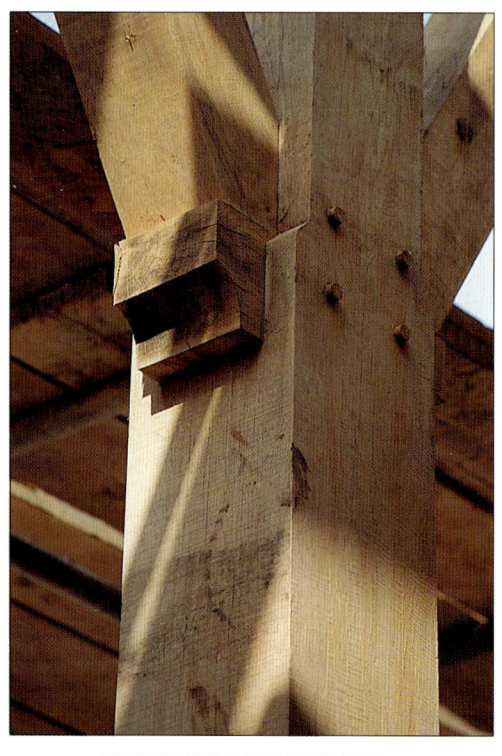

BELVEDERE FARM, BRACKET DETAIL

into myth: the demarcations of beginning and ending are commemorated as base and capital; the experience of load-bearing is made perceptible through the entasis in the shaft of the column; the chief beam, binding the columns together and imposing on them a common load, becomes the architrave; the syncopation of the transversal beams resting on the architrave is rendered visible in the figures of the triglyphs and metopes of the frieze; the projecting rafters of the roof, supported by the frieze, appear in the form of the cornice; finally – and most significantly – the whole tectonic assemblage of column, architrave, frieze and cornice becomes the ultimate object of classical contemplation in the idea of the Order.

The Order sets form over the necessities of shelter; it sets the myth of the tectonic over the contingencies of construction. The power of mythical fiction presides. It is the possibility of such an act of mythical fiction that constitutes the prime aesthetic subject matter of classical thought. Classical architecture constructs a tectonic fiction out of the productive level of building. The artifice of constructing this fictitious world is seen as analogous to the artifice of constructing the human world. In its turn, myth allows for a convergence of the real and the fictive so that the real is redeemed. By rendering construction mythically fictive, classical thought posits reality in a contemplative state, wins over the depredations of petty life and, in a moment of rare disinterestedness, rejoices in the power it has over contingent life and nature.

Mythical thinking, of course, it not necessarily primitive or prelogical as common opinion might maintain today. It is true thinking for it reduces the world to order. Its truth is no less than that experimentally verified by science. Today, if it appears that the mythopoeic mind cannot achieve objectivity (and should therefore be doomed as an irrationality that can never attain consensus) this is not because it is incapable of dealing with the world, but rather because contemporary industrial life is dominated by vulgar positivism. That is why architecture today is systematically denied its mythopoeic power. The vulgarity lies not in the search for objectivity but in the immanence with which consumer culture boasts of being the mere extension of production.

A version of this essay was first published in Architectural Design, *Vol 52, 5/6, 1982.*

NOTES
1 Théodore Jouffroy, Le Globe, *9 April, 1825, I, p 157, cited by Louis Hautecoeur in* Histoire de l'Architecture Classique en France, *A et J Picard, Paris, 1955, Vol VI, p 255.*
2 Theodor Adorno, Minima Moralia, *transl EFN Jephcott, New Left Review Editions, London, 1974, pp 76-77.*

NEW YORK PAVILION, AEOLIC CAPITAL

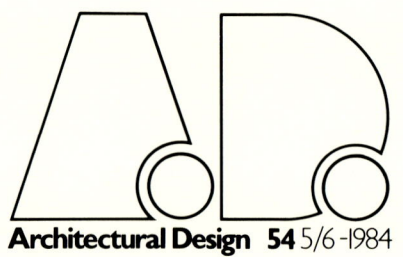

BUILDING & RATIONAL ARCHITECTURE

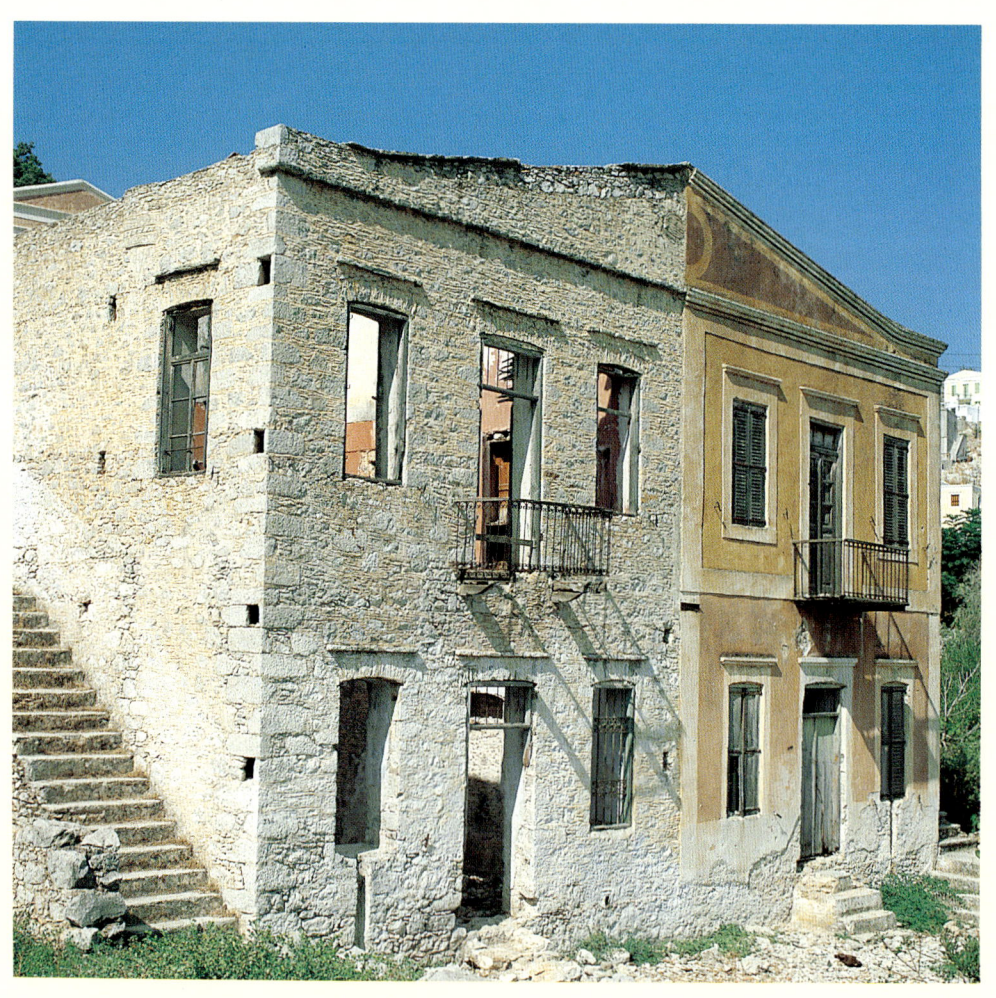

Guest-Edited by Demetri Porphyrios

BUILDING AND ARCHITECTURE

Since the early seventies, when the enthusiasm for it broke out in America, post-Modernism has become a mass phenomenon. From a historical point of view, however, the fact remains that it has contributed to a confusion that has become ubiquitous today. The confusion stems from the difficulty we seem to have in describing the scope of architecture. We may regard architecture as a focal point of our everyday activities but when asked to specify what architecture is, we become confused immediately.

Today, as always, it is important that we distinguish between building and architecture. Building refers to the craft of constructing shelter. It refers to the material techniques of construction, services, structure and functional disposition. Building comprises the knowledge and experience that man accumulates in dealing with the contingencies of providing shelter. Architecture, on the other hand, in the everyday use of the word, refers to the art of building. Architecture appears to be the product of an artistic intention, whereas building is the product of necessity. Nevertheless, we feel that architecture is not merely a supplement to building, but that building and architecture are interrelated experiences; one focusing on the experience of craft, the other on the experience of art. But what do we really mean when we say that architecture is an art and more precisely, the 'art of building'?

A work of art, writes Quatremère de Quincy, is a 'likeness of an original model . . . it is a picture, an image . . . that reproduces its original not as it is in itself, but as it appears to the senses'.[1] At first sight it may appear as a paradox that so venerated an enterprise as art turns out to be involved with the fabrication of reproductions. But it is precisely this preoccupation with imagery which gives art its distinctive charm and value.

Art and architecture do not copy their models in a servile manner but, by employing genius, they represent models freely and fashion them anew. The technique of imitation becomes in the hand of the artist a most inventive tool. When art and architecture imitate their models they do not reproduce them mechanically but they fabricate a sensuous image which invariably 'awakens' those ideas which the artist finds characteristic and essential to the model. Imitation, therefore, should not be understood as aping and mimicry but rather as the free production of a representation.

We should also note that all arts imitate their models in a partial and incomplete way due to the limitations set by their medium of execution. When an artist sets out to work, the material he chooses has a bearing as to whether he produces a painting or a novel, architecture or sculpture. If there

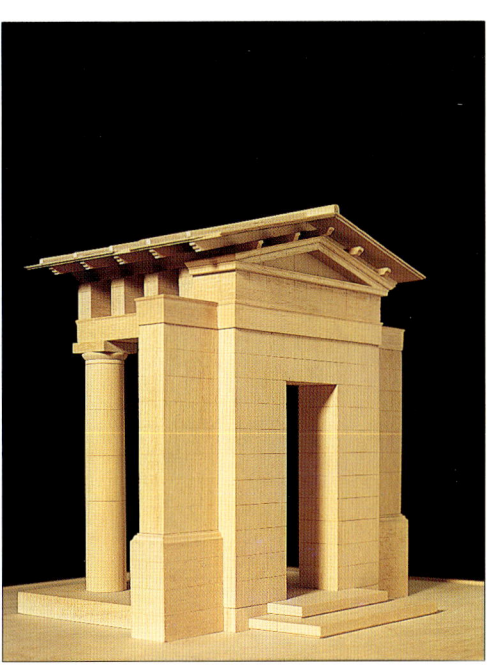

PROPYLON IN SURREY

are differences between painting, sculpture, architecture, music and poetry, that is so because each one of these arts imitates reality by means of a limited range of means, materials and techniques. Painting imitates reality by means of line and colour; sculpture by means of relief; architecture by means of tectonics; music by means of sound; and poetry by means of language. Of course, there might be overlaps between the various arts, but what I have in mind here is their essential, specific difference deriving from their medium of execution. A poem could be read aloud but that does not mean that its characteristic medium is sound; similarly, an architectural monument may use polychromy but that does not make it a painting. From this point of view the various arts are but so many different 'imitations' of reality: each one makes its claim to truth with the medium it knows best.

The problem of the means of imitation has been one of the greatest and commonest sources of confusion in both art and architecture. Setting aside any historical considerations, I will discuss the two major sources responsible for this confusion today.

First, let us look at Modernist architecture. Those who pursue its principles have little interest in the theory of imitation. Characteristically of a positivistic frame of mind, Modernist architects and critics have been openly contemptuous – as a matter of professional ethics – of artistic imitation in general and of the theory of architectural imitation in particular. They divide the history of architecture into a wholly irrational past and a wholly rational future. Questions of representation, figuration and ornament are ruled out as irrational and illegitimate on the assumption that twentieth-century man has outgrown such fetishes. Thus, in the aesthetics of Modernist architecture, the problem of representation assumes a new and different meaning. Figuration is said to have been superseded by abstraction; that is by a non-figurative 'mapping of essences'.

Putting aside for the moment all reservations concerning the dubious claim that abstraction is totally free of figurative schemata, when we come to examine Modernist architecture we find that its aesthetics of abstraction have yielded an outright realism. At first this might strike us as a paradox: how is it that an architecture of abstraction could ever be called realistic? And yet, the closer we look at Modernist architecture (especially its *Sachlichkeit* tradition), the more we realise that its principal formal aim consists of confounding abstraction with the raw immediacy and reality of the products of the building industry.

Let me illustrate this by a characteristic example. Reinforced concrete and the curtain-wall are to Modernist Dom-Ino technology what stone, timber and render are to classical technology. But whereas in classical aesthetics render imitates stone and stone imitates timber, in the aesthetics of Modernist architecture reinforced concrete and the curtain-wall remain what they are: facts of industrial production. The conception of Modernist architecture as dealing with facts and nothing but facts may seem rational enough but has nothing to do with abstraction. If anything, the 'facts' of technology carry an unmistakable realism that is dated and, therefore, not general enough to warrant the use of the term 'abstraction'. Let me not be

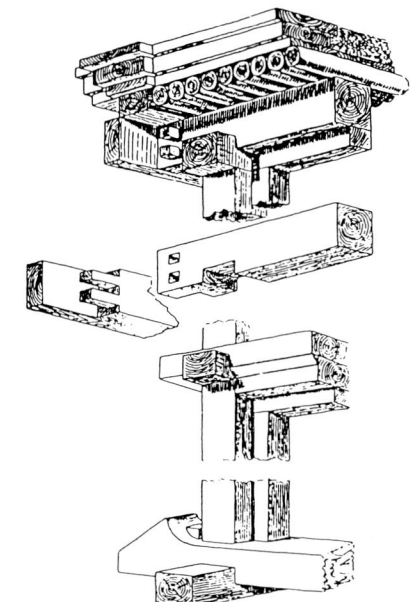

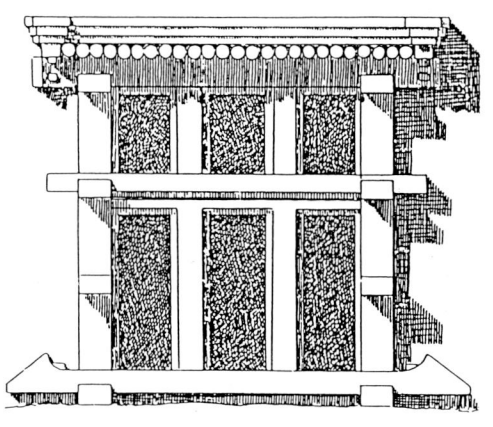

ARSACES TOMB AT MYRA

misunderstood: architecture always works with the 'facts' of technology. But the sympathy that architecture has with technology is not instanced by the literal adoption of technological 'facts'. Instead, architecture receives from technology 'facts' and returns to the world forms. It is in that sense that ornament is said to be the image of 'facts'.

Modernist architecture, however, views technology merely in a positivist manner. Unwilling to reflect upon the relationship between building and ornament, Modernist architecture mistakes ornament for mere caprice and crosses it out. *Sachlichkeit* and 'high-tech' Modernists alike have maintained (though for separate reasons and with different techniques) that 'pure construction is the basis and the characteristic of the new world of forms'.[2]

This constructional puritanism makes Modernist architects blind to the symbolic nature of architecture; it makes them forget that the true nature of architecture as art lies in the distance it establishes between itself and its model. The result has been a century of realism: the realism of industrial production, of the '*objet trouvé*', and of the misuse of construction and materials; all advanced under the platform of the aesthetics of so-called 'abstraction'.

If the aesthetics of realism of Modernist architecture led to a loss of symbolic form by underrating the importance of the principle of artistic imitation, by contrast, the aesthetics of multivalence of post-Modernism lead us today to an even more surprising sterility. This is the sterility that arises from increasing or multiplying the means of imitation.

To counter-balance Modernist architecture's lack of rhetorical eloquence, post-Modernism set out to describe 'the idea that an architect must master several styles and codes of communication . . . that he should be trained as a radical schizophrenic . . . (and that he should make) use of the full arsenal of communicational means, leaving out no area of experience, and suppressing no particular code'.[3]

Two fundamental principles soon become apparent: first, the conception that ornament and style are mere clothing; and second, the similar view that building materials and techniques are there only for their expressive, associational effect.

The first principle is meant to encourage architects to think 'cheap' and 'flashy': 'The detailing (ought to be) notional and symbolic, quickly conceived for spec builders'.[4] The second principle is meant to 'explode' the code of building techniques and materials; an attitude which, by its rampant inclusivism, endorses the whole wretched empirical reality encouraging the building industry toward the frenetic manufacture of waste products. 'Wood is warm . . . and full of knots and grain and so it is used domestically . . . (whereas) nylon . . . (and) the inflatable system is naturally pudgy, squashy, cuddly, sexual, and pleasant to touch . . . (and so they are used) in entertainment areas and other unmentionable places'.[5]

The post-Modern pleas for utilising the 'full arsenal of communication means' are being answered today by a Style Macaronique where anything goes. To paraphrase Adorno, 'superfluous jettisoning of meaning like ballast'[6] turns post-Modernism into an exercise of sterile inventiveness. The

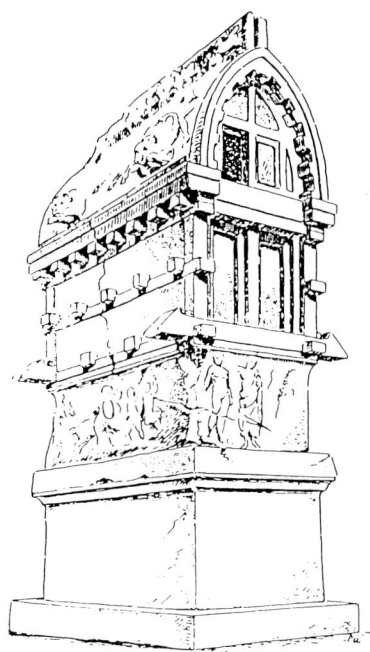

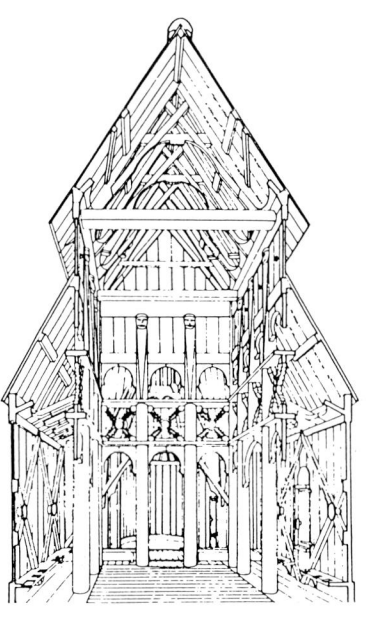

LYKIAN TOMB AND STAVE CHURCH

post-Modern mind invents so that things appear changing; and things change so that the mind appears to be inventive.

Modernist architecture discards imitation altogether. As a result, its forms are the raw 'facts' of industrial technology and materials it utilises. Such an extreme realism, therefore, short-circuits the possibility for an emergence of symbolic form.

Post-Modernism assumes that 'saturated' imagery enhances architecture's meaningfulness. By stepping into other branches like scenography and graphics, it loses sight of tectonics: architecture's distinguishing feature. Its indulgence in superfluous meaning leads ultimately to a travesty of architecture.

*   *   *

All along I have been speaking of the specific means of imitation proper to each one of the arts, but I have not as yet described the means proper to architecture. What are the means of architectural imitation and how have they developed? Have they been the intuition of one man or have they come into existence by natural habit and the accumulation of experience?

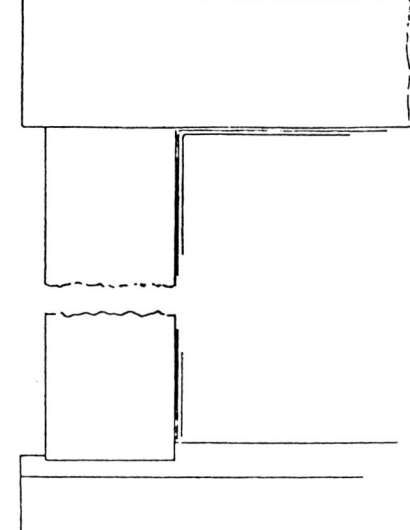

All historical, literary and formal evidence leads us to believe that the means of architectural imitation are to be found in the craft of building. Repetition and empirical judgement led builders to develop a habit of 'seeing' and 'judging' the constructional soundness and functional convenience of a particular solution. Over the years and centuries, a few chosen building solutions acquired a natural authority as truths. Such is the power of habit and consensus that soon this select number of building solutions became universal laws.

A select number of building solutions – such as that of the gable – are responsible, in the first instance, for the invention of form. Man, in contemplating these forms, recognises in them the cumulative knowledge, experience and genius of his species and thereby wishes to commemorate them. At that very moment, those select building solutions drop their use value and assume an aesthetic, symbolic value. The necessities of shelter are superseded by the aesthetics of tectonics; necessity is commemorated by means of symbolic form; building becomes architecture. 'It is not for pleasure but out of necessity that our temples have gables', wrote Cicero. 'The need of discharging rainwater has suggested their form. And yet, such is the beauty of their form . . . that if one were to build a temple on Mount Olympus – where I am told it never rains – one would still feel obliged to crown it with a pediment.'[7]

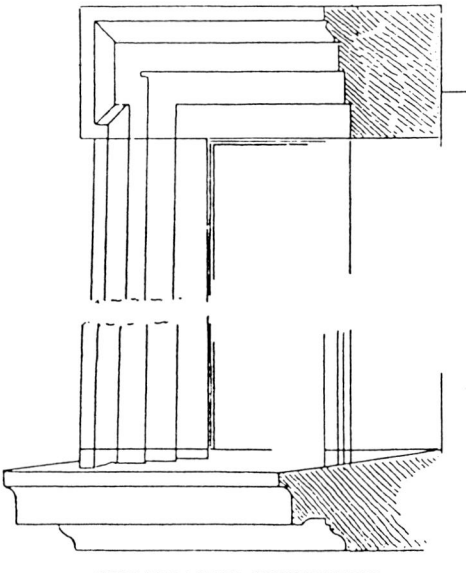

POST-AND-LINTEL CONSTRUCTION

It is in this sense that architecture imitates the constructional origins of its building craft. In the tectonics of classical architecture the experience of load-bearing is represented by the entasis of the column; the chief beam binding the columns together and imposing on them a common load becomes the architrave; the syncopation of the transversal beams resting on the architrave is represented by the triglyphs and metopes of the frieze; the projecting rafters of the roof supported by the frieze appear in the shape of the cornice; similarly the mutules, dentils, guttae, echinus, abacus, volutes, etc, all are images that imitate their respective constructional models.

It is not simply the tectonics of classical architecture that give evidence in support of this argument. All traditional architecture has derived its forms by means of imitating its building techniques.

The Sumerian temple retains memories of the reed construction with which houses were built. The rock-cut tomb of Arsaces in Myra imitates the constructional principles of indigenous timber framing. The Lykian tomb, now in the British Museum, is a representation in stone of the contemporary elements of building construction. The Egyptian tectonic order is an imitative representation both of constructional principles and of the lotus figure, the remembrance of which the columns commemorated. The half-engaged columns of early Romanesque architecture that subdivide the wall formalise in stone the round timber pales used in the construction of Norwegian stave churches, like that at Borgund. Finally, the applied order of the portico in the Forum Holitorium, Rome, shows the way by which Hellenistic and Roman architecture celebrates the constructional principles of both post-and-lintel and arcuated tectonics.

This list is only indicative and could draw its examples from primitive architecture, the architecture of early civilisations, of the Far East, or of our own western tradition.

I should stress yet again that the forms of all traditional architecture are not realistic copies but rather imitations of their respective constructional models. We can understand now why architectural forms are not a matter of individual fancy or invention. Their formal refinement and social authority cannot be fully developed in the lifetime of a single individual. Those who think otherwise have to pay the price of seeing their buildings being all the more readily confused with waste products.

A version of this essay was first published in Architectural Design, *Vol 54, 5/6, 1984*

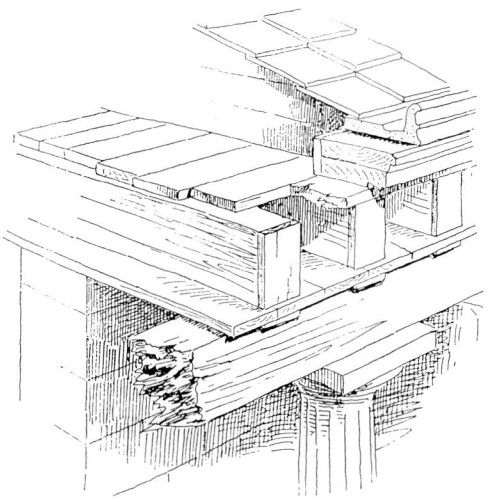

NOTES
1 Quatremère de Quincy, An Essay on the Nature, the End, and the Means of Imitation in the Fine Arts, *transl by JC Kent, Smith Elder and Son Co, London, 1837, p 13.*
2 Hannes Meyer, 'Building', 1928, in Ulrich Conrads, ed, Programmes and Manifestoes on 20th-century Architecture, *Lund Humphries, London, 1970.*
3 Charles Jencks, The Language of Post-Modern Architecture, *Academy Editions, London, first edition, 1977, pp 7 and 97.*
4 Ibid, p 78.
5 Ibid, p 82.
6 Theodor Adorno, Minima Moralia, *transl by EFN Jephcott, Verso Edition, 1978, p 141.*
7 Cicero, De Oratore, *L3, c 46, The LOEB Classical Library, Harvard and Heinemann.*

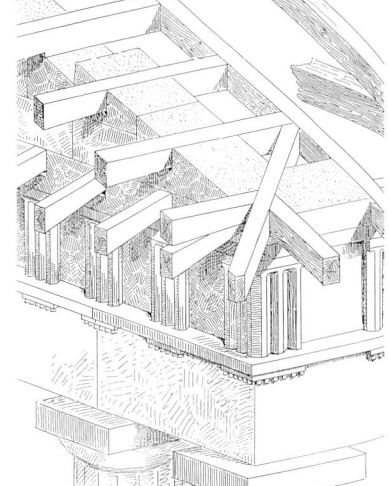

CONSTRUCTION OF DORIC TEMPLE, AFTER C. UHDE

CLASSICAL
ARCHITECTURE

DEMETRI PORPHYRIOS

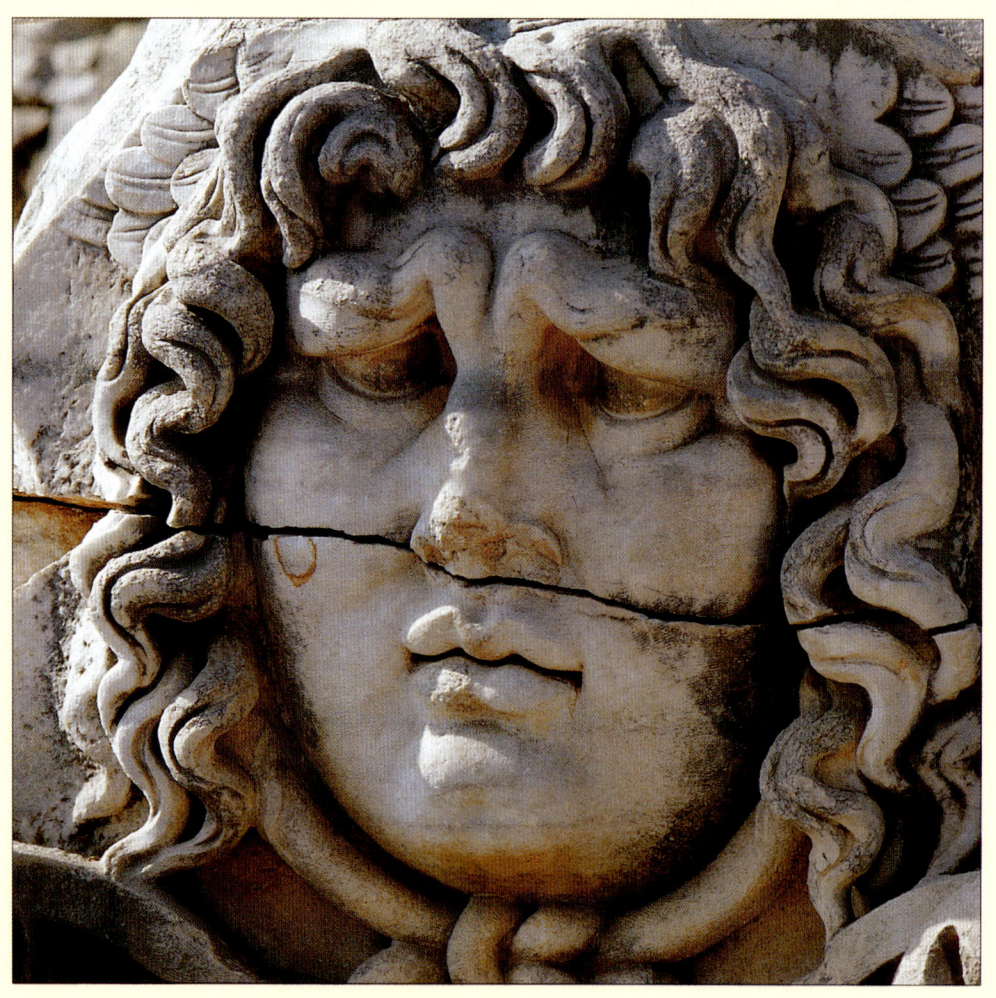

ACADEMY EDITIONS

TRADITION AND THE NEW

It is necessary to remember that the question of how tradition can be justified is not merely a contemporary problem but one which all historical periods have had to address. This problem of tradition as an awareness of the contingency of one's own period has been with us from the earliest times. Indeed this dialogue between new and old, often expressed as a desire to break with one's immediate past, always arises when a new claim is made against the tradition that has been guiding our everyday lives.

We have only to consider the founding legend of Western civilisation in its numerous versions from Virgil to the sixteenth century to see an example of this. Following the sacking of Troy, Aeneas escaped carrying his father and his household gods and eventually arrived in Latium. Years afterwards, his great grandson Brutus during his voyaging in exile founded Tours and Troynovant, the city of New Troy, which later King Lud was to rename London. The example of Brutus, the founder of both Britain and Brittany, was followed by the descendants of other Trojan princes who founded the various European nations. The story of the Trojan descent had a clear advantage over the biblical story of the descent from Noah. Aeneas of Troy became the cultural ancestor of Europe exactly because he represented an origin that had been already destroyed and which required the mediation of exile and reconstruction.

Or consider the position that Christianity adopted toward the pagan artistic traditions. By the ninth century, the iconoclastic movement which attacked the veneration of images was ultimately rejected. This decision to embrace once again the techniques of representational language gave a new impetus to Christian art. In the eyes of the Church, the use of the traditional language of representation was justified once again, this time because the pictorial narration of the Bible made the Christian message accessible to the illiterate masses.

Or again, we may use the example of the Renaissance humanists. They stressed the claim of their poets to choose their own models from antiquity rather than copy verbatim. In this way, they set out to reconstruct an antiquity that suited the fifteenth century, thereby controlling the transmission of tradition. For Policiano, Du Bellay or Alberti, the classical past lay in ruins and since each age is different from every other it was futile to copy mechanically the ancients. Had Alberti found an ancient sandal buried in Rome and worn it, that would not make him a Roman. Renaissance humanism, sensitive as it was to the relationship between tradition and anachronism, understood 'imitation' as an inventive transformation of the

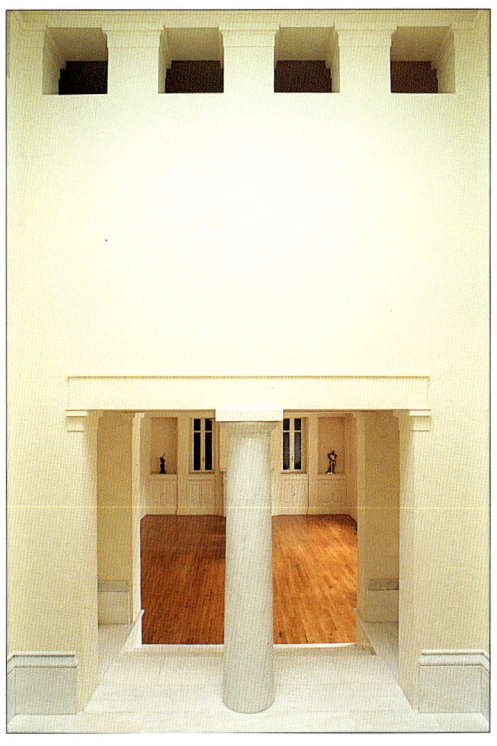

VILLA IN ATHENS, VIEW OF THE ATRIUM

ancients comparable to the Roman assimilation of Greece.

A most startling way of raising the question of tradition, however, and one that is closer to our perceptions today, is shown by the historicism of Hegel. What I have in mind here is Hegel's remark about art as 'a thing of the past'. When Hegel spoke of art as a thing of the past he meant that art was no longer understood as the revelation of the divine in the same unmediated and natural way in which it had been understood by the world of antiquity.

While for antiquity the divine was revealed in the very forms of classical art, this ceased to be the case with the arrival of Christianity. The infinite God of Christianity, Hegel argued, could not be adequately expressed by the finite forms of art. God's transcendent spirituality could never be represented by the materially wanting forms of art. Hegel's claim that art is a thing of the past points, therefore, to the realisation that with the close of antiquity art lost its divine authority and inevitably required justification. To say that art required justification was to imply also the reverse: that art inevitably now involved some prejudice. For it is only when we are suspicious of prejudice that we demand that a statement be justified or proven to us.

Historians of ideas tell us that the concept of prejudice acquired the negative overtones we are familiar with only with the advent of the Enlightenment. The Christian creed, incapable of universal verification, became an object of suspicion and was seen as an unfounded prejudice. Precisely because all men and women are rational, the Enlightenment argued, they can exercise their own judgement unfettered by tradition and without recourse to any sort of authority. To invoke tradition or pay allegiance to authority, therefore, was seen by the Enlightenment as an entrapment in prejudice.

A similar fate awaited the tradition of classical antiquity. A useful convention of cultural history has been to have the Enlightenment begin with the *Querelle des Anciens et des Modernes*, a debate which questioned for the first time the normative status granted exclusively to the art and literature of classical antiquity. I say 'useful convention' because this view grossly underestimates the contribution of other periods to the problem of break-versus-continuity with the ancients. Consider, for example, the practices of *inventio* in Roman oratory, of the *translatio studii* in Medieval scholasticism, of the Renaissance *renovatio* of antiquity, or of the sixteenth century Ciceronian Quarrel. They all bear precisely on the question of deciding whether absolute models can be selected from antiquity and to what extent tradition can be a source of inspiration or a futile constraint. But in spite of these qualifications, it remains true that the Enlightenment differed from all these attitudes in one characteristic way: it decided everything before the judgement of reason. The authority of the ancients, therefore, was seen as a source of prejudice. And though the Enlightenment's criticism was directed primarily against the religious tradition of the Bible, there was the general feeling that all tradition was indiscriminately tainted with covert guile.

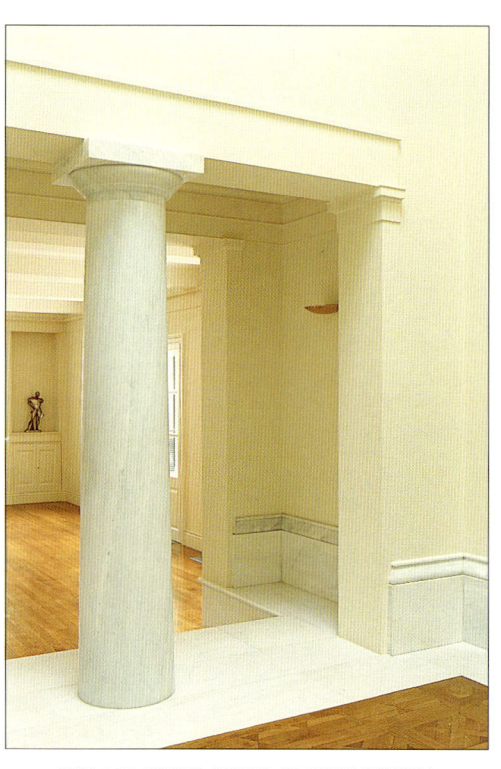

VILLA IN ATHENS, DETAIL OF DORIC COLUMN

This is where we find ourselves today and this is why I have examined the discrediting by the Enlightenment of all authority as prejudice. But let me go over this argument once again. The Enlightenment draws a distinction between faith in authority and faith in one's own reason. I suppose this distinction is legitimate; when authority tramples over reason then its claim is a perjury. But this does not mean that authority cannot also be a source of reason. And yet in the context of Enlightenment thought the concept of authority was vilified and blackened. Authority was given the meaning of blind obedience to power and force. Authority was made synonymous with authoritarianism. And all authoritative sources became authoritarian.

This is not, of course, the meaning of authority. Those who have authority base it ultimately not on the surrender of reason but on knowledge itself. When we say, 'he is an authority on brain surgery', we mean that he is superior to ourselves and everybody we know of in the knowledge of brain surgery. For this reason his judgement (on matters regarding brain surgery) takes precedence; that is, it has priority over ours.

Authority, in other words, cannot be bestowed but must be acquired on account of wisdom if someone is to lay claim to it. It is this passage into the social that gives meaning, say, to the authority of the teacher or the leader. Their authority has nothing to do with obedience and command but rather with reason and knowledge.

But is there another kind of authority that is different from those of the leader, the learned man or the teacher? At first sight it seems that the authority of tradition is indeed different in as much as it determines our everyday attitudes and institutions. And whereas all other authority answers to reason, the authority of tradition appears to be self-validating, at once imperious and natural.

I do not think, however, that such a 'natural' tradition exists or has ever existed. Even the most long-lived traditions in religion, in art or in science did not endure by nature because of habitual laziness or inertia. The authority of tradition does not rest on a *carte-blanche* code of trust. Instead, tradition has to be embraced and cultivated. The very idea of education itself hinges on this. For even though the teacher loses his authority when the pupil matures and forms his own insights, this passage into maturity does not mean that a person has repudiated tradition. On the contrary, he has made tradition his own. It is precisely in this passage into maturity that the 'wonder' of education lies. Education exists only when tradition is freely taken over.

What does it mean, however, 'to take over tradition freely'? It is true that in our attitude to the past we always stand within tradition. What I mean here is that we do not think of tradition as something foreign to ourselves, imposed as a means of censorship and control. Consider for a moment one's own language and the way it is handed down to us. It is not forced upon us against our will nor is it left over by accident or chance. Linguistic tradition is always given to us in the sense that we grow in it whether in the re-enactment forms of play, custom, speaking or writing. What tradition hands down to us is a sort of knowledge that allows us to relate to the world by

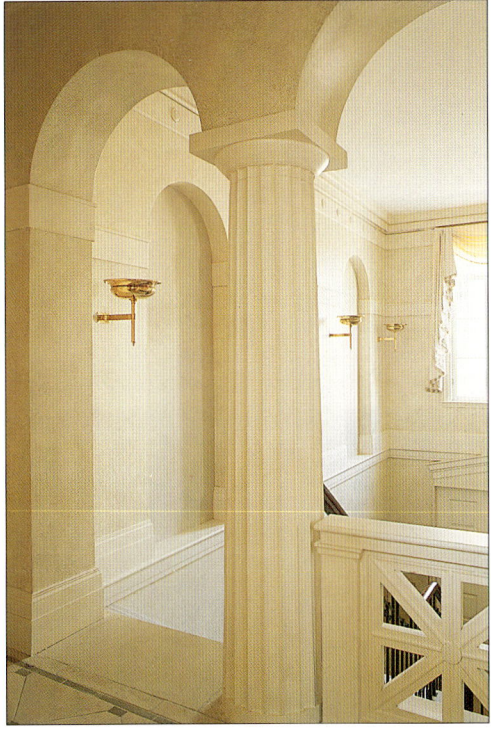

HOUSE IN KENSINGTON, DETAIL OF DORIC COLUMN

means of familiarity and recognition. In this sense tradition is always part of us for in it we recognise ourselves. Consider, for example, the case of learning a new language. In the beginning, French or Finnish is always something alien and outside ourselves; we stumble over it and it is an impediment to thinking. However, once we master a foreign language, we can hardly see it as an acquired knowledge but rather as a tradition that was always there. This is what I mean when I say that tradition is always part of us. This is the sense in which it could be said that in our everyday life we 'take over tradition freely', that is, of our own free will.

But what of those artistic traditions toward which we have developed a sense of loss and estrangement? Are such traditions irredeemably cut off from our understanding? Or can they be regained and, if so, what might be the relevance of such a new life?

Opinion here, as we know, is and has been divided. Broadly speaking two positions have been argued. There are those who maintain that if removed from its original context the work of art loses its significance. Being the product of a specific people and of a particular period the work of art can be understood only in terms of the conditions of its origin. Hence the theories according to which art is the reflection of its culture, and, hence, the studious search by historians for a total reconstruction of the past and for the re-establishment of the original context within which the work of art was first produced. According to this view, historical scholarship brings back what is lost and illuminates tradition in the sense of retrieving the circumstances of the past and restoring the world as it was in its full documentary significance. This version of historical understanding celebrates an enshrined world and invites us to rehearse it liturgically. Tradition is perceived as fixed beyond change and criticism as if it were a sacred original moment which we should all strive to regain by a ritualistic enactment. This attitude is generally known as revivalism. It promises the restitution of past life and, ultimately, it reduces history into cosy and pacifying fetishes.

In contrast, Hegel, in his *Aesthetics*, puts forward another attitude towards tradition. Hegel understood clearly the futility of revivalism when he wrote that the works of the Muses '. . . have become what they are for us now – beautiful fruit already picked from the tree, fruit which a friendly Fate has offered us . . .' All art belongs to the past: it remains 'fruit picked from the tree'. To re-create the historical context surrounding the production of a work of art does not give us a living relationship with art for '. . . the statues are now only stones from which the living soul has flown'. The miraculous dwelling of the spirit in the very forms of classical art is no longer possible in our romantic (modern) world. Scholarship cannot bring back the past; at best it can offer only a historical understanding. This understanding which art history affords us, argues Hegel, stems only from an external activity. The tradition which the art historian studies is always an external object of research. It is as if on one side there is tradition; and on the other it is us. We look at tradition from outside and we engage in historical research so that we may 'educate' ourselves about the past.

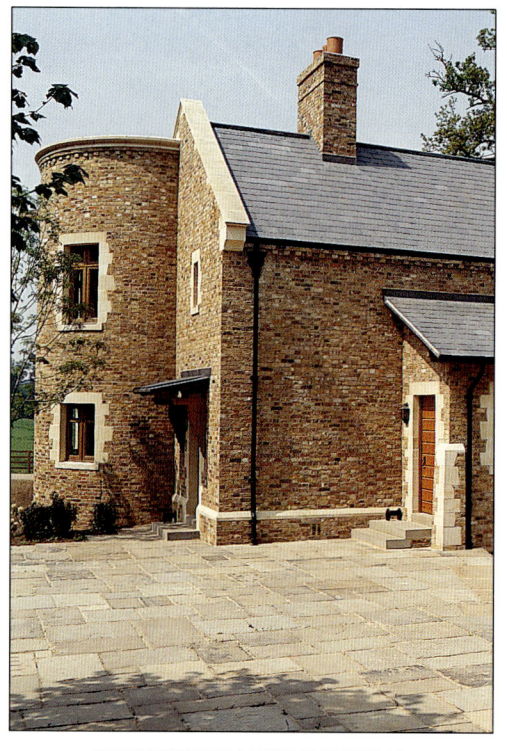

BELVEDERE FARM, VIEW OF THE HALL

Hence the extreme historicism and relativism of Hegel. Tradition becomes a self-referential system and soon history becomes historiography. We see this happening every day in most art and architectural history courses taught in our schools. And while art history students can at least graduate once they show proficiency in historiography, we architects are left totally bewildered. The Hegelian reduction of all history to historiography has made it impossible to integrate studio instruction with history courses in a significant manner. The student is presented with history as an objectifying process with no criteria of evaluation. He observes history, so to speak, from outside. The relevance of the historical models he studies is always a matter of arbitrary conjecture or simply of individual taste. It is understandable, therefore, why some repudiate tradition and concentrate on their so-called creative intuition, while the rest flirt with the history of civilisation indiscriminately as if it were a mere succession of charming styles.

My view on the subject of tradition is neither with those who preach revivalism nor with the advocates of historical relativism. To understand what tradition is (and specifically what is the meaning of tradition in architecture) we have to ask the question of the relationship of one building to another. Once we formulate the question this way, two considerations become important: convention and originality.

The study of conventions is based on analogies of form. It is clear that any classical building (and this applies equally to all architecture we speak of as enduring) may be studied not only as an imitation of the world and of construction, but as an imitation of other buildings as well.

Once we think of a classical building in relation to other classical buildings, we can see that a great part of creative design addresses the formation and transformation of conventions. All art and architecture is equally conventionalised, but we do not notice this because such conventions are always meant to appear natural and universal, otherwise their role as the binding 'cement' of society would be undermined. In fact, conventions can best be studied when one travels, for unless we are unaccustomed to the conventions of a country they do not stand out. The same is true with the conventions of art and architecture.

Today, however, the conventional element in architecture is elaborately disguised. As we all know, the market ethic of the original and the authentic is based on the pretence that every work of art is an invention singular enough to be patented. Ironically, this state of affairs would make it difficult to appraise an architectural tradition which includes, say, Palladio, much of whose architecture is paraphrased from others, or Schinkel, whose buildings sometimes follow their sources almost verbatim. The comparison between the Villa Malcontenta and that at Garches comes to mind. And though this particular example might be admirable exactly because it is so far-fetched, it is Colin Rowe who made us see that Le Corbusier's building remains in part unintelligible if we do not recognise Palladio in it. Similarly, if we turn to poetry for a moment I am reminded of Milton who asked for nothing better than to borrow the whole of the Bible.

Let me qualify this observation to avoid misunderstanding. Borrowing

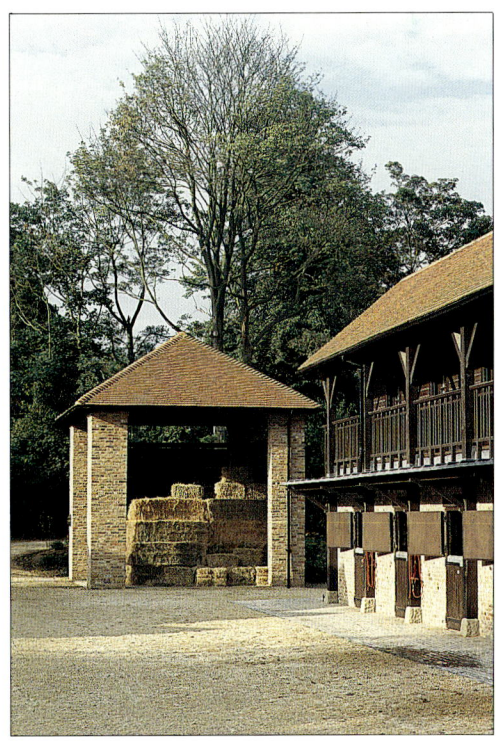

BELVEDERE FARM, VIEW OF THE HAY BARN

here does not mean reproducing. The distance between a new work and the model that has inspired it indeed always points out the contemporaneity of the work. Originality, and thus the modern itself, consists in this distance between the new and the model as the new emplots itself within tradition. Doubtless, some would argue that the new has no tradition whatsoever. Derrida's *itérabilité* for example, refers exactly to such an aimless 'drift' inherent in all language. Language, cut off from any sense of home-base, is a meandering away from any origins and from all cultural and social meaning. Neither the forms of art nor the words of language, however, are 'orphaned' (as Derrida would have them) but they always acquire a parenthood in the context of the tradition that adopts them. Out of the interplay between 'drift' and repetition each form acquires its unique itinerary. Art is situated exactly at this mid point: art deals neither with origins nor with creation *ex novo* but with the distance traversed between the model and its modern repetition. It is precisely this distance between the model and its imitative repetition that art quite consciously confronts and builds deliberately into the artefact. Art points to a dependence on the models that it conditionally overcomes so that it may formulate its own modernity. 'Imitate so that you may be original', has always been a working principle in art.

At the same time we should realise that the conception of a great architect entrusted with a heritage must become once again as elementary to us as it was to Alberti. And yet, such an attitude would seem to violate the principle of creation *ex nihilo* that most of us have been taught today.

Historically, of course, we have been told to believe that this 'fall' from the grace of tradition was triggered by a profound change in the social role of the artist/architect after the middle of the eighteenth century. With the fall of the Church, the State and the aristocracy that had sustained him for centuries, the artist found himself confronted with an anonymous public. This new client, we are told, he despised. Paradoxically, however, the artist demanded the public's approval even when it could not understand his art. This nineteenth century romantic attitude of the genius had much to do with the Modernist slogan 'down with conventions' and is still with us today, especially among the Neo-Modernist aesthetes.

But it is hardly possible to accept a view which imagines that a creative architect stares at a white board and designs *ex nihilo*. Human beings do *not* create in that way. Architecture may employ technology and it may be implicated with social and economic parameters; architects may read philosophy and novels and some may even be fascinated with fractal geometries and Boolean cubes, all of this is normal and human. But architecture is not made out of these things. Buildings can only be made out of other buildings. Architecture shapes itself. Its forms can no more exist outside architecture than the form of a sonata can exist outside music.

It should be evident by now that architecture takes up the challenge of tradition and makes us see something more than we already know. In that sense architecture elicits a sense of relevance from tradition. It makes us see the position we occupy within tradition by raising both the question of the ontology of art and of its historicity.

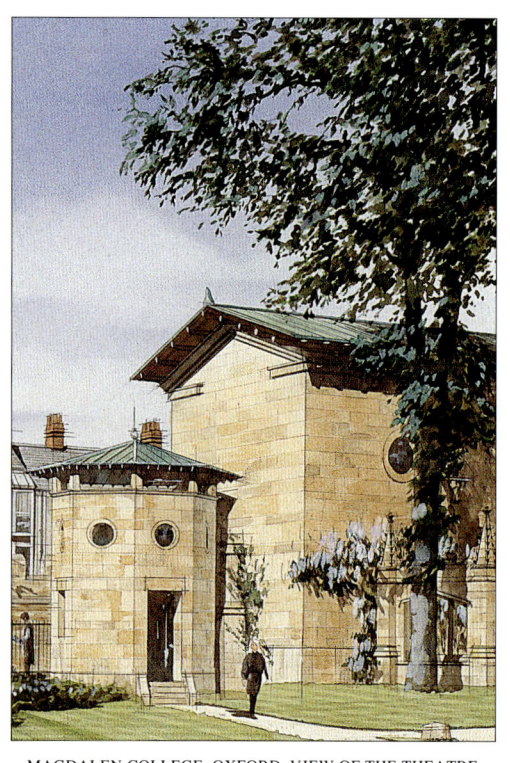

MAGDALEN COLLEGE, OXFORD, VIEW OF THE THEATRE

Nowhere is this seen better than in the achievements of classical art and architecture. In fact, since the Hellenistic period, the concept of the classical has had both a normative (ontological) and a historical side. The normative side of the classical refers to the achievements of a particular stage in the development of mankind: namely, Greek Antiquity. What we call classical, in a normative sense, is that which endures the contingencies of a changing political and economic life and of taste and fashion.

But insofar as this norm points to the past accomplishments of a specific people and age, the idea of the classical always has a temporal side which gives it a historical dimension. This historical side of the classical is tied up with the awareness of 'anachronism': that is, with the awareness of a distance from the norm and a sense of loss. Dionysus of Halicarnassus was perhaps among the first to have felt such an acute sense of loss. His polemics against the vitiated rhetoric of the Hellenistic era recall the Renaissance polemics against Medieval retrogression, the eighteenth century denouncement of Rococo as prurient as well as our twentieth century criticism of the duplicity of Modernism. It is not by accident, therefore, that the concept of the classical was formulated for the first time in the later years of the Hellenistic period exactly when deviation from the norm made the norm visible for the first time. Similarly, the stylistic concepts of Archaic and Gothic, or of Mannerism and Baroque, all presuppose a relation to the normative concept of the classical. Gombrich understood this clearly when he wrote in *Norm and Form* that 'gothic (referred) to the not-yet-classical . . . and baroque to the no-longer-classical . . .'

It is because of such an articulation between the normative and the historical that we can say that every new humanism has no ground other than the modernity it helps to actualise. The classical accepts the contingent and the historical as elements that supply it with the necessary distance without which its project of demonstrating the continuity of human life would not be possible.

Ultimately, this articulation of the normative and the historical means that the classical is that which speaks of tradition in a modern voice thus highlighting man's capacity for millennial continuity. The classical reaches across culture and time and, taking the risk of anachronism, it heals the estrangement which humanism constantly faces. The classical, then, is certainly the enduring and timeless. But this timelessness always takes the form of modernity; that is, it takes the form of the relevance of tradition.

A version of this essay was first published in D Porphyrios, Classical Architecture, *Academy Editions, London 1991.*

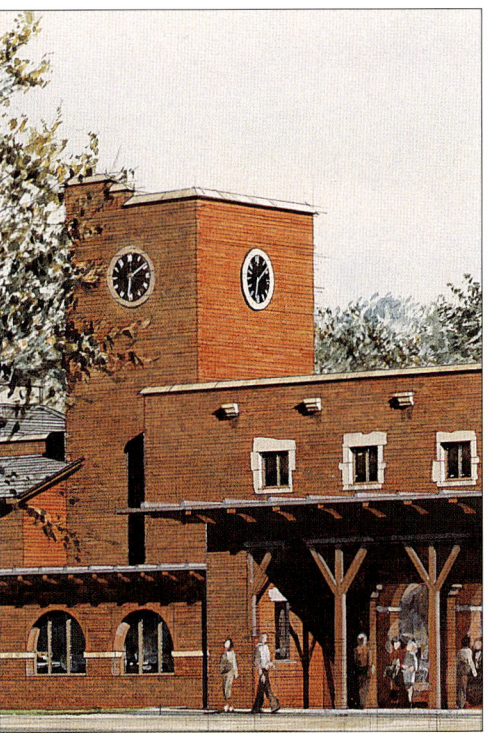

UNIVERSITY OF READING, RURAL HISTORY CENTRE

PROJECT CREDITS

PAVILIONS IN HIGHGATE
Design Team: Demetri Porphyrios (Design Principal), Andreas Zannas; Structural Engineers: Trigram Partnership; Contractor: Fox Engineering; Photography: D Porphyrios

BELVEDERE VILLAGE, ASCOT
Design Team: Demetri Porphyrios (Design Principal), Nigel Cox (Project Architect), Chris Britton, Victor Deupi, Melissa Pinsley, Peter Lorenzoni, Philip Doele, George Signori, Richard Economakis, Joanna Papathanassiou, Ian Fleetwood, Charles Bergen, Duncan McRoberts, Charles Addison; Structural Engineers: Upton McGougan & Partners; Quantity Surveyors: Davis, Langdon & Everest; Contractor: GJ Smith Bros; Modelmakers: Jordi Fontanals Modelmaking; Photography: Leigh Simpson

RURAL HISTORY CENTRE, UNIVERSITY OF READING
Design Team: Demetri Porphyrios (Design Principal), Nigel Cox (Project Architect), George Signori, Frank Green, Richard Economakis, Edwin Venn, David Anderson, Duncan McRoberts; Structural Engineers: Alan Baxter & Associates; Quantity Surveyors: Davis, Langdon & Everest; Client: The University of Reading

WORKSHOPS AND OFFICES AT POUNDBURY, DORCHESTER
Design Team: Demetri Porphyrios (Design Principal), Alireza Sagharchi (Project Architect), Mike Kennedy, Edwin Venn, Victor Deupi; Structural Engineers: Alan Baxter & Associates; Client: The Duchy of Cornwall

INLAND REVENUE OFFICES, NOTTINGHAM
Design Team: Demetri Porphyrios (Design Principal), Frank Green and Alireza Sagharchi (Project Architects), George Signori, Charles Addison, David Cox, David Anderson, Edwin Venn, Richard Economakis, Duncan McRoberts, Joanna Papathanassiou; Collaborating Architects: Renton Howard Wood Levin Partnership; Structural Engineers: The Waterman Partnership; Services Engineers: JR Preston and Partners; Landscape Consultants: Charles Funke Associates; Quantity Surveyors: Turner & Townsend; Client: Inland Revenue

BATTERY PARK CITY PAVILION, NEW YORK
Design Team: Demetri Porphyrios (Design Principal), Mike Kennedy (Project Architect), Ian Sutherland, David Cox; Structural Engineers and Engineers of Record: Tor, Smolen, Calini & Anastos; Contractor: Clark Construction; Client: The Battery Park City Authority; Photography: Scott Frances/Esto and D Porphyrios

MAGDALEN COLLEGE, NEW LONGWALL QUADRANGLE, OXFORD
Design Team: Demetri Porphyrios (Design Principal), Nigel Cox and Alireza Sagharchi (Project Architects), Victor Deupi, Chris Britton, Peter Lorenzoni, Charles Addison, Philip Doele, David Anderson, Edwin Venn, Joanna Papathanassiou, George Signori; Structural Engineers: Trigram Partnership; Quantity Surveyors: Beaufort Ellis Associates; Client: Magdalen College, Oxford

THE FITZWILLIAM MUSEUM EXTENSION, CAMBRIDGE
Design Team: Demetri Porphyrios (Design Principal), Alireza Sagharchi, Liam O'Connor, Frank Green, Thomas Karavis, Andrew Grossman; Structural Engineers: Trigram Partnership; Services Engineers: Max Fordham & Partners; Quantity Surveyors: Davis, Belfield & Everest

VILLA IN ATHENS
Design Team: Demetri Porphyrios (Design Principal), Alireza Sagharchi (Project Architect), Ian Sutherland, Joanna Papathanassiou, David Cox; Structural Engineers: Iris Ltd; Photography: Leigh Simpson and D Porphyrios

SHIPPING OFFICES, CITY OF LONDON
Design Team: Demetri Porphyrios (Design Principal), Alireza Sagharchi (Project Architect), Nigel Cox; Services Engineers: Max Fordham & Partners; Contractor: Morgan Lovell Ltd; Photography: Richard Cheatle

PATERNOSTER SQUARE OFFICE BUILDING
Design Team: Demetri Porphyrios (Design Principal), Frank Green and Alireza Sagharchi (Project Architects), Victor Deupi, Peter Lorenzoni, David Cox, David Anderson, Ian Sutherland, Joanna Papathanassiou, Chris Britton, Ian Fleetwood, Philip Doele, Mike Kennedy; Structural Engineers: The Waterman Partnership; Services Engineers: Jaros, Baum & Bolles; Quantity Surveyors: VJ Mendoza; Client: Paternoster Associates

HOUSE IN KENSINGTON, LONDON
Design Team: Demetri Porphyrios (Design Principal), Alireza Sagharchi (Project Architect), Ian Sutherland, Liam O'Connor, Nigel Cox; Structural Engineers: Cameron Taylor Partners; Quantity Surveyors: Gardiner and Theobald; Contractor: Redcon Contractors; Client: Balli Development Ltd; Photography: exterior by Nick Carter, interior by Tom Leighton

HOUSE IN CHELSEA, LONDON
Design Team: Demetri Porphyrios (Design Principal), Mike Kennedy (Project Architect), Joanna Papathanassiou, Peter Lorenzoni, Philip Doele, Richard Economakis, George Signori, Duncan McRoberts; Structural Engineers: Trigram Partnership; Services Engineers: Hanson Mendick Waring; Quantity Surveyors: John Webster and Associates

CHEPSTOW VILLAS, LONDON
Design Team: Demetri Porphyrios (Design Principal), Alireza Sagharchi (Project Architect), Ian Sutherland, Ian Fleetwood, Matthew Bradbury, Robert Wilson; Structural Engineers: Trigram Partnership; Contractor: Balli Development Ltd; Client: Balli Development Ltd; Photography: exterior by Mark Fiennes, interior by Tom Leighton

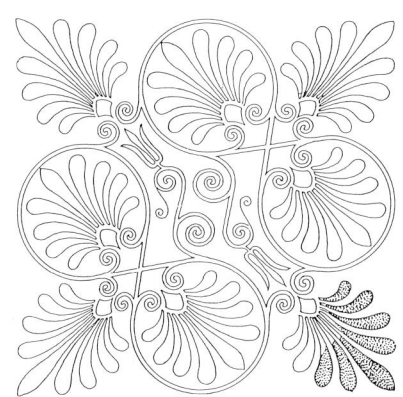